A SPIRITUAL DIRECTORS INTERNATIONAL BOOK

SUPERVISION

of Spiritual Directors

Engaging in Holy Mystery

EDITED BY
Mary Rose Bumpus and
Rebecca Bradburn Langer

morehouse

HARRISBURG • LONDON

Unless otherwise noted, the Scripture quotations contained herein are from the New Revised Standard Version Bible, copyright © 1989 by the Division of Christian Education of the National Council of Churches of Christ in the U.S.A. Used by permission. All rights reserved.

Morehouse Publishing, P.O. Box 1321, Harrisburg, PA 17105

Morehouse Publishing, The Tower Building, 11 York Road, London SE1 7NX

Morehouse Publishing is a Continuum imprint.

Cover design: Brenda L. Klinger

Library of Congress Cataloging-in-Publication Data

Supervision of spiritual directors : engaging in holy mystery / [edited by] Mary Rose Bumpus and Rebecca Bradburn Langer.
    p. cm.
  ISBN 0-8192-1994-0 (pbk.)
  1. Spiritual directors—Supervision of. I. Bumpus, Mary Rose. II. Langer, Rebecca Bradburn.
  BV5053.S87 2005
  253.5'3—dc22
                              2005001713

Printed in the United States of America

01 02 03 04 05 06 07 08 09   10 9 8 7 6 5 4 3 2 1

Contents

Dedication

To our parents,

Wilbur and Esther Knepper Bradburn and

Adrian and Marguerite Stewart Bumpus,

who first invited us to engage in holy mystery,

and to our students,

who teach us about God's outrageous surprise

Introduction

Supervision of spiritual direction is an ancient process within the Christian tradition. Informal conversations and correspondence among spiritual guides about issues related to those they accompany have been going on for centuries. As far as we can ascertain, however, what we think of today as the "formal" supervision of spiritual directors is a relatively recent phenomenon. It has arisen within the past three to four decades, as the desire for spiritual direction has grown in both Protestant and Roman Catholic traditions. The greater need for formal accompaniment of spiritual directors by competent supervisors has brought about more questions concerning the nature of supervision and the supervision relationship in a spiritual direction context.

This book is one of few written on the supervision of spiritual directors during this significant time. In conceptualizing and editing this work, it is our desire to honor those who have been engaged in the work of supervision and those who have written on the topic in recent decades. At the same time, we want to expand and encourage further conversation about the supervision relationship and process. We asked a variety of people gifted in both supervision and direction to write about their general understanding of supervision and particular issues worthy of our common attention. We hope the book produces a chorus of voices that stirs the minds, hearts, and imaginations of those doing supervision.

This book is divided into three parts. The first part addresses the question "What is supervision?" from three different perspectives. In chapter 1, Mary Rose

Bumpus suggests that supervision is a collaborative endeavor whose primary purpose is to assist "an absent directee" from a place of "respectful unknowing." James Neafsey, in chapter 2, asserts that the principal focus of supervision is on the "deep spiritual identity of the director." He proposes that a contemplative approach assists supervisors in seeing "beyond" and "through" to the primary charism of spiritual directors and their identity as persons in the eyes of God. In chapter 3, Rebecca Bradburn Langer defines the supervision task within an eightfold framework. She articulates basic precepts of supervision, such as preparation for supervision, growing in knowledge of God and self, attention to places of growth and healing in directors, and "referral with grace." These three chapters, while presenting different perspectives on the practice of supervision, all follow the basic assumption that supervision is engagement in holy mystery.

Part 2 deals with topics in supervision that we believe to be of particular import. We hope the four chapters provide practical and theoretical assistance to supervisors about the issues they cover. Chapter 4 focuses on issues that are common among beginning directors. Mary Rose Bumpus and Rebecca Bradburn Langer address areas that include supporting beginning directors, encouraging trust in God, "savoring" and "suffering," and appropriate forms of self-disclosure on the part of directors. In chapter 5, Maria Tattu Bowen looks at the various dimensions of the self that are used in the relationship and practice of supervision. She describes how the "physiological facts of our ongoing lives," emotions, and thoughts may each be revelatory of God in direction and supervision. She also gives examples of "encompassing, simultaneous experiences" that affect the whole of the human being and are often represented in desires and images.

From an essay on the use of all the dimensions of the self, we move to a more specific essay on sexuality and eros. Samuel Hamilton-Poore, in chapter 6, invites directors and supervisors to pay attention to human sexuality and God's eros, "given and gift" in spiritual direction and supervision, as well as problems in these areas. He suggests questions and exercises for reflection. Joseph Driskill, in chapter 7, speaks about human sexuality within the context of his reflections on ethical dilemmas encountered in the work of supervision. Driskill invites us to prevent "common quagmires" with "ethical forethought." He presents vignettes and highly nuanced remarks about familiar moral dilemmas and offers common-sense wisdom about how to deal with such issues in supervision.

Part 3 is meant to broaden the worldview of directors and supervisors. These final chapters represent movement in the supervision of spiritual directors. They challenge us to thoughtfully consider the social and cultural contexts within which we practice supervision, to learn the languages of our directors and directees, and to expand our vision of God's presence. In chapter 8, Elizabeth Liebert discusses the ways in which supervision expands the horizons of supervisors, directors, and directees. She visually portrays an "experience circle" that represents not only the dimensions of self through which we experience God, but also the arenas of life where we are confronted with the power and presence of holy mystery. The chapter challenges supervisors to see God's presence in the midst of all things—intrapersonally, interpersonally, through systems and structures, and within nature. Threads from one arena lead to another inviting us to explore and discover the simultaneity of God's grace in supervision and spiritual direction.

Cleo Molina and Hutch Haney also challenge supervisors. In chapter 9, they call for a greater understanding of the cultural assumptions and values that affect supervisors, directors, and directees in spiritual direction. They do this by inviting supervisiors, as well as the directors they serve, to engage in a process of co-cultural mapping that brings to light these assumptions and values and allows us to converse in meaningful and nonthreatening ways about different heritages.

In chapter 10, Susan Phillips describes supervising directors who are working with the disabled. Phillips places her remarks pointedly within the Christian religion's distinctive "commitment to those the world considers other-than-normal." She considers the contemporary social landscape, a landscape that is growing in its emphasis on "the personhood of those who bear some mark of difference" while its "orientation toward cure has eclipsed the place of care." She challenges supervisors and directors to stand in the light of Jesus' life and Passion in order to "come alongside others who are different."

This book has been conceived and written in an "in-between" space. We know the ideas suggested herein are all around us. We do not present this book as a first or final word on the topic of supervision. Rather, we hope it is a stimulus for further reflection, conversation, and expansion of horizons. We also hope it embodies some word spoken and given for the present moment in time. Ultimately, we hope it propels us to enter more fully into the reign of God, to recognize the presence and power of the Holy Spirit in supervision conversations and to glorify the incarnate God in all things—the ultimate purpose of all supervision.

Mary Rose Bumpus
Rebecca Bradburn Langer
Editors

PART ONE

What Is
Supervision?

CHAPTER ONE

Supervision: The Assistance of an Absent Other

Mary Rose Bumpus

I began doing spiritual direction when I was thirty years of age. At that age, I was too young and too foolish to be a director. But someone asked me to be his spiritual director (a "sure" sign I was called to this ministry), so I said yes. My first directee was a young man who was a student at a nearby university divinity school and a bright seeker. His first words to me were "I don't believe Jesus is the Son of God." I was stunned by the boldness of his statement, didn't have a clue about how to respond, and was silent in the face of it. I was grateful to have a good supervisor, who said to me, "So ask the young man how he does see Jesus in relation to God, what it is like for him to see Jesus in this way, and what his images of God are." I was grateful for the direct invitation and insight about what might be helpful. As a result, the young man and I began to develop more meaningful conversations about his life in God.

My second directee was an eighty-year-old woman. She rarely spoke of her "experience of God" or said anything about her inner life. I regularly invited her into this kind of conversation, but she just did not respond much. I was puzzled about how we could be engaged in the art of spiritual direction. One thing was clear to me: The woman was lonely. One day we discovered we had something in common—a love for music and joy when playing the piano and singing. We then embarked upon a very different mode of spiritual direction: Playing, singing, laughing, and rejoicing together became the rhythm of our sessions. We did not speak much of the inner life or of God. For a while, I wondered if what we were

3

doing together could properly be called spiritual direction. Yet I believe we grew in our capacity to be present to one another, and to life as a result of our encounter.[1] My supervisor strongly encouraged my way of being with this woman. She said that both of us had our Godward gaze expanded, even if we weren't speaking directly about it.

While I was seeing this woman and young man for spiritual direction, I was also studying the art of spiritual direction. There were ten of us—priests and sisters of a southern Catholic diocese. As part of our study, each member of the group served as spiritual director for another while the instructor and the rest of the group members observed and learned. When it was my turn, I was invited to act as a spiritual director for Sister John Mary, a Roman Catholic sister who was twenty years my senior. I was new, nervous about doing spiritual direction in front of the whole group, and I felt privileged to be the recipient of part of John Mary's story. Our time began in an ordinary conversational way, and we spoke together of things that were meaningful to John Mary. About twenty minutes into the conversation, John Mary said, "You know, I just don't trust God." It was a sacred and poignant moment—a moment of profound revelation. I was silent. We were all silent for a time.

John Mary did not speak further, and I found myself surprised, confused, and with no sense of how to respond. Finally I spoke to John Mary and the group as a whole, acknowledging my inability to respond and my need for assistance. The group facilitator asked if anyone in the group had a suggestion. The only suggestion forthcoming was that I try to pray with John Mary. Intuitively I knew there was something "not right" about this. But for lack of anything better to do or say, I did pray aloud for and with John Mary. As gracious and appreciative as she was at the end of this time of prayer, it was very clear to both of us that we were stuck.

Looking back on this twenty-five-year-old experience, a memory that has saddened me and aided in my reflection on spiritual direction and supervision, I know there are several kinds of responses I might have made and would make today. I might ask John Mary if there is some person in her life she trusts. If so, what does this trust look like? I might speak with her about the humanness of our moments of lack of trust in God. I might ask John Mary about how she would like to be in relationship with God. I might note her courage and ability to speak the truth in the group setting. A number of things come to mind. In the moment, the person of John Mary, our common humanity, and the presence of the Holy Spirit would guide my particular response.

In essence, I brought this experience to supervision by turning to the group for assistance, to no avail. I also could have taken this experience to an individual supervisor. The prevailing wisdom about supervision, then and now, suggests that the supervision conversation would be centered around my interior responses to the directee. Why was I surprised and confused by John Mary's assertion of her lack of trust in God? This conversation might have been a fruitful and beneficial one for me. But I suspect it would not have answered the fundamental question: How can I best be of service *to John Mary* in *her* journey with God?

Supervision: The Assistance of an Absent Other

Supervision is a conversation between peers that ultimately fosters the well-being of an absent other.[2] This notion of supervision puts the emphasis on the well-being of the directee, the one who is absent from the supervision conversation. It focuses most specifically on his or her *spiritual* well-being, though not to the exclusion of the physical or psychological realms of human reality; these cannot be completely separated from the spiritual. It also focuses on the *relationship between the director and the directee*, as this relationship directly affects the goals and well-being of the directee and is the place of encounter with the Holy Spirit in the direction session itself. By asserting that the primary function of supervision is to foster the spiritual well-being of an absent other—the directee—I am not suggesting that this is the only way for us to think about supervision.[3] But I am suggesting that we need to question and to enter into further conversation about models that are primarily focused on the inner life of the director as the substance of the supervision conversation.

I am putting forward another way of thinking about supervision, a way that does not focus so much on the inner life of the director. A director may speak with her own spiritual director or a therapist about this. Focusing on the inner world of the director leads one to think that stuck places between director and directee can usually be resolved by the inner work of one party or the other. This is often not the case and underemphasizes the highly social context of much of our spiritual journey. Models used to focus on the inner life of directors in supervision have been drawn largely from psychoanalytically based and self-help literature. In the hands of highly trained and competent psychoanalysts, psychoanalysis can be a significant source of human growth and transformation. Those of us not so highly trained in this arena tend to understand and employ psychoanalytically based concepts in their current cultural usage. This means they are employed in ways that are generally negative, and in ways that can be harmful to the representation of the director or the directee. I have done this myself. The following fictitious account of a discussion between two supervisors is a blatant, though not far-fetched, example.

Supervisor I: "One of the men I supervise came in today because he is having a very difficult time with someone he sees for direction. Sue [the directee] comes into her session with Tom [the director] and bolts out of the gate with lots of talk, moving rapidly from one topic to the next. Tom feels overwhelmed and can't get a word in edgewise. Before they know it, an hour and a half has gone by, and Sue is ready to be on her way. Tom is distressed. He cannot end his sessions with Sue on time and does not know how to deal with Sue's constant talk."

Supervisor 2: "So what did you do?"

Supervisor 1: "Well, Tom and I have had conversations about Sue before. Sue is thirty years old, came from an abusive family, and is obsessive-compulsive in her conversation and highly narcissistic. She is in denial about the significance of her childhood abuse and resists dealing with the pain of it. Tom has significant boundary issues, finds it difficult to set limits, and is angry at Sue's apparent inability to be more thoughtful in conversation. Tom and I began our conversation by discussing the roots of his anger." (and so the conversation goes . . .)

As I consider this conversation, I am aware that I now have negative images, caricatures actually, of both Sue and Tom—and no real sense of either person. Who are they? How are they in relationship with one another? Where is the presence of the Holy Spirit at work in each and in the relationship? I am wondering about some of the contemporary and underlying social and cultural assumptions that are directing this conversation. Does Tom really care if their sessions last for an hour and a half, or is he conforming to "the fifty-minute hour" rule? Is God inviting Sue to reenter the pain of her childhood abuse, or is this what the supervisor strongly believes is necessary in the process of healing and growth toward wholeness? Is Tom able to follow and keep up with Sue? What would it be like for Tom to interrupt Sue or ask her to slow down? What kind of assistance does Sue need from Tom? What are Sue's spiritual goals? Is Sue comfortable with her conversational style? What might Tom do or say that would assist Sue in being the woman she is in God's eyes while maintaining his own sense of self?

Assumptions and Beliefs

The notion that supervision is a conversation that fosters the well-being of an absent other rests upon particular assumptions and beliefs that are important to name in order to further this conversation. I believe that all spiritual directors who are authentically called to this ministry want to assist directees in realizing their spiritual goals or desires—growing in relationship with God, entering into discernment regarding a particular decision, righting a relationship with another, discovering the presence of God in the ordinary, learning how to pray, or living a life of greater justice and compassion. Whatever the spiritual desire of the directee, the God-given "necessary dissatisfaction,"[4] spiritual directors want to assist their directees with these endeavors. This desire is admirable and fundamental to the call of spiritual directors.

Furthermore, as a spiritual director, I want to know how I, being the person I am, can assist my directee, being the person she is, in realizing her spiritual goals. I want to do this without being or becoming a different person. Or to say it more aptly: How do we as supervisors work with spiritual directors toward the spiritual well-being of absent directees without asking the spiritual director to become a different person than he or she is in the eyes of God?

This desire is rooted in my belief that each spiritual director is different. Each does direction coming out of his or her *unique person*. Our directees tell us this is the case, and they are sometimes smarter about these things than we are. Directees seek out directors they like, with whom they believe they will be comfortable, and they choose people they believe can assist them on their spiritual journeys. They are often very astute in their sense of themselves and their sense of the other, even when they are not very articulate about choosing someone as a director.

I had someone approach me about direction once. He had seen me in a small-group setting on two occasions, and we were having our first one-on-one conversation. He said to me, "I want to ask you to be my spiritual director." I was surprised at this and asked him to tell me more. He said, "I want you to be my spiritual director because you are the kind of person who would not hesitate to say 'that's bullshit!' to my blather, my evasions, and my delusions." Little did this fellow know he was speaking to a "genteel southern woman" (not that I took exception to his language; I did not). I said, as gently as I could, "You know, if this is what you are looking for, I think you really want someone else." For me, this was a moment of *great consideration* for the person who asked and a moment of *freedom and self-awareness* for myself. A week later, after several more encounters with each other in a group setting, the fellow came back. This time he said: "I was not correct about what I wanted when we last spoke. When I watch you work with others, how you are and the way you are, this is what I would like for myself in a spiritual director."

Directees approach directors whom they consider to be a good fit. Directors approach supervisors in the same way, and we all do direction and supervision coming out of our own person. In the work of supervision, we use our inner and outer senses to perceive and experience the director, his or her directee, and their relationship in and with God. We use our common sense, good judgment, personal and communal experience, expertise in the field, and knowledge of the tradition. We are particularly attuned to signs of life, freedom, compassion, justice, solidarity in suffering, enhanced self-identity before God, ability to stand in the truth, invitation, consolation, or a new word spoken as we encourage the director and foster the well-being of the absent directee. And we do this work of supervision within the confines of our personal gifts, strengths and limitations, and social and cultural contexts.

As with supervisors in supervision relationships, spiritual directors are invited to be themselves in direction relationships. I am not suggesting here that it is permissible to be oneself in a way that is harmful to a directee. Quite the contrary! But we can do only what we are able to do in a direction relationship. Or to put it a better way: We ought to do what we are able to do in our work with our directees and supervisees, being who we are in the eyes of God.

Supervision by Difference

Just as directees instruct directors about their desires, so spiritual directors instruct us, their supervisors, about their goals and desires—what they want to learn about themselves, how they are grappling with and responding to the endeavors of their directees being the persons they are, what they want to learn from us, and so on. I believe we do *supervision by difference*. This is not unlike what we know and do in our ordinary lives and relationships. Let's say, for example, I've gone to someone's home for dinner, and I come into the kitchen and ask, "How can I help?" Jim might respond by asking me to go to the store for something he needs. Someone like my mother would have said, "You can help best by staying out of the kitchen." (Not an easy one to hear, I might add, as a real way of helping.) Theresa might say, "Sit here and have a glass of wine with me; I hate cooking alone." Or one of my siblings would say, "How about if you mash the potatoes while I finish the salad?"

In supervision, we let the persons we are supervising instruct us about their goals and desires in our work with them. The practical implication of this is that I find myself doing supervision in significantly different ways with each person I supervise. And when I ask about the supervision work of others, I am amazed at the stories I hear about the different ways in which people approach the supervision process and each director they meet.

Models of Supervision

In the fields of psychotherapy, counseling, and pastoral care, there are a variety of models of supervision.[5] Allen K. Hess, professor of psychology at Auburn University, delineates six different models of psychotherapy supervision: Lecturer, Teacher, Case Conference, Collegial-Peer, Monitor, and Therapist. He also cites K. Watson, who suggests a similar typology: Supervisory Group, Case Consultation, Tutorial, Peer Group, Tandem, and Team.[6] Other practitioners and theoreticians suggest models or stages more specific to the supervisory relationship itself: inception, skill development, consolidation, and mutuality for the supervisee; beginning, exploration, and confirmation of supervisor identity for the supervisor.[7]

Models represent particular theoretical assumptions. Our assumptions are often based on what we believe about how human beings learn. Sometimes our foundational beliefs are simply based on notions near and dear to our hearts. A spiritual direction supervisor who is psychoanalytically oriented might look at the motivation of a director's conduct with a directee and then offer an analysis or interpretation of such conduct. A spiritual direction supervisor who uses a "client-centered" approach might encourage and teach a director certain beneficial listening responses.[8] Much of the work done in contemporary spiritual direction supervision is based on a particular psychotherapeutic model, whether consciously or unconsciously espoused. In spiritual direction supervision, models also conform to what we believe about how human beings are transformed in the direction of God.

I have already noted several of my own theoretical assumptions and beliefs underlying supervision with spiritual directors. Given what I believe about *supervision by difference*, I have no specific model of supervision to offer to supervisors. I would like to offer three scenarios in which my focus is centered on assisting an absent directee. In each of these instances I was led to do something different or to be present in a different way. In these encounters, the Holy Spirit seemed to be present and at work "simultaneously" on behalf of the absent directee, his or her spiritual director, and their relationships with one another and with God.

The Playful Imaginative Work of God: Learning through Doing

I have been a supervisor for and with other spiritual directors for about ten years. As the former administrator of a program in the art of spiritual direction, I have read hundreds of remembered snatches of dialogues between directors and directees. I have listened to directors describe directees and name what struck them. I have paid attention as directors have given accounts of their inner and outer responses to the direction conversation. Most important, I have been present as directors have tried to discern the presence and activity of the Holy Spirit in the life of the directee and the direction session. One thing I have noticed is that moments of freedom, insight, and transformation often occur in supervision in imaginative and playful ways, instructing both directors and supervisors about just what is needed.

Once, under appropriate circumstances, I was approached by a fellow staff member about a student spiritual director.[9] He told me that Jane was a strong person and others were intimidated by her strength. I knew Jane and found her to be open, straightforward, a somewhat circular thinker, and an amiable person. It so happened I was meeting with Jane the next day to review her supervised spiritual direction dialogues. One of Jane's remembered dialogues with a directee named Clare went like this:

Jane: I am learning something about imaginative experiences of God and how to take an imaginary walk toward Jesus. Would you like to try this with me?

Clare: Yes, I think I would.

Jane: Close your eyes and find a relaxed and comfortable way of sitting. . . . Take a few deep breaths. . . . Now let's imagine you are outside walking amidst beautiful trees going along a trail. . . .

Clare: Okay.

Jane: There's a river off to the left, and you are enjoying the sound of the water as it accompanies your footsteps. . . .

Clare: Uh . . . uh . . . You know, I'm not sure I really want to do this.

Jane: Let's keep on going. I think you will find it helpful.

Clare: Okay, but I'm not sure about this.

Jane: Let's go back to the trail, the beautiful trees and the lovely sound of the water. . . . Now you see a cave up ahead. You go in and wander around. . . . You find yourself drawn toward a light at the end of the cave, where Jesus stands, waiting to greet you. . . . What does Jesus look like or say to you?

Clare: I'm not sure what Jesus looks like. I don't see him, and he's not saying anything to me. . . . This doesn't feel real to me.

Jane: How about trying . . .

Clare: (interrupting) I would like to talk about work. You know how my boss has been lately.

Jane noted how Clare had shifted the conversation to the arena of her work life and continued to speak in this vein. She then asked me: "Why did Clare keep resisting me? What do you do when your directee keeps resisting you like this?"

My first concern in this situation was for the freedom of the absent directee and the label of "resistance" being placed upon her. My second concern was Jane's insistence on going down a path about which Clare seemed so uncertain. The latter concern could have been acknowledged, analyzed, and explored for a long time. But we did not discuss this. We began with conversation about the appropriate use of the imagination in a spiritual direction session. We spoke about the difference between directing the experience of the directee and exploring the meaning of the directee's own experience. What happened next was surprising and an utter gift. I suddenly found myself saying to Jane, "Let's try something different here." Jane agreed, and here is what happened:

Mary Rose: Jane, suppose you hold up your arm and hand as if you were going to give me a high five.

Jane: Okay.

Mary Rose: (holding up my hand in a similar position about a foot away from Jane's) Now suppose you take your hand and press it as hard as you can against mine.

Jane: (pressing her hand against mine) Okay.

Mary Rose: (pressing back) See if you can press harder.

Jane: Okay.

Jane presses harder and so do I. After twenty or thirty seconds of this, I let my hand simply fall back on its wrist. Jane's hand spontaneously fell back as well. Both of our hands were open and curved, with a small space in between, looking like the outer petals of a flower, ready to receive whatever was given as a gift. We were both quiet for a moment, only noticing and experiencing. Finally I said: "So you see? The next time you sense your directee is resisting you like this, you fall back and see where your directee wants to go."

Jane sat in silence, and the tears began to stream down her face. She spoke about how she had experienced "resistance" earlier in the day, only in this instance, she was the directee. In a small-group experience, a director-in-training had asked her to believe something about herself she knew to be untrue, and there had been a significant tug-of-war between them. As Jane ended her story, silence filled the room. She knew well what it was like to be in the place of Clare, her directee, and no more needed to be said. Jane and I had learned. We learned by doing. We learned through the imaginative, playful, and powerful presence of the Holy Spirit. In the future, Jane would know how to conduct herself, being the woman she is, with her directee named Clare.

The Slow Work of God: Patient Waiting and Readiness for Learning

There are moments when supervision seems to be filled with miracles. More often than not, however, it calls for a lot of patient waiting and attentive reliance on the steady and slow work of God.

John is a very competent spiritual director.[10] He is the pastor of a large Presbyterian church, a capable administrator, and an outstanding preacher. John exhibits great care for the church community and its individual members. He has been doing spiritual direction for many years. It is always a treat to see John, and he is a very fine spiritual director. His recollections of his direction conversations are a clear indication of his capacity to listen to others and his ability to notice the presence of God's Spirit.

John came to see me for supervision after several years as a spiritual director. In the beginning, he seemed somewhat fearful. He said it was difficult for him to hear much about his work as a spiritual director or accept encouraging and supportive comments. In supervision, John and I read dialogues of his spiritual direction conversations. John always opted to take the role of the director, and I read the remembered words of the directee. After a first reading and some conversation about John's stated desire for our work together, we would invariably read the dialogue a second time. This time, I would move into the actual role or person of the directee. Virtually, we would reenter the spiritual direction conversation. If John noticed something he would like to do or say in a different way, something he would like to underscore, something he had missed that he would like to pick up on in the future, or something he wanted to celebrate, he would tell me about it. I encouraged and supported John, and he grew in confidence.

About a year into our work together, I let John know that he was an outstanding listener, wonderful at summarizing, and had a gift for discovering and speaking about the presence of the Holy Spirit in the life of the directee. He was adept at conversation with others about their ongoing struggle to live in love, truth, justice, and fidelity to the Word of God. I also noticed that there was very little appropriate self-disclosure in John's responses to his directees. This made it difficult for John to accompany others in the midst of great suffering or joy. We had a conversation about the importance of particular kinds of self-disclosure to a spiritual direction relationship. Yet John's supervision dialogues changed very little in the months ahead.

Two years later, in a supervision session around a particular dialogue with little or no appropriate self-disclosure, John said to me in a timid voice, "I am afraid of intimacy, and I don't know how to be or what to say to my directees when I feel this way." I immediately and spontaneously replied to John: "Intimacy was once frightening to me, too. But I discovered that as soon as I began telling my directees my felt responses to them and to their stories, it became easy, and I felt fine. I think you will be fine, too." John hesitated for a moment, then sat back in his chair and said, "I wish you had told me this two years ago." (Ah! I thought to myself.)

All of us have things to learn about life, work, relationships, and the ways of God. Like directees, directors and supervisors learn these things in good time. In the work of supervision, we are often called to wait patiently and trust in the slow work of God.

Collegiality and Respectful Unknowing:
Remaining Together in God's Hidden Mystery

Supervision is a collegial affair. The terms *supervisor* and *supervisee* belie this reality in some respects. A supervision relationship includes significant, respectful, and mutual storytelling and disclosure—the kind of storytelling and disclosure that are beneficial to the absent directee.

Not long ago, a director named Jim stopped by to have a supervision conversation. Jim was concerned about Susan, a woman he had been seeing for spiritual direction for many years. Susan is a Roman Catholic laywoman. In the context of Spirit-filled discernment, Susan's call to become an ordained minister within the Roman Catholic tradition was affirmed. Susan received a master of divinity degree from an excellent Roman Catholic school of theology, yet she cannot be ordained. Jim bemoaned the state of affairs in the Catholic Church. He felt that Susan's call was authentic but was convinced nothing more could be done. He felt that he and Susan were stuck going over the same distress and difficulties again and again.

As a supervisor, I didn't know the answer to Jim's dilemma, but I could respectfully share a similar story with him. I began to tell Jim about a Roman Catholic sister I know named Jean Marie. Jean Marie had an authentic call to ordination within the Roman Catholic tradition. She, too, had a master of divinity degree from an outstanding Catholic school of theology. I told Jim that I also got discouraged about the structures and governance of the Church. I then told him a bit more about Jean Marie's ongoing discernment process. After graduation, Jean Marie found a parish willing to accept her as a deacon (the step just prior to full ordination to the priesthood in the Roman Catholic Church), if she should be ordained as such. She gathered together letters of recommendation from former seminary faculty members, parishioners, and friends. She wrote to the bishop of the diocese, sent him the letters of recommendation, and asked to be ordained to the diaconate. The bishop ultimately refused her request. But the public and prophetic witness she gave to so many people in the Church was remarkable.

After I recounted this incident, Tom and I sat in silence for a while. Then Tom said: "I'm very glad to hear that you, too, get discouraged about the Church. . . . Susan and I have had several conversations about how she might use her master of divinity degree now that she has graduated. But we have not asked whether there is some next step she is being invited to take toward ordination. I don't know how Susan might respond, or where God is leading her, but I think I now have some sense of how to assist her in continuing her journey in faith, hope, and love."

Supervision is a collegial process. Storytelling and appropriate self-disclosure on the part of the supervisor assists directors and absent directees. Supervisors are not experts on the spiritual lives of others—directors or absent directees.

They cannot know the fullness of the relationship between the director and directee, and they cannot know what spiritual directors ought to do or say to their directees. But they can know *how to know*. Supervisors can assist directors with various processes of discernment. They can help directors and their absent directees give voice to the range of their spiritual experiences. They can support the unique and mysterious personhood and God-directed lives of both.

Ultimately, supervision requires of us a respectful unknowing, a willingness to remain within God's Hidden Mystery. This is not an easy stance. It requires prayer for those we supervise, considerable discernment, and trust in the ongoing life of God. The guidance of the Spirit enables us to discern when a supervisee needs to be shown how to do something, when to wait patiently, when to be supportive, when to nudge in a different direction, when to tell stories, and when to be appropriately self-disclosive. In the end, we enter into supervision in order to be of assistance to others—absent others moving in the direction of God.

Notes

1. It is hoped that direction relationships foster connection between director and directee as well as with God and foster life.

2. I am indebted to Eric Greenleaf, Ph.D., and our many conversations about supervision for my present understanding of the goal of supervision for spiritual directors. Greenleaf is the author of *The Problem of Evil* (Phoenix: Zeig, Tucker & Theisen, Inc., 2000), a work that addresses what can be done in the aftermath of the sweep of evil into people's lives.

3. See Maureen Conroy's excellent work on the supervision of spiritual directors as a process of "Looking into the Well." I believe it is the best work to date from this particular perspective. Maureen Conroy, with a foreword by George Aschenbrenner, *Looking into the Well: Supervision of Spiritual Directors* (Chicago: Loyola University Press, 1995).

4. Philip Sheldrake, *Befriending Our Desires* (1994; Toronto: Novalis, 2001), page 58 of first edition.

5. As various theories of psychotherapy have developed, a variety of parallel models of supervision have been devised and advocated. See C. Edward Watkins Jr., ed., *Handbook of Psychotherapy Supervision* (New York: John Wiley & Sons, Inc., 1997). This work, and several other works on supervision in psychotherapy, offers chapters on supervision in psychoanalysis, in dialectical behavior therapy, in rational emotive behavior therapy, in cognitive therapy, in client-centered therapy, in gestalt therapy, and so forth. Each model of supervision is based on the assumptions and dynamics of the particular therapeutic mode in which its therapists are engaged.

6. See Allen K. Hess, "Training Models and the Nature of Psychotherapy Supervision," in *Psychotherapy Supervision: Theory, Research, and Practice*, Wiley Series on Personality Processes, edited by Allen K. Hess (New York: John Wiley & Sons, 1980), 15–25. See also Elizabeth Liebert's essay on the assumptions, differences, and possibilities of a psychodynamic model versus a pastoral circle model of supervision in "Accompaniment in Ministry: Supervision as Spiritual Formation," *Journal of Supervision and Training in Ministry* 18 (1997): 20–31.

7. This typology is suggested by Allen K. Hess, "Growth in Supervision: Stages of Supervisee and Supervisor Development" in *Supervision and Training: Models, Dilemmas, and Challenges*, edited by

Florence W. Kaslow (New York/London: The Haworth Press, 1986), 51–68. See also Janet Ruffing's description of the three stages of the supervision relationship as "Building the Alliance, The Working Alliance, and Concluding the Alliance," in "An Integrated Model of Supervision in Training Spiritual Directors," *Presence* 9, no. 1 (February 2003): 24–30.

8. See Hess's description of this phenomenon in the supervision of psychotherapy and counseling in "Growth in Supervision," 51–52.

9. This story is told with permission of the then spiritual-director-in-training. All names are fictitious.

10. This is a composite story of a number of directors with whom I have been in conversation about their ministry of spiritual direction.

CHAPTER TWO

Seeing Beyond: A Contemplative Approach to the Supervision Relationship

James Neafsey

What's really at the heart of the relationship between a supervisor and a spiritual director? What's supervision like at its best? When I asked myself these questions, a variety of ideas and images came to mind. A single sentence from Paul Scott's novel *The Towers of Silence* kept surfacing again and again. One of the characters in the novel, a retired missionary named Barbara, expresses her appreciation for her friend Sarah in these words:

> She looks at my old fond foolish face and sees through it, I think, sees below the ruination, hears behind the senseless, ceaseless chatter, sees right down to the despair but also beyond to the terrific thing there really is in me, the joy I would find in God and which she would find in life, which come to much the same thing.[1]

These words brought to mind some of my own cherished memories of being seen and seeing others in a contemplative way in marriage and friendship, in spiritual direction and supervision. These memories marked moments of trans-formation, sacred moments in which the mystery beneath surface appearances was revealed. Barbara's description of Sarah's gaze also spoke to my desires. It became clear to me that I want to be seen in this way by my own supervisor and that I want to bring this kind of deep, affirming vision to my practice of supervision. The compassionate, contemplative vision described in Scott's novel lies at the heart of the supervision relationship at its best. I am aware that such vision cannot be achieved simply by an act of will or by mastering a technique. The kind of seeing that Barbara describes comes as a gift, as pure grace. Though I can't invoke this kind of vision simply through an act of will, I can desire and seek this gift and welcome it when it comes.

Overseeing and Seeing Beyond

The centrality of vision in the supervision relationship is suggested by the word *supervision* itself. It is a compound formed by the root word *vision*, meaning "sight," and the prefix *super*, meaning "over, above, beyond, to an especially high degree." *Super-vision*, then, literally means *over-sight*, a meaning reflected in the dictionary definition of *supervise*: "to oversee (a process, work, workers, etc.) during execution or performance." This definition suggests a model in which the supervisor looks down from above, from a perspective of more knowledge, experience, or skill, at another's work or performance. In the context of spiritual direction, the task of the supervisor would be to oversee the work of the director, to help the director perform more wisely and skillfully in the direction relationship. In such a model, the director approaches the supervisor with the expectation that the supervisor's higher perspective will help solve problems, point out mistakes, affirm good performance, offer information and advice, and suggest helpful tips or techniques for improving the quality of direction.

This understanding of supervision is common in business and professional contexts, and many spiritual directors bring this perspective explicitly or implicitly to the process of supervision. Though the supervision of directors can and does involve overseeing performance, sharing information, and offering advice regarding specific problems and how to handle them, I do not believe that this model of supervision gets to the heart of the supervision relationship.

The prefix "super" means not just "over and above" but also "beyond, to an especially high degree." These alternate meanings suggest a different model of supervision, one that involves seeing beyond ordinary appearances or seeing with a high degree of vision. Barbara's description of Sarah's gaze, for example, focuses on Sarah's capacity to see *through* and *beyond* appearances, to see in an especially high or deep way. "She looks at my old fond foolish face and *sees through* it, I think, *sees below* the ruination, *hears behind* the senseless, ceaseless chatter, *sees right down* to the despair but also *beyond* to the terrific thing there really is in me. . . ."

There is something much deeper going on here than overseeing performance. Sarah's vision penetrates beyond physical appearance, external behavior, and even the depths of despair. Ultimately, Sarah sees beyond to Barbara's spiritual core, the place where she experiences joy in God. Sarah's spiritual vision does not exclude or ignore other levels of Barbara's experience. She sees Barbara's physical face marked by age and perceives her unique personality with all its gifts, flaws, and underlying emptiness. All dimensions of Barbara's experience are embraced in a contemplative vision that sees her particular qualities within the comprehensive spiritual horizon of her identity in God. Sarah's gaze sees beyond Barbara's personality to her spiritual height and depth in a way that allows room for the whole of who she is.

If the capacity to "see beyond" is central to supervision, then the primary focus of supervision will be the deep spiritual identity of the director, who he or she is in God, rather than correct or incorrect performance at the behavioral level. The supervisor's role is not so much to measure the director's behavior against extrinsic standards of right and wrong, but to behold the unique image of God at the core of the director. Within this open, spacious spiritual horizon, attention can be given to whatever level of the director's experience needs attention at the moment, including issues of performance and skill.

Ira Progoff's description of the vision required of a depth psychologist sheds further light on what "seeing beyond" in supervision entails:

> On the surface of the personality one will see the disturbances and conflicts which could easily be misanalyzed as the symptoms of pathology. It is necessary to feel beyond these to what is present but latent in the depths of the person. It is necessary to reach through to what is there but has not yet disclosed itself . . . to reach and affirm that seed of meaningful life in the other person even while it has not yet made itself visible. This is why it is basically an attitude of love. . . . He who feels the beauty of the tulip while it is still in bulb covered by the snow has love for the tulip.[2]

Progoff acknowledges the disturbances and conflicts that manifest at the surface level of personality, just as Sarah recognized Barbara's neurotic chatter and saw her underlying despair. He cautions against viewing and analyzing these disturbances with a clinical eye, however. Instead, he urges the depth psychologist to see with a contemplative eye, to "feel beyond" to the inner beauty of the person just as Sarah did when she saw the "terrific thing" there really was in Barbara. Progoff notes that seeing beyond is basically an attitude of love in which one intuits the goodness and beauty of a person's deepest self. Seeing and feeling beyond help call that self forth into realization.

A Gospel Account of Seeing Beyond

The encounter of Jesus with the rich young man in Mark 10:17–22 offers a scriptural example of the power of seeing beyond to the inner depths of a person. A wealthy young man approaches Jesus, seeking to know what he must do to inherit eternal life. The man addresses Jesus as the "good teacher," the expert who has a higher perspective, more experience and wisdom, the one who can presumably tell him what to do to reach his goal. Jesus appears uncomfortable with this role and with the request itself. He directs the man's attention away from goodness as a personal possession to God as the ultimate source of goodness. Then Jesus recommends that the man keep the commandments.

So far, the dialogue has remained at the surface levels of correct behavior and the conventional social roles of teacher and student. When the young man insists that he has kept the commandments since his earliest days, however, Jesus seems to sense an opportunity for a deeper level of relationship. Mark writes, "Jesus looked steadily at him and loved him . . ." (10:21).[4] Jesus then invites the man to let go of his former life, sell his riches and distribute the money to the poor, and join the company of his disciples. The young man, at least for the moment, is unable or unwilling to accept the invitation. The cost is too high, and he goes away sad.

This story can shed light on the contemplative nature of the supervision process. Like the rich young man, directors often come to supervision in search of answers or advice from a "good teacher" about "what they must do." Perhaps they have tried to practice the commandments of good spiritual direction but have come to sense in an obscure way that there is more to spiritual direction than simply doing or saying the right things. When directors come for supervision, their supervisors face a choice. Supervisors can respond as good teachers who oversee performance and make recommendations about correct or incorrect performance, or they can see beyond to the wholeness and spiritual freedom of directors and take the risk of meeting them at that depth.

It is not always the supervisor who initiates a shift in the level of relationship. Often the director will spontaneously move into the depths, and the supervisor will be faced with the challenge of letting go of conventional wisdom and the security of a well-defined role for a more real and creative personal encounter. What will happen if the director and supervisor both take the risk? No one knows, but the story suggests that both the cost and the potential rewards are high. Supervision grounded in seeing beyond is shaped and informed by the commandments of good direction and professional ethics, but it is also open to following unique and unpredictable paths when the call to do so occurs.

The agenda of supervision in this model is set by the demands of the emerging seed of spiritual selfhood in the director rather than by extrinsic norms of performance. Still, performance and person, law and grace, formation and transformation need to be held in creative tension in the supervisory relationship. There is a place in supervision for learning objective dos and don'ts, but at its best, the supervision relationship challenges both supervisor and director to deep intuitive knowing and surrender to the surprising invitations of grace. In my experience, the most powerfully transforming moments in supervision have occurred when both director and supervisor have met at a depth beyond social roles and extrinsic norms.

Supervision and the Discernment of Foundational Identity

To see beyond surface appearances to the intangible spiritual identity at the core of oneself or another is the most fundamental task of spiritual discernment. Discernment is usually defined as the process of distinguishing or sifting through interior movements to discover whether their origin is from God or some other source, such as one's own ego, cultural conditioning, or a spirit of evil. Discernment can also refer to the process of weighing alternative courses of action in order to choose the one that seems most congruent with God's will.

Before one can discern inner movements or outer choices, however, one must have a reliable touchstone, a felt sense of one's authentic identity in God that can serve as a fundamental criterion of discernment. As Wendy Wright states: "[Discernment] is not simply about resisting what is evil, self-absorbed, or destructive. It is about foundational identity. It is about who we know ourselves ultimately to be."[3] This core identity is not static. It seeks dynamic expression in the world and implicitly contains a sense of call or mission. For example, when Jesus saw through to the spiritual core of the rich young man and loved him, the man was challenged to become the new self he had discovered himself to be in the gaze of Jesus, even before Jesus explicitly articulated his call. The young man's sadness arose from his refusal to follow the call to realize his foundational spiritual identity.

There is an organic relationship between discernment of foundational identity and discernment of interior movements and courses of action. This relationship between identity and action can be seen in the stories of the baptism and temptations of Jesus. At his baptism, Jesus discerns his foundational identity as the Son of God in a revelatory moment at the river Jordan. He experiences God's deep love for and delight in his core identity. In the temptations in the desert that follow the baptism, Jesus begins to work out the implications of his identity in terms of interior movements toward specific actions and roles in the world. Satan frames his temptations in terms of the God-centered sense of self that Jesus experienced at his baptism. "*If you are the Son of God*, tell these stones to turn to bread . . . fall at my feet and worship me . . . throw yourself down from the temple" (Luke 4:1–13).[5] Jesus rejects these possible courses of action as incongruent with his foundational identity as God's Son that he experienced at his baptism.

The stories of the baptism and temptations of Jesus suggest two important and related tasks in the supervision of spiritual directors. *First supervisors help directors see and experience their foundational identity in God; then supervisors help directors distinguish authentic and inauthentic expressions of that identity in the actual practice of direction.*

Charism: The Expression of a Director's Foundational Identity

The dynamic expression of one's unique spiritual identity in relationship to others is called a *charism*, a word derived from the Greek *charis*, meaning "favor" or "gift." According to John Haughey, a charism is "the specific way one concerns oneself with another's or the community's good. It is the specific way one loves others."[6] Charisms, then, are spiritual gifts that make their recipients into distinct and original manifestations of God's love and grace in community. This does not mean a charism is simply a particular type of action. "A charismed person, it would seem, is rather a matrix of gifts, with virtues mixed with graces, with character traits, with genes, with talents—all sublated by the Spirit, which bundles these together into a giftedness that is *sui generis.*"[7]

The term *sublated* means that natural gifts, talents, and traits are raised to a new level that includes and preserves all their natural properties, yet also carries them forward to fuller realization in a broader spiritual context. For example, a person gifted with a cheerful temperament might find that gift sublated by the Spirit into the charism of spiritual joy. A person blessed with keen intelligence and good judgment might have that natural gift sublated into the gift of spiritual discernment. The individual's experience of God suffuses natural temperament through his or her charism, a gift or talent with a particular spiritual efficacy that makes God present in that individual in a unique and original way.

Spiritual direction itself is a charism, but within that broad category there are many individual ways of expressing that gift. When I reflect on the charisms of experienced directors that I know, I am aware that each has responded to a common call to spiritual direction, and yet each expresses that call in a uniquely personal way. One manifests a charism for insight, discernment, and clear articulation. Another exudes a sense of compassion and nurturing care. Another manifests a quality of simplicity and vulnerability. Still another has a provocative style that speaks truth forthrightly and with love. These charisms are closely related to distinctive personality traits that were no doubt present in these directors from childhood, but their natural gifts have been integrated as adults into their relationship with God. One feels God present in and through their particular personal qualities. By authentically being themselves, these directors mediate God's presence and implicitly encourage their directees to find and be their own unique selves in God.

Supervision: Drawing Forth the Charism of a Director

One of the fundamental tasks of supervision, then, is to recognize, affirm, and draw forth the particular charism of the director. For example, a supervisor might encourage a director to notice and reflect on his or her individual strengths, special talents, and personal qualities. Or the supervisor might invite a director to explore where he or she feels the most joy, passion, freedom, or ease in the direction relationship. It is not necessary, or perhaps even possible, for supervisors and directors to name charisms in a succinct verbal formula as I did above. It is more important for directors to get a feel for when they are living and speaking from their authentic selves, even if they cannot define what this means in a clear and distinct way.

In one supervision session, a director spoke of how he finally understood what spiritual direction was all about. He compared his new insight to learning how to ride a bike as a child. Just as he once discovered from experience the way to maintain balance on a bike, so he had learned through personal experience in a particular direction session how to lean back into God and trust the spontaneous guidance of the Spirit. The subtle sense of self-consciousness and anxiety about performance that had characterized his mode of direction until that point seemed to simply disappear. He was now more at home with himself. His natural gifts for compassionate listening and intuitive perception were at the service of the Spirit in a freer, more spontaneous way.

Without being able to define exactly what he had discovered, it was clear to this director that he had touched his charism, his unique way of being himself and loving another in the context of spiritual direction. He was visibly more relaxed, humble, grateful, and confident. This experience became a touchstone that helped him discern whether he was living and acting out of his authentic charism or whether anxiety and self-consciousness had taken over in some subtle way.

Development of Charisms

The charism of a person is intertwined with deep psychological and genetic roots, as well as with an individual's foundational spiritual identity. Therefore, the charism itself does not change essentially over time. Nevertheless, it does grow and develop according to its own inner dynamism in interaction with the demands and opportunities presented by changing external circumstances. In "The Father Confessor," Hermann Hesse tells the story of how the charisms of two desert fathers developed over a lifetime.[8]

One of these two men, Joseph Famulus (Latin for "servant"), withdrew to the desert at the age of thirty. Over the course of many years of prayer and fasting, Joseph discovered and developed a unique charism of listening.

In Josephus . . . a gift slumbered, and with the passing years, as his hair began to gray, it slowly came to flower. It was the gift of listening. Whenever a brother from one of the hermitages, or a child of the world harried and troubled of soul, came to Joseph and told him of his deeds and sufferings, temptations, and missteps, related the story of his life, his struggle for goodness and his failures in the struggle, or spoke of loss, pain, or sorrow, Joseph knew how to listen to him, to open his ears and his heart, to gather the man's sufferings and anxieties into himself and hold them, so that the penitent was sent away emptied and calmed. Slowly, over long years, this function had taken possession of him and made an instrument of him, an ear that people trusted.[9]

Joseph's reputation spread, and gradually more and more pilgrims and penitents came to him, drawn by his charism of compassionate listening.

Hesse writes that Joseph was sometimes mentioned in the same breath as another great hermit named Dion Pugil (Latin for "boxer"), who was blessed with a quite different charism:

> Father Dion was celebrated for being able to read the souls of those who sought him out without recourse to words. He often surprised a faltering penitent by charging him bluntly with his still unconfessed sins. . . . Father Dion was also a wise counselor of erring souls, a great judge, chastiser, and rectifier. He assigned penances, castigations, and pilgrimages, ordered marriages, compelled enemies to make up, and enjoyed the authority of a bishop.[10]

The charisms of these two men were at opposite ends of the spectrum. Joseph the Servant operated out of a gentle, nondirective model of spiritual direction that emphasized silence, listening, patience, and compassion in response to penitents. Dion the Boxer, on the other hand, operated out of a directive, confrontational model. He was gifted with an acute sense of discernment and demanded honesty and accountability from those who confessed to him. Despite their radically different styles, both monks were revered for their holiness and were eagerly sought out by penitents.

After many years of ministry, Dion and Joseph simultaneously reach a point of spiritual crisis. Both begin to doubt their call as the limits and shadows of their particular charisms become increasingly evident. As doubt deepens into despair, each is moved to leave home to seek out the other for advice. At an oasis midway between their hermitages, Joseph meets an old monk and explains to him the purpose of his journey without realizing that he is speaking to Dion. Dion realizes that if he tells Joseph that he, too, has reached the point of despair, the younger monk will surely be lost.

Dion reveals his identity to Joseph and hears his confession, but chooses to conceal his own struggle with despair. He then invites Joseph to join him at his hermitage to help with everyday tasks and hospitality for the penitents. Gradually Dion draws Joseph back into the ministry of sacred listening. Years later, shortly before his death, Dion confesses his secret to Joseph. By this time, both men have been transformed through wrestling with inner darkness and by their relationship to one another. Dion is noticeably more gentle and often listens patiently to penitents rather than bluntly chastising them for their sins. Joseph is now painfully aware of the harsh judgments he secretly entertains concerning some penitents. Through dialogue with Dion about these troubling thoughts and feelings, Joseph gradually comes to greater self-knowledge and freedom. Each monk slowly learns from the other how to confront the limits and shadows of his particular charism, as well as how to develop the qualities that complement his natural strengths.

Hesse's story makes clear that a director's charism is a living thing that grows and matures over time. Discovering one's charism and acting out of one's strengths is the first phase of a lifelong unfolding of one's call. Later phases may include painful discoveries about the limits of one's strengths and the nature of one's weaknesses. A director may eventually be driven by dissatisfaction to leave his or her comfort zone and begin a long journey into unexplored territory for the sake of further development and renewal. Finally, there remains the important task of developing a sustained, life-giving relationship with one's shadow. A supervisor's role, then, involves more than simply helping directors discover and affirm their charisms. The supervisor also challenges directors to face the limits and shadows of their gifts. The integration of this kind of self-knowledge into a director's personal life and practice of direction is at the heart of the transformational process of supervision.

The Supervision Process

So what does the transformational process of supervision look like in practice? How does a contemplative stance of "seeing beyond" actually unfold in a supervision session? Each situation is unique, but the following imaginary supervision dialogue may help ground the ideas presented above. In this session, Dion the Boxer discusses with his supervisor his responses to his initial direction session with Joe the Servant.

Dion: I just have to tell you right off the bat that I am really frustrated! I have this new directee, I'll call him "Joe," who just sits there, quiet as a mouse. Hardly says a word. Directing him is like pulling teeth! I feel like we're both wasting time!

Supervisor: Dion, I hear your frustration and anger. Tell me more about what's going on.

Dion: That's just it—nothing is going on! I ask a question. He sits there . . . thinking . . . real quiet. Then he comes out with a sentence or two. Then silence again. I can't get this guy to talk!

Supervisor: Let's take a look at what's going on in *you*. You clearly have some very strong responses to what's happening.

Dion: Yeah . . . well, I'm angry. I feel like I'm doing all the work, like
             it's all up to me to keep the session going. That seems to be the
             story of my life. I feel like I'm surrounded by passive, incompe-
             tent people who expect me to take control and lead the way. Joe
             is just the latest in a long line of them. Frankly, I'm getting tired
             of it! *Real* tired of it.

Supervisor: So, you're angry . . . not just with Joe, but at the role you've
             played, the story you've been in, for your whole life. And not
             just angry, but tired, real tired.

Dion: Yeah . . . the role of the strong one, the one who takes the ini-
             tiative, gets things going. . . . It's wearing thin, getting old. I
             resent being put in that position all the time. I'm just losing
             interest in it. I guess Joe just triggered all that.

Supervisor: Triggered the feelings of resentment and loss of interest?

Dion: Yes . . . resentment that others still expect me to carry the ball
             all the time.

Dion came to supervision full of anger and frustration at what he perceived
as Joe's passivity and silence. The supervisor gently redirects Dion back to what
is going on inside him. He invites Dion to stay with his anger and not simply
project it onto Joe. The supervisor acknowledges the anger without judgment
but sees beyond it. He senses there is more to come and invites Dion to explore
further. Dion rather quickly sees that his anger is directed not so much at Joe,
but at the constricting story that has shaped his life. Dion believes he must play
the role of the strong, independent leader who takes initiative and responsibility
because passive, incompetent people around him are unwilling or unable to do
so. The supervisor reflects back to Dion his anger and frustration, as well as his
dissatisfaction and weariness with this story and the role he plays in it. As the
dialogue continues, he next invites Dion to explore his experience of dissatisfaction more deeply:

Supervisor: Tell me about your dissatisfaction.

Dion: Hmmm. . . . (speaking more slowly now) Well, I just don't seem
             to care like I used to. It used to be really important to me to be
             strong and competent and respected . . . even feared. But like I
             said, that's wearing thin. It feels more and more like a burden, a
             weight I'm always carrying around.

Supervisor: I can sense the heaviness of it as you speak. What would it feel
             like if you let the burden of being the strong, competent,
             respected one go?

Dion: (after keeping silent for a moment) I was going to say I'd be relieved, but actually what came up inside was a feeling of fear . . . but I can't get a hold on what that fear is.

Supervisor: Take your time. Stay with it. See what comes up about that fear . . .

Dion: (pauses) I don't know . . . that's part of what makes it scary. If I let go of being the strong one, I don't know who I would be. I want to let go of the burden . . . but then . . . who would I be? What would I do? When I face that "not knowing," I feel fear in the pit of my stomach.

Supervisor: What's at the heart of that fear? Stay with it and see what comes . . .

Dion: (after waiting in silence for a while) Oh my God! What came up was an image of Joe! I'm afraid if I let go of being in charge, I'll end up like Joe! That I'll be seen, or see myself, as weak and passive . . . and that feels . . . well . . . *contemptible* is the word that comes to mind. I feel like this is what I've been running from, this is what I've been afraid to look at. Maybe this is why I was so upset with Joe!

In this portion of the dialogue, Dion begins to contemplatively explore his dissatisfaction and the ambivalence it evokes. He wants to let go of the burden of always being strong and competent, but he also fears the unknown that letting go would open up inside. As he stays with these uncomfortable feelings, an image of Joe emerges that represents his fears of appearing weak and passive and contemptible. Dion begins to make connections between his own feelings of ambivalence about exploring these feelings in himself and the intensity of his reaction to Joe in the direction session. His supervisor again refrains from judging these emerging feelings and insights as he gently encourages Dion to open up to what is spontaneously revealing itself.

Supervisor: So Joe is an image for that scary, contemptible place of weakness and passivity inside. See if you can allow some space for those feelings inside. See if you can stop running from them and actually welcome them.

Dion: (after silence for about one minute) Underneath the fear, I feel a deep weariness and sadness. I feel like I have pushed and pushed and pushed myself for so long. I am just so tired . . . and sad that I have been running and pushing for so long. But the sadness isn't a bad thing. . . . There's a feeling of . . . tenderness . . .

and vulnerability. When I actually let it in I feel a kind of soft-ening inside. . . . And I feel peaceful . . . not so afraid. I've always labeled these feelings as weakness or passivity, but they are really not so negative at all. They have a kind of fullness to them . . . and a sweetness that feels . . . well . . . satisfying.

Supervisor: A satisfying fullness, a sense of sweetness and peace . . .

Dion: Yes . . . I feel like I am in touch with something holy, something sacred. And to think it has always been there waiting on the other side of my fear and weariness!

Supervisor: Something holy and sacred just on the other side of fear . . .

Dion: Yes . . . something holy. God is in this place . . . and I never knew it. . . . This changes everything.

Supervisor: Changes everything? In what way?

Dion: I already see Joe in a different light. I get a sense that he knows something about what I've just experienced, that he knows this tender face of God in a way that is new to me. I've labeled him as passive and dependent, just like I labeled part of my own self that way. But maybe that's not who he is at all. I have something to learn from him. I think I can be a little more patient with his silences. I want to approach Joe next time with more respect . . . even reverence. There's something deep and holy and mysteri-ous going on.

Supervisor: Let's talk about "next time." Do you have a sense of how you might integrate this new awareness into your next session with Joe? . . .

When Dion actually experiences the weakness and passivity he has feared, his feelings begin to transform. His weariness and sadness change gently to tender-ness and vulnerability. He experiences a sense of peace and fullness and sweetness as he allows these feelings into his heart. He begins to touch his deep spiritual core, where a sense of sacredness and reverent love begin to well up spontaneously. Dion has moved through his deep fears and darkness to the "terrific thing" there really is in him, the tenderness and compassion that can deepen and complement his natural strength and assertiveness. Having touched these deeply human and holy qualities inside, he sees his relationship to Joe in an entirely new way. Dion, with the help of his supervisor, has seen beyond his conditioned personality to his own sacred core. He is now open to seeing beyond superficial labels to Joe's sacred core as well. An overall shift in perception and felt experience has taken place. Where judgment and rigidity existed, there are now reverence, humility, and openness. Within this new perspective, the supervisor invites Dion to address specific ways he might respond to Joe.

This account is a condensed version of a process that may unfold over many sessions of supervision. Similar dialogues may need to occur several times in various contexts for the fundamental shift described here to really take root. Not every session will include important breakthroughs or intense experiential shifts in perception and identity. Some sessions may focus more on the practical implications of a transformation in perception. The director and supervisor may discuss the choices a director faces, such as when to speak and when to remain silent, whether to share one's own experience, where to focus attention, or how to ask evocative questions. The imaginary dialogue above, however, exemplifies the spontaneously unfolding process that is the central focus of a contemplative approach to supervision.

Supervision as a Guest House

The poem "Guest House," by the Sufi mystic Rumi, offers several images that capture the contemplative spirit and dynamic process of supervision as understood in the "seeing beyond" model I have been describing.[11] If one were to substitute "supervision" for "being human" in the first line, the poem would offer a rich and evocative description of a contemplative approach to supervision.

The Guest House

This being human is a guest house.
Every morning a new arrival.

A joy, a depression, a meanness,
some momentary awareness comes
as an unexpected visitor.

Welcome and entertain them all!
Even if they're a crowd of sorrows,
who violently sweep your house
empty of its furniture,
still, treat each guest honorably.
He may be clearing you out
for some new delight.

The dark thought, the shame, the malice,
meet them at the door laughing,
and invite them in.

Be grateful for whoever comes,
because each has been sent
as a guide from beyond.

The image of the guest house suggests that the supervisory relationship can be thought of as a safe haven in which the director and supervisor welcome the moment-by-moment unfolding of the director's immediate experience. We can imagine a supervisor standing with the director "at the door" between the relatively familiar realms of the conditioned personality and the unknown realms of "the beyond." Together they focus attention on the "new arrivals" that appear in the form of spontaneous experiences of joy, sorrow, depression, shame, meanness, and malice. Though these visitors are unexpected, the sequence of their appearance carries a thread of meaning and direction. It is as if another intelligence and a deeper purpose wiser than one's conscious mind is at work. As Rumi puts it, "Each has been sent as a guide from the beyond."

Dion and his supervisor welcomed the unexpected visitors of fear, vulnerability, sadness, weariness, tenderness, and peace. Each feeling swept part of Dion's house empty of the furniture of old assumptions and expectations, allowing space for the next feeling or insight to arise. Neither Dion nor his supervisor attempted to anxiously figure out what was happening. To do so would have interrupted the stream of experience that arrived in a gradual but steady flow. Only in retrospect does the wisdom carried by the succession of unexpected guides from the beyond become apparent.

The stance of the supervisor and director is essentially one of hospitality toward whatever thoughts and feelings arise. Rumi advises us to "be grateful for whoever comes," to "welcome and entertain them all," and to "treat each guest honorably." Even when dark thoughts, shame, and malice appear, Rumi tells us to "meet them at the door laughing, and invite them in." This is easier said than done. When unsettling thoughts and feelings threaten one's deep sense of self, it is difficult to welcome them with gratitude and humor. Fear and dread are more likely to be the initial responses. It can help enormously at such moments to see oneself through the eyes of a supervisor who has learned to welcome such unexpected guests as integral aspects of wholeness. This is precisely what Sarah's gaze did for her friend when Barbara looked into her eyes and saw herself loved and accepted for the whole of who she was. Sarah's gaze allowed Barbara to say yes to her dark thoughts of despair, as well as the deep joy within her. At its best, the supervisory relationship can provide a welcoming guest house for the whole of a director's experience. It can help the director see beyond surface appearances to the mystery at work in the depths.

Notes

1. Paul Scott, *The Towers of Silence* (New York: Avon Books, 1979), 175; cited in Alan Jones, *Exploring Spiritual Direction: An Essay on Christian Friendship* (New York: Seabury Press, 1982), 26.

2. Ira Progoff, *The Symbolic and the Real* (New York: McGraw-Hill Book Company, 1963), 62.

3. Wendy Wright, "Passing Angels: The Art of Spiritual Discernment," *Weavings*, vol. 10, no. 6 (1995): 10.

4. Biblical citation taken from The Jerusalem Bible.

5. Author's paraphrase.

6. John Haughey, *Revisiting the Idea of Vocation* (Washington, D.C.: The Catholic University of America Press, 2004), 14.

7. Ibid., 12.

8. Hermann Hesse, *Magister Ludi (The Glass Bead Game)* (New York: Bantam, 1982), 454–83. "The Father Confessor" is one of three short stories that appear at the end of *Magister Ludi.*

9. Ibid., 455–56.

10. Ibid., 457.

11. Rumi, *The Essential Rumi*, translated by Coleman Barks with John Moyne, A.J. Arberry, Reynold Nicholson (HarperSanFrancisco, 1995), 109.

CHAPTER THREE

Seeing with Clarity:
Defining the Supervision Task

Rebecca Bradburn Langer

Assumptions are often an unspoken guide to one's work as a supervisor, and articulating them is key to having a clear sense of how you work as a spiritual director. In 2002, in preparation for a workshop on supervision sponsored by the Program in Christian Spirituality at San Francisco Theological Seminary, my colleagues and I conducted a workshop for supervisors. These are the basic assumptions that Mary Rose Bumpus, Joan Currey, and I chose as grounding for supervision work:

- God is the prime mover in a session, so the goal, of supervisor and supervisee together, is to be attentive to the movement of God.
- Supervisors are seeking for themselves and their directees to "grow into their unique God image," discovering both their challenges and gifts.
- Supervisors assist supervisees by means of their own unique being in God.
- God loves both the supervisor and the supervisee, just as they are.
- It is the supervisee and God's spirit that determine the agenda of the meeting, grounded in human experiences, desires, feelings, resistances, and longings.
- The process is contemplative.

Because your own assumptions about supervision are foundational for the supervisory process, you are urged to examine your assumptions around the call you have to supervision.

In my training as a supervisor, I was fixated on how to do supervision right. How could I facilitate a session where the heavens would open and the supervisee miraculously be transformed? I am exaggerating. I was not nearly as focused on "me" as I was on "them." But I viewed supervision more as a "change agent," not as a way of embracing directors right where they are. I was not grounded in my own "belovedness," but led more by my nervousness concerning what it was I didn't do well in a particular session. Although we can improve our supervision skills by being more aware of that which evades or sidetracks us from the movement of God in each session, we are, first and foremost, beloved of God. That raises a question: Is supervision something we do or something we are?

My first experience with supervision was one of being thrown into leadership of a group as it was doing a form of peer supervision. At that time, I had little firsthand experience of supervision and wasn't clear about where to focus. I felt unsure, frightened, and out of my league. After that start, it has been hard for me to accept my own giftedness in supervision. Only in the last few years, after twenty years of doing direction, have I found real freedom as a spiritual director, let alone as a supervisor. As is often the case, because of my doubting spirit, it took one of my colleagues to see something in me that might engender a good supervisor and invite me to teach supervision.

I accepted my colleague's challenge because I know God is often the voice behind an appeal to risk. Besides, I have this ever-gnawing desire for continued self-growth, skill, and confidence for myself as director and supervisor. I want to be all God has called me to be, not only as a director and supervisor, but most especially as a daughter of God. So I have a sense that perhaps supervision isn't so much something I do as something I am. I seek to ground myself in God's everlasting love and affection and supervise from that place. Perhaps that is why you are reading this book.

The Task of Supervision

Clearly understanding and reflecting on what you hope to attend to in supervision will enable you to more carefully assess your growth toward these goals. The following areas are important to achieve clarity regarding the task of supervision:

- An understanding of how consultation fits into the role of supervision.
- A clear definition of the supervision task for oneself, along with a clear focus by supervisees on what they desire to explore in their time.
- Careful attention to how to prepare oneself as supervisor and hold the space for the person who comes for supervision.
- Basic precepts that sustain and root the practice of supervision.
- Attention to possible places for growth and healing for oneself, as well as the supervisee.

- Articulation of what definitely is not supervision.
- Referral with grace as part of the art of the discipline, and clarity about times when one simply should not proceed with a supervisee without the assistance of outside expertise.
- Continual grounding in God and focusing on God's Spirit at work in the supervisee, and celebrating God's mystery revealed, both in the supervisee and in one's role as supervisor.

Consultation

In consultation, the *focus* shifts from the supervisee to the directee. A definition of consultation is "all that focuses on the *directee's* story," as well as "discussion that helps the supervisee grow in specific skills to enhance the supervision process." For example, the supervisee may ask: "How do I do a closing session with someone who is moving from the area? I want to evaluate and celebrate our time together." The supervisor might suggest a type of examen of the supervision sessions, with questions such as these: "Tell me about a time that you want to savor as you recall our sessions. Tell me about a time that was a challenge."

The supervisor's "toolbox" for assisting directors and valuing the sacredness of their time together is enhanced by learning a variety of ways to approach situations. Consultation questions such as "How long should my sessions last with the directee?" or "What do I do when the directee misses three sessions in a row?" are typical. Discussion with an experienced person helps the supervisee gain confidence and perspective. Consultation is an invaluable part of supervision, particularly in helping build what I call a "toolbox," which collects some possible ways to explore an issue. It also encourages and supports supervisees in claiming their own voice in particular direction sessions. For more on this topic, you may want to look at Maureen Conroy's summary of consultation in her classic book on supervision, *Looking into the Well*.[1]

Prayerful Preparation and Accountability

Supervision is an act of being accountable not only to those we serve, but also to the faith community at large. We are not out there on our own, but bound to those with whom we live and work. As supervisors, we are morally and ethically responsible for how we foster the art of supervision.

Supervision is not done in a haphazard way. A phrase I hear in spirituality circles is that "you cannot go where you have not been." In other words, we must venture into our own realm of prayer and practice before we can be someone else's companion there. Our own growth will be reflected in the growth of those we serve.

To be accountable as supervisors, we must be engaged in our own journey of faith and self-reflection. A personal rule of life, including the specific disciplines of doing justice, praying, and engaging Scripture, intertwined with practicing the presence of God each moment of each day, sets a framework for our spiritual well-being. What inhibits our spiritual well-being? Perhaps the greatest danger for supervisors lies in believing we can be truthful and honest without examining our lives in the presence of others. We can assess our own self-growth using questions such as these: Am I duly attending to my faith journey with a spiritual director and supervisor? Is prayer a part of my daily discipline? Do I truly believe I am a son or daughter of God, forgiven, blessed, and loved infinitely by God? Do I take time in solitude and retreat, listening for God's voice in my life?

Part of the excitement of engaging in supervision is the grace of personal growth. God, the "hound of heaven," lovingly pursues us. God delights in us and in our desire to be open to self-revelation. Our world is transformed as we more fully embrace our gifts and graces, as well as our shortcomings. This personal spiritual preparation is a gift we offer the supervisee in order to be faithful to the supervision process.

In addition to our personal spiritual preparation, supervisors create safe, inviting space for the supervision session. We need a place that slows the hustle and bustle of daily life and helps us move into a space of centered attention. The space should be free of clutter and completely void of items that will result in distraction, perhaps with just a few pieces of art, something from nature, or a simple candle. The space should speak of hospitality, inviting supervisees to leave behind the busyness of the day and be present to God and the experience they bring.

Strict Confidentiality

Supervision provides a wide, spacious, safe space, and confidentiality is essential to keeping it that way. The supervisee may enter the space full of ambivalence and confusion. Supervisors offer a confidential place where supervisees can safely relay what happened within them as they reflect on their experience with a directee.

Confidentiality is the bedrock for trust. Being able to speak and be heard in confidence can be a doorway to freedom. It also provides supervisees with a place to grapple with issues that confound them in sessions. It is truly a gift to have a person who listens, full of mercy and compassion, receptive to whatever is spoken, but holding it in strict confidence. Often a deep intimacy develops in the supervisor-supervisee relationship because of the gift of honest, confidential sharing.

It is not easy to provide strict confidentiality when supervisees live and work in a place where other directors or supervisors are acquainted with the parties involved. In a small community, it is likely that people know who is being seen by whom. It is an injustice to those we serve if we reveal even a hint of personal detail about them to another. Serious consideration must be given as to how best to maintain confidentiality. In some circumstances, supervisors may advise supervisees to consider getting away from the place where they reside and see a supervisor who has little knowledge of people in their communities. Supervisees may have to travel an hour or so out of the area, but it is a way of truly honoring the seriousness of the confidentiality pledge.

Growing in Knowledge of God and Self

Amazing transformations take place as folks come to intimately know themselves. This often occurs as supervisees recognize that nothing they say will shock the supervisor. The truth about oneself can be said and is received openly. So often we are our own worst inquisitors, and to speak aloud those things we hold so closely can result in real freedom. John Calvin writes about self-knowledge as related to knowledge of God when he says in the first chapter of *Institutes of Christian Religion*, "Nearly all the wisdom we possess, that is to say, true and sound wisdom, consists of two parts: the knowledge of God and of ourselves. But, while joined by many bond which one precedes and brings forth the other is not easy to discern."[2]

As we learn about ourselves, we learn about the God who created us. Supervision is a vehicle in which the supervisor explores with the supervisee who the supervisee is as God's beloved.

One of my favorite stories is about Rabbi Zusya, which comes in a variety of versions, but all with the same proclamation relating to our divine, "one of a kind being" created by God.[3] As he ages, Rabbi Zusya, a wise and good man, tells his friends of his distress. Zusya realizes he must go before God soon. He worries that he will be asked, "Why were you not Moses?" or "Why were you not like Joshua?" But his friends assure him that when he goes before God, God's only question will be "Why were you not Zusya?" So it is with us; our call is to become all that God has called us to be, unique and graced in our own way. How exciting as a supervisor to help someone grow into deeper awareness of the power and beauty of his or her real self! And as the mystery of God would have it, we gain self-knowledge in return.

One Asian supervisee achieved this type of self-knowledge as he explored a group direction session with a church group. He felt something missing in the session. As he reflected, it became clear to him that it was time for him to directly engage more of his own cultural heritage, rather than follow the process set out by the class instructor. He understood the "something missing" as needing to embrace his cultural heritage. He desired to involve his whole self, cultural heritage and all, as he directed. This discovery sent him out the door glowing with a new truth about his role as director.

Humor and Humility

One of the greatest privileges I have is doing supervision with students of spiritual direction. Critical to this relationship is the gift of humor. Where I work, I often hear great bouts of laughter coming from rooms where supervision is happening. This speaks to me of both the ability to hold things lightly and the profound goodness of laughing at one's humanness. Humor can help us let go of things that impede our work as directors and have a stranglehold on our very being. It can reduce an overinflated sense of responsibility for that which belongs to God. The ability for us to accept our humanness frees us to allow our foibles to be part of a transformed life.

Humor and laughter cannot be prescribed. They arise as spontaneous and often surprising responses to the paradoxical, the ambivalent, the ambiguous, or the plain unadulterated truth. Nevertheless, supervisors can foster such appropriate lightheartedness by pointing out and laughing at their own occasional foibles or missteps, by describing humorous situations in which they have found themselves, and by helping supervisees appreciate the inadequacies and limitations we all experience. Although humor and humility are not the same, they are often related.

The word *humility* comes from the Latin *humus* and refers to the "earth which is beneath us." As an English term, it refers to "the knowledge we have of ourselves as we truly are." Humility, then, evokes an image of one who knows in truth who he or she is and where he or she stands. In supervision, we are often presented with the gift of humility as our supervisees come to greater awareness of themselves.

One spiritual director, who has been doing direction for about five years, noted a growing awareness of his desire to move the spiritual direction session along with advice giving. He spoke to his supervisor of this discovery in the following words: "So, what is underneath this unwillingness to wait? It can be none other than spiritual hubris. My concern for the directee stems from my desire to help. When their distress continues at length, the underlying message I hear is that I've not helped them adequately or in a timely manner. This evidences that I think I'm so helpful and capable that I take on their pain personally. That is where the hubris enters and my concern crosses the line from responding to the heart of their matter to my own. It's a challenging issue. It requires that in faith I recognize my own skills (and their limits) as a director in order to allow freedom in the directing space. Without faithful confidence (in humility), I risk becoming self-attendant."[4]

Careful Attention to Places for Growth and Healing

God is always doing something new in people's lives. Supervisors should attend to particular comments made by supervisees. Certain types of responses or feelings can signal that more exploration is warranted:

- I become bored with the conversation.
- I am overly moved to tears or feel no emotion whatsoever.
- I become angry or anxious at what the directee is telling me.
- I feel sexually aroused.
- I notice I'm very sleepy or unable to stay attentive to the conversation.
- I am reminded of an experience that I find difficult to bracket.
- I notice a great joy that I want to celebrate.
- I have a particularly strong bodily reaction to something said.
- I want to savor something said much longer than the directee does.
- I become overly involved with my directee's life and story.
- I feel a strong urge to "parent" or give advice.

This by no means exhausts the list of comments that should lead to gentle exploration, but such things should alert the supervisor to areas that need more contemplative attention. For example, Sam realizes his eyes were filled with tears during almost the entire session with a directee.[5] He couldn't understand what was happening. When he had time to explore this with his supervisor, he realized the directee kept referring to his mother's death. Sam's mother was in her final days. As Sam watched his mother slowly lose her strength, this prompted a deep sadness in him. His ability to name this sadness unlocked his sense of grief. Sam realized he needed to be more aware of how his personal grief affected his direction.

Power in the Supervision Relationship

An imbalance of power is intrinsic in supervision, and the potential exists for a supervisor to abuse that power. As supervisors, we have power as a result of such factors as our education, our age, our experience, or our position. Sometimes we hold the potential for giving a student a passing or failing grade. We who supervise must be very careful not to infringe on the rights of those we see. As supervisors, we are privy to confidential information that must remain confidential. We must never cross either sexual or ethical boundaries. Our boundaries must be kept clear and clean. Even though we desire mutuality in relationship with our supervisees, there is still an imbalance of power, and the supervisor is the responsible party in this power relationship. It is our duty to uphold the high standards out-lined in the Spiritual Directors International *Guidelines for Ethical Conduct.* [6]

Before, During, and After a Session

Both supervisors and supervisees should engage in concrete preparation for a supervision session. At San Francisco Theological Seminary, we have found that having supervisees work from a Contemplative Reflection Form (CRF) and write up a verbatim dialogue according to a particular format is helpful (see Appendix A for a completed CRF, Appendix B for a sample verbatim, and Appendix C for an explanation of the CRF). These forms invite supervisees to be cognizant of their own feelings, thoughts, and body reactions, and the body reactions observable in their directees. Supervisees send these forms to their supervisors a week before the supervision conversation.

Supervisors also should come well prepared to a session. They must leave enough time before the session to become centered, in order to spread a table of hospitality where the truth of what is happening in the life of the supervisee can meet the light of God's grace. In this light, the Holy Spirit may reveal the power and majesty of God at work. As supervisors, it is important that we come to a session as alert and alive as possible. Irenaeus said, "The glory of God is the human person fully alive, and the life of the human person is the vision of God."[7] The glory of supervision is a supervisor, fully alive, ready to use his or her total being—body, mind, and spirit—to graciously embrace the truth laid out before one.

As supervisors, we read verbatims and CRFs ahead of time in preparation for our supervision sessions. Read the verbatim dialogue as a holy text, prayerfully considering where your attention is drawn. It is like doing a *lectio divina* process. Ask yourself: What shimmers in this dialogue? What feelings, thoughts, or body reactions do I note that might need to be explored? What clarification do I need from the supervisee? The Spirit is at work in the service of the supervisee as the supervisor prepares for his or her arrival.

Begin the actual supervision session with silence or a prayer. Then ask the supervisee what he or she notices at this moment about what is recorded in his or her dialogue. It is helpful to read the dialogue aloud, with the supervisor and supervisee each taking a part. Is there more to be explored than was first noticed? Is the focus of the session clearly defined by the supervisee so that exploration and probing can proceed? (See question 7 in Appendix A.) The focus in supervision is to explore whatever supervisees bring from any arena of their lives, notic-ing where God appears active or absent. Sometimes defining the focus is the biggest challenge. During the session, supervisees can go back to their dialogues and get in touch with where the reactions or feelings for them are the strongest, the most puzzling, where they feel void of any personal affect, and so on. This provides a focal point for the supervision conversation. It is worth investing time to be clear about what the focus issue is the biggest challenge.

Within the supervision conversation, the supervisor has the privilege of going alongside the supervisee and celebrating a particular joy, peace, freedom. If your mind is in the "what is wrong" mode concerning either the supervisee or his or her process with the directee, you could easily dismiss the abundant grace inherent in many supervision sessions. Once a supervisee brought a focus issue concerning a strong physical sense of euphoria he had as the directee talked. The more we probed this, the more he noticed that this was the same sense he has when he feels particularly close to God. He realized that they were both "sitting in the Presence," and he had missed the opportunity to savor and celebrate with the directee.

If you are trying to analyze your supervisee, you miss the mark. It is a natural tendency to analyze, because we live in a society of armchair analysts. But our goal is to sit with supervisees contemplatively, noticing the movement of God in them and the other, as they recall the direction session and how it affected them. A supervisee named Harry noticed that as his directee kept going back to a particular part of his story, he, as director, felt very impatient. Since Harry tended to be a patient person, his reaction was out of character. In supervision, we spent a long time prayerfully noticing what this impatience meant for him. It turns out that Harry was impatient with many things in his own life, and his story was mirroring the life of his directee.

Another director named Sally had a directee who talked on and on about this wonderful tranquil place. Sally reported a deep pit of what she called "longing" in her stomach. As we examined this, she uncovered a deep longing on her part to go to that place too. Sally was going through a divorce and felt she badly needed the peaceful presence of Christ.

Those who come to us are not coming as problems to be solved, but as great mysteries to be plumbed and celebrated. The gift of vulnerability, offered to us by supervisees, is not to be taken lightly. It takes great strength on the part of anyone to lay bare what it is that stirs within him or her, both that which is embraced and that which is ignored. In the naming of what is churning inside, there is great risk. The process of supervision should be gentle but truthful, lovingly delivered in a manner that does not shame. Supervision of the director is done in a contemplative manner, leaving time to ponder and savor what is happening in the moment. Psalm 131:2a implies this kind of quiet attentiveness when it says, "But I have calmed and quieted my soul, like a weaned child with its mother."

What Supervision Is Not

In addition to understanding clearly the different aspects of supervision, it is also important to be aware of what supervision is not.

Supervision Is Not Puffed Up

Supervision is about building up rather than tearing down. The verses from I Corinthians 13 aptly describe the mood for operation as we attend to a supervisee. This loving attitude is paramount for those doing supervision. No noisy gongs or clanging cymbals. Supervisors should not be "puffed up." On the contrary, since God is the prime mover, a supervisor's aim is to be filled with a God-like, loving, attentive spirit. There must never be a hint of harassment on the part of a supervisor, only the reflections of a humble, open servant.

Forget Advice Giving

One of the hardest things for supervisors to avoid is problem solving. People come seeking answers, and supervisors quite naturally want to be helpful. It is assumed that those who come for supervision desire to do God's will, but sometimes they expect the supervisor to be the vehicle for quick solutions. Unfortunately (or fortunately), we are not. This doesn't mean that we don't pray with and for someone seeking discernment for an issue, but it does mean that we steer clear of trying to fix the problem or the person. We may help supervisees list a number of ways to approach something, then invite them to prayerfully discern what is the most fitting way to proceed, considering who they are as directors and who their directees are. At the end of the supervision session, it is helpful to have supervisees explain how they want to work with their directees in a new way and where they understand the spirit of God to be at work in them as directors. Note that these are the decisions or discernments of the supervisee, not the supervisor. It takes time as a director not only to develop confidence in oneself, but even more to recognize the impact of the power of God at work in the sessions.

It's Not about Control

The process of supervision is not about controlling anything or anyone. We need the humility to admit that we don't have the answers for someone else. Supervisors, like everyone else, have their own biases and assumptions—about theology, about the human being, about how the world works and how it ought to work, about how spiritual direction should be done. We need to understand our biases and assumptions so they do not get in the way. Do we have favorite images of God? Do we cling to beliefs that might preclude embracing another person's belief system? Knowing our assumptions and understanding our prejudices allow us to use them on behalf of supervisees or let go of them so that they will not get in the way.

Supervisors also should offer a place for supervisees to explore their belief systems, assumptions, and prejudices, and to discern what is right for them and helpful for their directees. We don't know what is right for another. For example, a supervisor might hope that a particular director would be more open to people who are gay and lesbian, have a more conservative theology, or hold a female image of God. The supervisee, however, will evolve in that understanding as God leads him or her. Growth around images and understandings of God needs to come from within, not be pressured from without, even by a supervisor.

It's Not about Being Nice

The process of supervision is not about being nice. That doesn't mean we aren't kind and compassionate. It is of service to the supervisee to explore all areas that may lead to greater freedom, so we should be honest and open with what we notice, although we should not engage in faultfinding. The biblical phrase "speaking the truth in love" aptly applies. Sometimes this is a challenge for supervisors. We desire to be liked and be helpful, and it can be difficult to bring up what someone may be avoiding, find difficult, or simply is missing. We need to be honest and forthright with those we serve.

Supervision Is Not Therapy

Supervision is not a therapy or counseling session for the supervisee, in which the focus is on solving a particular problem or situation. At the same time, supervisors need to know when to refer a supervisee to a therapist. When should you refer in a supervision relationship? There are some clear indications, such as when a person comes month after month and is clearly getting deeper into depression. You should refer such people to a counselor. I always have on hand names of at least two counselors I know personally who do quality work. I try to support the person by saying something like this: "Jean, I noticed in the last few months you seem more and more depressed. I think it would be helpful for you to see a counselor. We can decide if you would like to continue working with me at the same time. What do you think?"

If you are an intuitive person, the sense of needing to refer may come in the form of a feeling in your gut of something just not being right. For example, Margaret comes to you regularly for supervision for two years. She is faithful in her supervision and lets you know if she has to cancel an appointment. All of a sudden, Margaret misses a scheduled supervision appointment. After the second missed appointment, you call her and establish a meeting. When she arrives, she is tense and looks very tired. Out of the blue, it surfaces that her significant other is an alcoholic and abuses her. She kept forgetting the supervision appointment because this issue is so painful for her. The issue surfaced when her directee talked about abuse in their direction session. Margaret was embarrassed and bewildered as to how to help this person, and this issue was extremely difficult for her. There are two referrals you should make for Margaret: one to a domestic violence center and another to Al-Anon. Explain why you are referring her to each place, and make sure she is in no immediate physical danger.

Another time to refer a supervisee is when he or she needs help beyond your expertise. Certainly, if someone is talking of suicide, refer. He or she needs to see a counselor immediately! Sometimes a supervisee unearths something that he or she did not recognize previously, such as unresolved grief. If it is chronic and blocks the supervisee's ability to be present to self and others, then help from a professional is desirable. If an issue surfaces that is harmful to any party, then a referral is necessary. Any time the quality of life is threatened or severely distorted, such as when the supervisee is engaging in an illicit affair, the supervisor needs to discern with the supervisee the course of action. If illegal or unethical experiences are reported to you, such as sexual abuse, you have no recourse but to let the proper authorities know immediately. You should tell your supervisee that you are reporting the matter to the proper authority.

Those You Should Serve with Caution or Not at All

It is important to recognize when you are not the best supervisor for a particular supervisee. Sometimes personalities or your personal experiences are in conflict with the directee and hamper the ability for you to provide open, honest space. For example, I must be very careful when I am supervising anyone who is dealing with reported experiences of alcoholism. Because there is alcoholism in my family history, it can be a place of blindness or even too deep a pain for me. Some folks feel they cannot work with people who are radically liberal or conservative in their views. Others believe that working with either males or females could be problematic for them. Knowing yourself and what is uncomfortable to or threatens you is important.

When setting up a supervisory relationship, it is helpful to suggest a trial period so that you both can "try on" the relationship. If you find that it won't work for you, you need to be open and honest with the supervisee. Let the person know that the problem lies with you, not with him or her, and provide names and phone numbers of two or more other supervisors for referral. If you are honest, you have to admit that there are people you just don't particularly like. It is unfair to attempt to be present to such folks. There also may be cases in which a person's cultural background, theological worldview, or socioeconomic situation is so different from yours that it limits your ability to comprehend and aid him or her. As much as I like to think I'm an open, embracing person, I am not always knowledgeable or free enough to be a good guide for some people. Honesty on your part is better than deceiving yourself about having a global ability to work with all people.

If the supervisee chooses to exit the relationship, it is helpful to find out why, if possible. Sometimes people decide not to reveal their reasons or simply stop coming without notification. In such cases, humble acceptance is necessary.

God takes all of who you are and all of who the supervisee is, embraces both of you, and calls forth the true identity of God in each of you. As I looked over the evaluations of the supervisor workshop I helped conduct, the most outstanding comments from those who attended were from people who realized the power in being their true selves as supervisors. Supervision supports the ability for both the supervisor and the supervisee to stay rooted and grounded in God. This prevents each individual from straying easily from the heart of the matter. We celebrate all that is revealed by God, places of maturity and places of immaturity. My prayer as a supervisor is to be open to the presence of God, grow more profoundly into myself, and be of service to those who grace me as we grow more fully into sons and daughters of God.

Notes

1. Maureen Conroy, *Looking into the Well: Supervision of Spiritual Directors* (Chicago: Loyola Press, 1995), 156–57.

2. John Calvin, *Institutes of Christian Religion*, ed. John T. McNeill, trans. Ford Lewis Battles (Philadelphia: The Westminster Press, 1960), 35.

3. Abraham Buber, *Tales of the Hasidim* (New York: Schocken Books, 1975), 251.

4. Thanks to David Evans, DASD graduate, for allowing me to use this piece.

5. All names of people in this document are changed. The reported information has been graciously granted from participants of supervision with their permission.

6. *Guidelines for Ethical Conduct* (Spiritual Directors International, 1999).

7. Irenenas, *Adversus haereses IV*, 20, 7 (SC 100): 648.

PART TWO

Specific Topics in Supervision

CHAPTER FOUR

Supporting Beginning Directors: Participating in the Dance

Mary Rose Bumpus and Rebecca Bradburn Langer

Our image of beginning spiritual directors is one of slowly but surely moving into a dance. Beginning dancers tend to feel clumsy and awkward. They wonder if they are stepping on the other's toes, and they often sense they are too stiff in their responsive movements. As supervisors, we assist such beginning dancers by pondering how we learn to dance, being continually aware of the basic posture of the dance, and teaching the kinds of steps that will help new directors feel free enough to enjoy the dance.

When we learn to dance, we *first* listen to the music and hear its rhythm. *Then* we learn the moves that help us respond to the rhythm, the melody, the mood, and even the lyrics of a musical piece. Educators and mentors in the art of spiritual direction first encourage beginning directors to develop the charism of "holy listening," by using all their inner and outer senses to perceive the presence and activity of the Holy Spirit. Then they teach them particular skills meant to help these new directors respond to the dynamic movements of a directee's life in God.

What often happens in practice, however, is that beginning directors tend to focus on the steps of the dance. They spend a lot of time thinking about what they are doing. This kind of self-conscious reflection and overly focused attention on skills and appropriate responses, natural in the beginning, inhibits a director's ability to see and hear the actual movement and presence of God.

Our God is a God of surprises. Moses did not anticipate seeing or experiencing God in a burning bush. Elijah did not expect to hear God in a "still small voice." Mary never dreamed she would be overshadowed by the Holy Spirit, and Mary Magdalene could not have imagined that the tomb would be empty. In our human experience, the presence of God unexpectedly arises and surprises us.

As supervisors, we want to help beginning directors be prepared for unanticipated surprise. This is probably the *greatest* challenge supervisors of beginning directors face, and it is one of the most significant paradoxes of our work. On the one hand, we encourage new directors to incorporate new skills, practice what they are learning, be attentive to their inner responses, and look at how they are doing things. On the other, the fundamental attitude that fosters the experience of our God of surprises is one of "unknowing." As supervisors, we want to encourage in beginning directors a certain kind of "not knowing," a kind we find ourselves continually invited to enter. We want to wait in anticipation of the unfolding mystery of the directee and the ultimate mystery of God. We want to rest in the knowledge that every dance with God is different and unique to each direction relationship. We want to acknowledge with certitude that we are not experts on another's life. This kind of "unknowing" frees directors to be guileless and therefore able to be surprised by mystery, perceive God's life, be surprised by God's song, and move in freedom to the rhythm of God's dance.

Supporting the Person and Gifts of New Directors

Supervisors of beginning directors are in a particularly privileged place. They bear witness to the enthusiasm, compassion, and joy of new directors as they enter their first spiritual direction relationships. They are privy to the verbatim dialogues, reflections, and vulnerabilities of new directors who struggle to take their first steps and savor their first gifts of encounter. Supervisors of beginning directors experience the openness, fears, and great desire to learn that new directors manifest and express.

From this privileged place, we begin the work of supervision by inviting new directors to be who they are and do what they already do well *in assistance of their directees*. We do this by lifting up and enhancing the particular abilities and gifts of each new director and suggesting or demonstrating how such gifts can be used on behalf of directees. For example, a supervisor named Janet is supervising a beginning director named Terry. Reflecting on Terry's initial dialogues, Janet points out that Terry is highly attuned to her own physiological sensations. While Terry is aware of this, she had not reflected on her body as a particular source of wisdom, or how God might be at work through this body awareness. Janet worked with Terry to discern how her physiological responses and ability to notice the somatic reactions of her directees could be used as a tool in her practice of spiritual direction.

John, a new director, plays the flute. He is particularly informed by the gift of music, and his connection with God is deepened through playing and listening to music. Maria, John's supervisor, suggests that John listen to his directees for the presence of God as he would listen to music. John begins to hear the melody of the directees' life and discovers "the heart of the matter." He feels the rhythm and begins to notice the presence of God in all the arenas of his directees' lives. John, with the help of Maria, also learns to help his directees give expression to their relationship with God in and through the arts.

Amy is particularly good with the use of images. She receives much of her guidance from God through her imagination. Amy is good at offering her directees images that summarize their felt senses, values, and thoughts. Amy's supervisor, Jim, builds on this gift. He encourages Amy to become more aware of the naturally occurring metaphors and images her directees employ. He then shows her how to explore such images to discover the gifts of God they potentially represent. Beginning directors have a variety of gifts, sensibilities, and skills. As supervisors, it is important that we *see* such gifts, support and strengthen developing skills, and encourage the innate sensibilities of these directors.

Giving Trust Where Trust Is Due

Beginning directors also come to spiritual direction with different levels of confidence. Those who are overly confident may miss the more subtle ways of letting directees discover for themselves how God is at work in their lives. More frequently, however, we meet new directors who are nervous and overly focused on what they are doing, and therefore miss the movement of the Spirit. It is easy enough for this to happen, especially when the movements of the Spirit are subtle, and it is a common and understandable phenomenon among new practitioners of this art. Supervisors are of great assistance to such directors by keeping the question of the presence and activity of the Holy Spirit in the forefront of the new director's thoughts and at the heart of the supervision conversation.

As part of a reflection process on a particular direction session (see Appendix A), we ask new directors to respond to the following question: "Of all the things you could notice during the direction session, where did you see glimpses of the gifts, fruits, or movement of the Holy Spirit?" To help them reflect upon this question, we also present a list of some possibilities: "signs of life, freedom, joy, compassion, solidarity in suffering, justice, enhanced self-identity before God, ability to stand in the truth, invitation, consolation, a 'new word spoken.'" As supervisors, we consider this to be the *most important* question we ask new directors. It reminds beginning directors, as well as experienced supervisors, that trust in God is the most essential posture of a spiritual director.

Whereas some new directors miss the activity of the Spirit because they are overly focused on what they are doing, others get caught up in adhering to the letter of the law. We often hear comments such as the following from new directors: "My professor taught me never to do spiritual direction with a parishioner," "I was told never to do direction with a friend," "I know I shouldn't meet with people in my home unless I have a designated place," or "I see that many people don't charge a fee for doing spiritual direction, but . . ."

These statements are representative of guidelines we have taught beginning directors in our spiritual direction programs. These guidelines were developed to address concerns of which any director should be aware. At the same time, such guidelines need to be examined in light of the unique circumstances of new directors and their directees.

James is the pastor of a congregation of six hundred people. Clara, an eighty-year-old member of this community, asks James if he would assist her as her spiritual director. James's immediate inclination is to say no. But before responding to Clara, James consults his supervisor. Together, James and his supervisor clarify the potential pitfalls of such a relationship and listen for the promptings of the Spirit. The supervisor works with James to discern what is best for all involved—Clara, the congregation, and James himself. In this instance, James decides to accompany Clara. He does so to the delight of others in the congregation, to the benefit of Clara, and in response to the promptings of the Holy Spirit. As beginning directors become more aware of the unique and often subtle movements of the Spirit, they grow in trusting God to be active and present in the life of the directee and in the direction session itself. As their trust in God grows, new directors begin to trust themselves as well.

Common Struggles

In addition to working with supervisees around these foundational attitudes and postures, supervisors attend to a number of pragmatic struggles that beginning directors have in common, whatever the source of such struggles may be. Several spiritual direction programs in the United States and beyond offer an excellent education in the art of spiritual direction. Additionally, much of what is taught, theoretically learned, and practiced in small-group settings is embodied in new directors as they do direction with the support and assistance of good supervisors. In reviewing hundreds of verbatims and serving as supervisors for individuals and groups of new directors, we have noticed certain common struggles that persist beyond an initial education and introduction to the art of spiritual direction. We have also become aware of dilemmas new directors face that generally are not addressed in the spiritual direction programs. We have spoken with a number of supervisors about how they assist new directors with such dilemmas and offer here some reflections and suggestions.

Transitions and Dead-End Questions

Beginning directors have a good sense of the purpose and tenor of their first encounters with new directees, as well as what needs to be accomplished. During this time, supervisors sometimes help new directors discern whether they and their directees are an appropriate fit.

As beginning directors move into regular or ordinary sessions with directees, however, they often have difficulty with an important transition: They do not have a sense of how to move from the greeting and initial conversation with directees into the substance of the direction conversation. As supervisors reflect with new directees on their attempts to make this transition, significant pragmatic and theological concerns come to the fore. Some new directors abruptly interrupt the flow of initial conversation and call for silence and prayer in a way that is stilted and awkward. They make a dramatic shift away from an informal and naturally conversational tone to a more formal, serious, and ponderous tone. As they make this move, beginning directors report thinking such things as "We had better move into spiritual direction now" or "Am I doing spiritual direction yet?" Susan, Tom's supervisor, sees such behavior and thought reflected in Tom's verbatims. She invites Tom to reflect theologically on his understanding of what constitutes "the spiritual." They enter into a fruitful conversation that gets at the heart of some of Tom's assumptions about how and where God is present and active within the direction conversation itself. In exploring a similar dynamic, Sandra and her supervisor come to realize that Sandra is not clear about the role of prayer *within* the spiritual direction relationship. She and her supervisor speak about her desire to pray for her directees and whether her directees desire to pray during a direction session itself. When a directee desires to have formal prayer as part of the direction session, Sandra's supervisor suggests ways in which such prayer may become a natural outgrowth of the direction conversation.

Beginning directors are taught to ask "open-ended questions," among other skills, but it is difficult for them to know when and where to use such skills. Some new directors, after greeting their directees, almost immediately ask a broad, open-ended question about a topic from their previous direction session. One beginning director reported asking her directee, as they were moving across the room to be seated, "How is your relationship with your husband going these days?" Director and directee were off and running, only to have the same conversation they had in their previous session.

Imagine how you might help this director. There are many humorous, interesting, and enjoyable ways to assist new directors in learning how to greet directees and make the transition into the substance of the direct conversation. You might have a conversation about the differences between "open-ended" and "dead-end" questions and suggest alternative introductory questions for this director: "How was your drive over here today?" "Did you see the roses blooming outside the office door?" You might invite the director to role-play this situation with you and enact various ways of making the transition into the substance of the direction conversation. Show him or her how to move into a natural silence with the directee or suggest a more general question such as "What shall we talk about today?" However you imagine working with this new director, it is important to help him or her learn to make the initial transition in such a way that the informal and conversational tone of the direction session is not lost.

Silence

It is not uncommon for beginning directors to be uncomfortable with silence in the presence of another. In the clamorous culture of the United States, it is difficult to find places where silence abounds. Boom boxes blast away at us from noisy street corners, and car radios blare. Department stores and offices are filled with elevator music and loudspeaker announcements. Even worship services are full of music and words. When there is a pause, a moment of silence, community members move about in their seats, acknowledging their discomfort and inability to be present together in the absence of sound. When we are not being bombarded with external noise or sound, we often find ourselves struggling with inner disquiet. Thoughts assault us. Voices repeat again and again in our minds.

In addition to the more obvious cultural and personal difficulties directors might have with silence, beginning directors find it hard to distinguish among kinds and qualities of silence. Although silence may generally be defined as the absence of noise, speech, or sound, qualities of silence vary tremendously. Silence may feel to some people like punishment, as when a child is sent to his or her room for a "time-out." Similarly, when one person in a relationship denies another access to feelings or information needed for the relationship, the quality of silence may be forbidding or imposing. Silence may be poignant, compelling, hopeful, or loving. It may be a sign of reverence, awe, disdain, or lack of respect. Or it can be fearful, vindictive, secretive, or reserved.

Here is an exercise that can be helpful for beginning directors in preparing to be silent in the presence of their directees. In group supervision settings, new directors can move into dyads, where they take turns as director and directee. One person, acting as the directee, describes an experience that invites natural places of silence, and then moves into such silence as the Spirit moves him or her. The directors attend to the directees and move into the places of silence with them. According to new directors, such practice has been helpful to them. New directors also might consider becoming members of *lectio divina* or contemplative prayer groups. Silence is common in these groups, and new directors get a sense of the growing and pervasive quality of this silence as the group continues to pray together.

Directees are better at assessing the quality of a particular silence. They know how a particular silence feels to them, and this is what is important in the direction conversation. In one-on-one supervision, it is helpful to the beginning director for the supervisor to read the directee's part of a verbatim, enter into the experience, and then give the new director a sense of the quality of the silence in this conversation.

Savoring

Sometimes directees speak with directors about particularly powerful or poignant life-giving experiences infused with the ineffable Spirit of God. Such experiences are difficult to describe because of the nature of language, particularly the English language, which is oriented toward action rather than relationship. Such experiences are also difficult to articulate because we cannot grasp or hold or contain the ultimate mystery of God. Thus, directees often speak metaphorically about these life experiences and then lapse into silence. In the telling of such experiences, directees are inviting directors to savor and appreciate these moments, to give praise, thanks, and blessing for the gifts of God's graciousness, mercy, and love.

For some beginning directors, savoring is difficult. Words are inadequate to express our thanks and praise for the mystery of a new birth, the beauty of a sunset, or an experienced moment of truth or justice. Savoring invites directors into the silence of gratitude, reverence, or joy. At the same time, it invites verbal responsiveness and exploration.

Beginning directors often hear the good news of directees and then immediately move the conversation to a different topic. One way supervisors can assist new directors with the process of savoring is by becoming their directees for part of the supervision session. Think of a recent simple experience that was surprisingly infused with the Spirit of God, one that you would like the new director to enjoy and savor with you. Recount this experience, and then assist the director in responding, asking such questions as "What would you say if a friend were telling you this?" "What is your spontaneous felt sense as you hear me speak of this?" "What kind of wonderment are you as director experiencing?" "Ask me what it is like to be given such a gift." These questions and others help new directors get a sense of how to savor the mystery and wonder of God's activity in their directees' lives. Acting as good directees for new directors is something we do often in a variety of settings. This posture enhances new directors' fundamental stance of unknowing, inspires confidence, allows us to draw upon their innate sensibilities, and gives us an opportunity to offer appropriate thanks and praise for their helpful responses and ways of being with us.

Responding to Human Suffering

Whereas some beginning directors find it difficult to savor certain experiences of their directees, others do not know how to be present and respond to the revelation of suffering and human anguish. Suffering is an inevitable consequence of our human identity. Human beings experience the pain and anguish of the loss of others, ill health, moments of darkness, doubt and despair, death itself. Such suffering is inevitable. We also experience suffering as a result of the mistreatment of others, economic disparity, societal injustices, and cultural marginalization. Most beginning directors are good at discerning whether their directees are suffering as a result of the oppressive practices of others or the inevitable consequences of human life. When directees suffer from the preventable mistreatment of others, directors should take an active role in direction sessions, intervening where appropriate according to ethical guidelines. In such situations, supervisors have helped new directors work against religious and cultural attitudes that blame victims for such suffering.

Suffering from the inevitable consequences of human life is somewhat different. When directees speak with directors of their experiences of inevitable suffering or past suffering from oppressive practices, a variety of stances and emotions are evoked in both directors and directees. In the face of great suffering, directors and directees find themselves in places full of sadness and sorrow, anger and despair, compassion and kindness. In these places, directees are inviting directors to accompany them in the midst of and through their suffering.

Some beginning directors struggle mightily with this. It is difficult to know how to be present or what to say in the face of the mystery of human suffering. As supervisors, we have found ourselves working on several levels with new directees around these concerns. We attend to the theological assumptions new directors have about human suffering, and we foster and encourage stances and responses that can be helpful in the midst of suffering. The Judeo-Christian tradition has much wisdom to offer us about both. A few beginning directors idealize the faith of Jesus in a way that all but precludes his humanity. We encourage such directors to listen to the cry of Jesus on the cross, "My God, my God, why have you forsaken me?" (Mark 15:34), and hear it as a real expression of the faith of Jesus. We also encourage them to be present to their own or another's experience of suffering and consider what this experience is really like. It can be helpful for new directors to reread the book of Job, pay close attention to the three friends as examples of what *not* to say and do, and view Job as an example of how one might speak to God in the midst of suffering. Calling to mind the incredible range of felt responses to suffering expressed by the Psalmists, we have entered into conversation with new directors about their ability to give expression to their many feelings that correspond to human suffering. We also invite new directors to imagine Jesus, for a moment, as a directee rather than a director. The gospels give eloquent witness to the quality of silence and kind of presence desired by directees in times of great suffering.

> Then Jesus went with them [the disciples] to a place called Gethsemane; and he said to his disciples, "Sit here while I go over there and pray." He took with him Peter and the two sons of Zebedee, and began to be grieved and agitated. Then he said to them, "I am deeply grieved, even to death; remain here, and stay awake with me." (Matt 26:36–38)

Jesus asked his disciples to stay awake, remain present, and be with him through his suffering. Directees often ask the same things, one way or another, of their directors.

Directees know directors cannot determine or change the outcome of human suffering. But they invite directors to stay awake, remain present, and be with them as they go through it. Spiritual directors serve as a sign of God's presence in the midst of the suffering of directees. They offer hope in times of fear and a sense of God's compassionate accompaniment. Supervisors serve beginning directors as a sign of the presence of the Christian community and faith tradition. They assist beginning directors by encouraging them to remain with directees in the midst of suffering and reminding directors they are not alone. They, too, are accompanied. They are accompanied by their supervisors, the communion of saints, the living Word of God, and a faith tradition that has much to say about consolation and desolation in the face of human suffering. We also encourage beginning directors to be responsive listeners to directees who are suffering.

Responsive Listening

Many books and treatises on spiritual direction speak about the director's role as a listener and the power that listening and attentive loving presence play in the spiritual direction relationship. These basic stances are foundational and true of good spiritual direction. It is also true that the forms of our listening, as well as our responses to what we hear and perceive, are conveyed both verbally and nonverbally to directees. Students of various fields study what contemporary psychology and counseling literature call "active listening skills." That is, we learn how to actively communicate to others *what* we are hearing and *that* we are listening. The following are typical skills associated with active listening: the use of probes such as "hm," "ah," "um," or a nod of the head; the employment of open-ended questions; summarizing the content of a directee's communication; and primary accurate empathy—noticing and naming the feeling of the directee and the heart of the matter being communicated by her or him. These skills are taught to beginning spiritual directors in a number of spiritual direction programs. They help new directors attend to their directees and empower them to tell their stories.

Beyond such basic skills, instructors and supervisors assist beginning directors in developing their own gifts for a kind of listening that literature in spirituality generally calls "contemplative." Contemplative listening, more appropriately understood as contemplative perceiving, involves what Neafsey has described in chapter 2 of this book—seeing the particularity of the other, seeing the whole of the other, seeing the surface, and seeing beyond. Walter Burghardt speaks of this kind of perceiving as "a long loving look at the real."[1] Beginning directors learn various processes of discernment in order to help them see and notice the reality, presence, and activity of the Holy Spirit in the life and person of directees.

The explication of such active and contemplative listening is often accompanied by a list of don'ts: "Don't parrot a directee." "Don't give advice." "Don't respond with biblical platitudes." "Don't sit in silence when directees have revealed something central and surprising about their identity." "Don't analyze." "The focus of the spiritual direction conversation is on the directee and the Spirit, not on the director." The list is endless. This list of don'ts and the singular focus of active and contemplative listening on the directee and the Holy Spirit lead beginning directors to assume that they basically facilitate a process of God-directed *self*-discovery for their directees in which they have little to say or to offer.

We see verbatim after verbatim in which beginning directors convey on paper what they are thinking, feeling, imagining, and sensing in response to their directees. But they share very little, if any, of this information with the directees themselves. Rather, they tend to ask exploratory questions, a practice that makes the director the determiner of the course of the conversation. As supervisors, it is common for us to say to such beginning directors, "What kept you from telling your directee how you felt at this moment in response to this sharing?" or "Why did you not offer this wonderful summarizing image to your directee?" So in addition to encouraging the use of active and contemplative listening skills and sensibilities, we encourage beginning directors to be engaged in a kind of responsive listening to directees. Responsive listening acknowledges the social, communal, and interpersonal dimensions of spiritual direction, and it allows for the director-directee relationship to unfold in the most natural of ways. We encourage beginning directors to listen responsively by sharing specific types of noticings with directees and by using appropriate self-disclosure.

Noticings

Over time, beginning directors grow in their ability to notice. In practice, they often start by focusing on the external, nonverbal signs and behaviors of directees. It is important for directors to be aware of the shifts in tone of voice and body language of directees. These provide significant clues about how the direction conversation is going at any given moment. However, verbalizing these noticings can make directees highly self-conscious—an effect that is generally not desirable in a direction conversation. (There is a significant difference between feeling self-conscious and becoming self-aware; the latter is desired in a spiritual direction conversation.) As new directors grow in the art of spiritual direction, they find themselves using such noticings sparingly.

Good spiritual directors more commonly offer directees a different kind of noticing. These noticings might be described as affirmations or confirmations of the self—something real the director sees in the person of the directee in the telling of his or her story. Such noticings are important and significant for directees and are verbalized by directors as they get to know their directees. They may also be indications of the presence of the Holy Spirit at work in the person of the directee. "I am struck by your courage in the face of this difficult situation." "You were a very good neighbor to Mr. Smith the other day." "That kind of perseverance requires real fidelity on your part." "You bring such joy to those around you." "As you speak about this, I am struck by your love for holy mystery." Such noticings assist directees in discerning the activity and presence of the Holy Spirit in their lives and lead them to greater self-awareness. This kind of noticing is not easy for beginning directors. New directors tend to get caught up in the story of the directee, as we all can, and fail to notice the person who is telling the story. Supervisors can assist beginning directors with this by asking them to describe their directees. "What qualities or virtues does this directee possess?" "How has this person lived his (or her) life?" "Of whom is this directee aware, and how does he (or she) respond to others?" "How does this directee act in the world?" These and similar questions assist beginning directors in getting a picture of the whole person of the directee.

Images and Biblical Narratives

At times in direction sessions, a summarizing image occurs to the spiritual director. This kind of image pulls together various threads of a directee's story. At other times, a directee's story will remind a director of a particular biblical narrative or a passage from a classic text on the spiritual life. For some directors, images or biblical texts come to mind often as directees speak. These directors have to be particularly attentive to whether such images and texts represent a nudge from the Holy Spirit to offer them to directees.

Generally in spiritual direction conversations, directors should work with images that come from the minds and hearts of directees. But occasionally the presentation of a summarizing image by the director can powerfully assist a directee in drawing the threads of his or her story into a coherent whole.[2] On other occasions, directors will remind directees of a biblical text akin to his or her story. This can be an effective means of bringing to consciousness the way a particular directee's story is connected to the larger Christian story or the paschal narrative and event. Supervisors can assist beginning directors in discerning when it is or is not appropriate to make such connections for directees. They also can help new directors let go of offered images when directees have found them unhelpful or not accurate to their experience.

Appropriate Self-Disclosure

Many of the common struggles of beginning spiritual directors could be remedied with the proper understanding and use of appropriate self-disclosure in the spiritual direction relationship. The following conversation is a familiar example of what often happens when directors fail to be appropriately self-disclosive. Cynthia, the directee, has been seeing Steve, the director, every three weeks for a year for spiritual direction. At the end of the last session of the year, Cynthia has this conversation with Steve:

Cynthia: Steve, I want to tell you how much I appreciate the way you have accompanied me during this past year. It was not an easy year for me. I am grateful for your presence, your assistance, and your wisdom along the way.

Steve: Uh, well, Cynthia, this is God's grace, powerfully at work in your life and our time together. I am grateful to God for all that has happened.

Cynthia: Steve, I am grateful to God too. But I also wanted to let you know that I like you. You have made a difference in my life and relationship with God. I am happy to have you as a spiritual director.

Steve: I think of this as God's work. Our time together has been blessed. God has been gracious and merciful.

Cynthia: Steve, I love you and want you to know how much I appreciate you as a director . . . (she continues with similar sentiments as expressed above).

Steve brought this verbatim to a group supervision session. He began by saying he was afraid because his directee Cynthia had told him she loved him. In the context of peer supervision, Steve came to realize that he was unable to accept Cynthia's appreciation and praise. In addition, he was uncomfortable being self-disclosive and did not know how to respond to Cynthia's initial statement. Here is an example where self-disclosure not only would have been appropriate, but also would have prevented the escalation of the conversation and discouraged the greater possibility of transference and countertransference. In the above conversation, it would have been helpful to both Steve and Cynthia if Steve had said something like this: "Cynthia, I like you too, and I enjoy our work together. I am looking forward to our future spiritual direction conversations." Steve came to this realization as the supervision group noticed the tenor of his responses, asked what he was feeling at the time, and pointed out what was missing from his reply to his directee.

We have read many spiritual direction dialogues of beginning directors that are absent of appropriate self-disclosure. In the reading of such dialogues, we are often struck by our sense of the *absence of self* on the part of the director. Spiritual directors are not psychologists. Nor are they blank slates upon which directees project all of their feelings, attitudes, experiences, and beliefs about God. As contemporary literature in almost every field of study suggests, directors are not objective observers who have no effect on directees or their relationship with God. Spiritual direction is a relational encounter among the directee, the director, and the Holy Spirit. Everyone has to show up for spiritual direction in order for it to be fruitful for the directee. As Thomas Merton asserts, "The first thing that genuine spiritual direction requires in order to work properly is a normal, spontaneous human relationship."[3] In a normal, spontaneous spiritual direction relationship, certain kinds of self-disclosure are essential for the well-being of the directee.

Storytelling

In a spiritual direction relationship that is human and spontaneous, a certain kind of storytelling on the part of the director is appropriate. Such storytelling needs to be suitable to the direction relationship, evidence the quality of mutuality, and be of assistance to the endeavors of the directee. It may not take the place of the directee's story or be of such a nature that it could cause discomfort or disturbance to the directee.

We overheard one such story in a spiritual direction demonstration. The directee, a woman named Sarah, was speaking with her director, Alex. Sarah came in to the session speaking about her serious concern over her "addiction" to cherry cola. Sarah was drinking too much of it, and she knew she was jeopardizing her health in a number of ways. Alex, who had grown up in Brooklyn, began to speak about "egg creams," the chocolate soda fountain drink he'd been fond of as a boy. Alex told stories about the soda fountain shop and the former concentration camp victims who owned and ran the place. Sarah told stories about her days playing the organ for three worship services every Sunday morning. One of the highlights for her, among many, was getting to go to the soda fountain shop for a cherry cola in between worship services. Before they knew it, Sarah and Alex were laughing aloud over egg creams and cherry cola. At the end of their storytelling, Alex said, "Now, let's see what we (director, directee, and God) can do to substitute something for this cherry cola." God was clearly present in this conversation—in the laughter, the joy, the acknowledgment of the fun and great taste of childhood treats, the mutual storytelling. In the end, Sarah did not feel so awful about her "addiction" to cherry cola. She did not feel alone in her misery, and she was ready to hear what she was being called to do about it.

Cooperative Conversation

In addition to certain kinds of storytelling, it is appropriate and sometimes necessary for directors to share their felt responses and thoughts to a directee's communication. It is not unusual for directees to wonder what their directors are thinking as they communicate more and more of themselves and their life in God to their directors. Directees will ask directors questions such as these: "What are you thinking about all of this?" "How do you see this situation?" "What do you think of me now that I have said this to you?" When directors do not answer such questions, or revert to answering such questions with another question, directees often begin to feel paranoid. In addition, they will tend to fill in the space of the unanswered question with a mental response of their own: "He can't think well of me after I said this." "She must think I'm crazy thinking this way about things." "She must not think I am a very spiritual person having confessed all of these doubts to her." The lack of communication on the part of directors in such circumstances can create significant difficulties for directees and in their relationships with God. As supervisors, we advise beginning directors to answer a directee's questions in a way that is both true and helpful to the directee.

Directors also communicate their felt responses to directees and their stories. This aspect of appropriate self-disclosure is one of the most important forms of communication from the director to the directee. Directors and directees are in relationship with one another as well as with God. The relationship should be a sign of the incarnate Word, of the Spirit-filled presence of God. Lack of acknowledgment of the relationship between director and directee creates greater difficulties for directees than the honest communication of the self of the director in response to the self of the directee. We have heard good spiritual directors say to directees things such as the following: "I have such a sense of reverence and awe as you tell me about this." "I am angry that you were mistreated in that way." "I am filled with gratitude at such a blessing." "I am missing some of what you are saying. Would you slow down a bit?" "I am so saddened to hear of your loss." "I like you and enjoy our time together." "When I doubt God, I sometimes feel inadequate. What is it like for you?" "My own feeling about the church is very mixed." The list could go on and on.

What is imperative about this kind of self-disclosure is that directors claim their thoughts and feelings *as their own*. This promotes open dialogue and cooperative conversation rather than competitive, combative, or adversarial conversation. Thoughts and feelings are legion and worldwide. They are "in the air," so to speak. As directors and directees enter into cooperative conversation around them, they develop interesting notions and are able to discern God's presence in ways that neither is able to do alone.[4]

Ironically, appropriate self-disclosure on the part of the director also supports directees in differentiating themselves and their relationships with God from that of the director and others. In addition, as directors communicate themselves to directees where appropriate, directees feel less isolated, alone, crazy, or distressed—feelings that are common in particular kinds of faith invitations—and much more at ease with themselves and aware of the presence of God. (We see this as both paradoxical and incarnational.)

When beginning directors are not appropriately self-disclosive, they can appear to directees as either detached observers or experts on the matters of the directee's spiritual life. Such attitudes militate against the notion that directors and directees wait attentively in a place of unknowing for God to be made known, and against the understanding that both director and directee are unexpectedly surprised by the presence and activity of God in the directee's life.

As supervisors, we spend a lot of time assisting new directors in learning the art of appropriate self-disclosure. Such disclosure is indicative of a number of important realities. It indicates that directors know what they are feeling, thinking, imagining, and sensing during the direction conversation. It indicates that they trust their directees enough to be able to say how they are responding to them. It indicates that they have the courage and willingness to be self-disclosive. And it indicates that directors know when and where to be appropriately self-disclosive. This is another place where it is very helpful for supervisors to serve as the directees for new directors during part of a supervision session. In a recent supervision class of new directors, one of us told a poignant story and asked the new directors to tell us how they felt in response. There were six students in the class, and there were six different felt responses. This was wonderful. It gave us the opportunity to demonstrate several things that may happen when directors respond to directees from the place of their own felt experience. One of the new directors, a very astute and wise woman, walked out of the class saying, "Boy, do we have a lot to learn."

As supervisors, we are always learning from our work with beginning directors. They teach us how to be present with them in ways that are meaningful and helpful to them in their work with their directees. Inevitably, they introduce us to beautiful melodies, encourage us to participate in old refrains, and invite us to participate in the dance of supervision.

The Rhythm of the Dance

In those moments in educational settings when we get to observe a really fine spiritual director at work, it is clear that spiritual direction is an art form. There is a rhythm in the direction relationship—between silence and sound, between savoring gifts and lamenting losses, between director, directee, and God—that is akin to the rhythm of music. In the familiar "Hallelujah Chorus" from Handel's *Messiah*, this is seen or heard immediately. Melodies and harmonies are punctuated throughout by rests, places of quiet, the absence of sound, and all are supported by rhythms of stability and particularity. This is what makes the sound so arresting and part of what makes music an art form.

In supervision, we help beginning directors get acquainted with the various rhythms, sounds, and silences that pervade a particular spiritual direction relationship. The more attuned they and we become to such music, the more fully we are able to enjoy and participate in the dance that God leads. It is a privilege to support beginning directors. It is a graced experience of God's cosmic dance.

Notes

1. Walter Burghardt, "Contemplation: A Long Loving Look at the Real," *Church* (Winter 1989): 15.

2. See Maria Bowen, "Dimensions of the Human Person in Relationship and the Practice of Supervision," chapter 5 in this book, on working with various dimensions of the self in spiritual direction.

3. Thomas Merton, *Spiritual Direction and Meditation* with *What is Contemplation?* (Wheathampstead, Hertfordshire, England: Anthony Clark Books, 1950), 19.

4. This understanding of cooperative conversation comes from dialogues about such matters with Eric Greenleaf, Ph.D., author of *The Problem of Evil* (Phoenix: Zeig, Tucker & Theisen, Inc., 2000), a work that addresses what can be done in the aftermath of the sweep of evil into people's lives.

CHAPTER FIVE

Dimensions of the Human Person in Relationship and the Practice of Supervision

Maria Tattu Bowen

Every moment we live a miracle. Fueled by food and air, we reason, feel, perceive, as we develop relationships with ourselves, with our world, and with the God who suffuses and sustains all. Our mere physiology is a source of amazement. Our brains coordinate most biological processes completely outside our awareness. Unless we live with conditions like asthma or lung disease, we think only occasionally about breathing; unless we exercise vigorously or have heart trouble, our hearts' continuous beating remains mostly secret to us. Certainly, we must cooperate by eating, sleeping, exercising, and eliminating wastes, but barring ill health, if these needs should slip from our awareness for an extended period of time, gentle reminders arise from somewhere outside our consciousness to prompt the required actions. In God we live, move, and have our being (Acts 17:28), and what a wondrous symphony, a precious grace our living is. Contemplate it: the Holy Spirit dwelling with us, in us, animating our lives and our world, when we are conscious of it and when we are not.

Not only the physiological facts of our ongoing lives can speak to us of God; so, too, can our experiences of ourselves and of the world, as most spiritual directors and supervisors well know. Yet there are many ways to think about ourselves and our experiences in relationship to the world and to God, just as there are many ways to practice spiritual direction. Each has its own strengths and weaknesses, and each yields its own implications for the supervision of spiritual directors. This chapter explores one way of understanding ourselves and our relationships with the world, drawing out some implications of this understanding for relationship with God and for the practice of supervising spiritual directors.

I did not invent the concepts used in this discussion, though in some cases, I have adapted them. Rather, my understanding, grounded in the Christian traditions, owes much to my colleagues and students, past and present, in the Diploma in the Art of Spiritual Direction program at San Francisco Theological Seminary in San Anselmo, California, most especially to theologians Elizabeth Liebert, Andrew Dreitcer, Mary Rose Bumpus, and Rebecca Langer. These concepts rely also on the teaching of John Mostyn and the writing of Elinor Shea, colleagues at the Center for Spirituality and Justice in the Bronx, New York.

Assumptions

This chapter rests on several key assumptions about God, human beings, and the world:

- God dwells in us and in our relationships and wants to reveal God's self to us. God does so in and through our relationships with ourselves and with the world.

- The incarnation of Christ and the presence of the Holy Spirit testify to the goodness of the world and to God's desire for us to know God in and through relationship with the world, even as the incarnation acknowledges the existence of evil and the ongoing need for human beings to participate in the reign of God.

- God is always present and at work in our lives and in the world, even during those times when we do not perceive God's presence.

- As we grow more conscious of the intellectual, emotional, and physical responses we have to ourselves and to the world, our ability to perceive God's presence and work in the world increases, as does our willingness to participate ever more fully in the reign of God.

This chapter also assumes the following about the supervision of spiritual directors:

- The primary purpose of supervision is to serve directees' growth in relationship with God by aiding their spiritual directors.

- Supervision sessions focus on particular details supplied by spiritual directors about specific direction sessions.

- Skilled spiritual directors and supervisors use their bodies, minds, and emotions as instruments that resonate with the relational dynamics of their sessions.

- Supervisors facilitate directors' growth in consciousness about the relational dynamics of their sessions and the ways in which directors' personal psychology and experiences influence their interpretation of these dynamics.

- Supervision aids directors as they seek to recognize the movement of the Holy Spirit in their sessions.

- Supervisors model skills that directors wish to learn by example and through role playing.

- Supervisors discuss with directors consultation questions that arise.

- Supervisors help directors recognize and celebrate what they are doing well.

Dimensions of Human Experience

Sometimes God seems to communicate to us directly, in a flash of inspiration, an open, enlivening moment when we are alone and not particularly conscious of ourselves or our surroundings—say, when we awaken spontaneously, consoled in the dark at 3:00 A.M. We recognize such times of grace immediately, and they become cherished moments in the history of our faith, moments we can contemplate and savor again and again. One cannot count on spontaneous and overwhelming consolations to occur regularly, however, and many people likely hunger for them yet do not receive them. More often, human beings must rely upon the ordinary moments of daily existence to reveal God's loving, transforming presence. How, then, can we contemplate these quotidian experiences until they emit for us a whiff of the sacred?

Our relationships with people, environments, social structures, and culture can reveal God's presence to us in the course of our daily lives. Though God imbues the entire world with divine presence, we seem to experience this reality only sporadically. Sometimes when God startles us into noticing, we feel shaken alive, awash in divine mystery; then, as the poet Gerard Manley Hopkins writes, "The world is charged with the grandeur of God."[1] More often, though, if we want to experience God, it is incumbent upon us to seek to perceive God's presence in daily life. One way of doing so is to pay careful attention to how our relationships challenge and move us, to the impressions they make on us, with the expectation of meeting God. If we gaze at the world through the lens of faith, engage it in hope and with God in mind, when our relationships challenge and move us, we can find ourselves noticing and responding not only to them, but also to the divine.

At times like these, we are present to ourselves, to our relationships, and to God. Theologian Karl Rahner (1904–84) suggests that it is precisely this ability to be present to ourselves in the midst of being present to others that makes human experience spiritual experience.[2] For example, we may say that we experience God while praying with a congregation, talking with a friend, or gazing at a painting. Each of these is a very different kind of interaction from the others: One involves us with a community, one with an individual, and one with a work of art. What all of these interactions have in common, however, is that they invoke *in us* a sense of God's presence. When we notice that our attention is drawn to God either during experiences like these or when we recall them later, say, in prayer or in spiritual direction, we grow in relationship with ourselves, getting to know ourselves more fully by noticing and reflecting on our own experiences. We also grow in relationship with God by perceiving more thoroughly how God invites, inspires, and moves us. It follows that continuing to hone our awareness of ourselves, and helping those who come to us for supervision to do the same, can lead to ever more conscious experiences of God's presence, inspiring ever more abundant faith.

What may be instructive to spiritual directors seeking supervision, then, is a detailed examination of the means by which we can notice our own experiences of ourselves and of the world with an eye toward experiencing God. In short, what kinds of data do we notice in our bodies, emotions, and minds when we sense God's presence and when we feel blocked from doing so? Also, what do we notice about the body language of our directees, and about what they report about their own bodies, minds, and emotions when they try to sense God's presence and when they feel blocked from doing so? Such questions are central to spiritual direction and to those supervising spiritual directors. This living, breathing body of ours, whose very processes invite attention to the holy, is also the exquisitely sensitive instrument used by spiritual directors as they attend to those who seek direction and by directees as they seek God's presence in their lives.

Since the brain, generator of thought, seat of emotion, controller of nervous systems, is part of the body, feelings and thoughts are as much about the body as sensation is. It becomes impossible, then, to set body in opposition to mind or mind in opposition to emotion, as was the temptation in earlier generations. Indeed, researchers can now use brain imaging to locate emotions, thoughts, and sensations precisely in the body. For example, research conducted at the University of London found that simply observing a loved one experiencing the physical sensation of pain registers pain in the observer, specifically in areas of the observer's brain responsible for emotion.[3] We really do feel one another's pain, and this empathy registers in our bodies. Of course, a thought, emotion, or sensation experienced in one context may mean something entirely different in another. But before attempting to discern what our thoughts, emotions, and sensations mean, we must first become conscious of them.

Sensations

When spiritual directors and supervisors consider the role of the body in direction, they tend to think most often of body language, perhaps because the body language of director and directee alike provides a considerable amount of useful data. Even most beginning directors have noticed something akin to the slumping directee with downcast eyes who says weakly, "Everything is going well," and have responded by mentioning to the directee the dissonance between his or her body language and words. Most directors have also wondered about their own body language—what it might mean, for instance, when they find themselves folding their arms across their chests and straining against the back of their chairs whenever they meet certain directees. Even spiritual directors well aware of body language, however, may not take note of sensations mentioned by their directees or those that they themselves experience during a session, each of which can provide data useful to the spiritual direction conversation.

Sensations Reported by Directees

Some directees seem aware of their sensations and report them often in spiritual direction. Others are conscious of them but don't realize that it might be helpful to mention them in direction. Still others rarely notice them.

When directees freely recount their sensations—a twinge here, a constriction there—while in the midst of discussing other things, this information can stymie some directors, who avoid responding because they simply do not know what to say. In such cases, supervisors might encourage directors to simply communicate what they notice to the directee. The director might say something like "I notice that you've mentioned more than once that your throat feels constricted" or "I notice that your awareness today is drawn often to your sensations." Such statements invite directees not simply to notice their current experience, but also to reflect on it. This opens more possibilities for them to experience God's presence.

Conversely, if a director notices that a directee rarely, if ever, mentions sensation, he or she might probe gently to invite the directee's sensations into the conversation. For example, a director might ask, "If you were to imagine that thought as a bodily sensation, what might it feel like?" or "If you were to locate that feeling somewhere in your body, where might it be and how might it feel?"

Another challenge for directors is that on occasion directees might be held in the sway of their sensations. A girl I taught in high school two decades ago insisted that a boy she liked must really love her, because "if he didn't, he couldn't kiss me like that." She let the delightful sensations she experienced while kissing the boy convince her of his love, not allowing herself to notice for quite some time that he did not treat her well. Nor are adults immune to such behavior. If directors notice directees becoming inordinately attached to the realm of sensation, they can counter this by investigating what the directees perceive about their own thoughts and emotions as well.

Sensations Experienced by Directors

Directors would do well during sessions to attend not only to sensations reported by their directees, but also to their own, because they can make use of their sensations as they listen and discern. For example, if one's back aches during direction, it may be due to an uncomfortable chair or an injured back, but a director with back pain may also be able to discern other reasons for it. Perhaps this sensation of pain is instead (or also) about some heaviness in the session, and perhaps the weight that is sensed burdens him or her. Not every sensation one experiences while directing is relevant, however, and paying attention to more than a few of them could be counterproductive. Nevertheless, if directors who aren't in the habit of doing so practice checking for sensations during sessions, they will discover that just as their thoughts and feelings can register significant occurrences during direction, so, too, can their sensations.

Sensations in Supervision

Whether or not a particular sensation opens us to God's presence is, like everything else in spiritual direction, dependent on context and subject to discernment. For me, tensed muscles, a pounding heart, and butterflies in my stomach can signal a knowing that God is truly present in a particular moment, or it can simply indicate that I'm about to give a speech or arrive at a party full of strangers. Like emotions and thoughts, sensations are subjective. Not only their meaning, but also the circumstances that prompt them can vary greatly from person to person. Feeling embarrassed might cause your face to flush, but in someone else, a reddened face might indicate a feeling of shame. And whereas feeling nervous may cause beads of sweat to appear on your brow, a directee's sweating brow may indicate a fever.

Even for the same person, the meaning of particular sensations can vary. Indeed, each of us evinces a unique lexicon of sensations and their diverse meanings. Today a constricted throat might mean that I can't find my own voice, but if my throat constricts tomorrow, it may indicate fear or exhaustion.

In supervision, it is often helpful to query directors about which sensations they were experiencing during the sessions they bring for supervision. When our hearts and minds are perplexed, contemplating sensations can help us better understand the dynamics of a session. It also can be helpful for supervisors to invite directors to note, in general, which of their sensations they notice regularly and which most often attend their experiences of God. In addition to tensed muscles, pounding heart, butterflies, and tingling, some relatively common sensations that can signal the holy include sighs, tears, a sense of coursing energy or warmth, shivers, goose bumps, and flushing.

Now for a caveat: Sensations don't always generate clear and specific meanings for director or directee during, or even after, sessions. The specific meaning of a sensation isn't always crucial, however; simply acknowledging that you feel your skin tingling may be all that's needed to open you to the mystery of God.

Not only can a sensation mean more than one thing, but its meaning may change over time. In this sense, interpreting sensations seems analogous to interpreting dreams. For example, I experienced an ache in my stomach repeatedly during the first year after my mother's death. This was, coincidentally, also my first year of doctoral studies. I felt a profound sense of loss when my mother died, often awakening during the middle of the night and physically aching for her. It wasn't until I sat in a seminar several months later, when my attention moved yet again to the ache in my stomach, an ache that had by this time become acute, that an interpretation more accurate to that particular moment occurred to me: "I bet this isn't sadness at all—it's probably an ulcer!" Thankfully, I didn't have an ulcer, but I did have a condition that required medical attention. In retrospect, I believe that the ache in my stomach did have something to do with the sadness that arose when my mother died. Over the course of several months, however, that ache became more about my stomach and less about my feelings about my mother's death.

Emotions

Particular dimensions of knowing seem to gain favor at different times and among different populations. Today religious people from a variety of traditions tend to favor emotions. Ecstatic medieval mystics appear to have emphasized emotions as well, whereas figures from the enlightenment often seemed to regard thought most highly. Among poets from the romantic period, emotion reigned supreme. More recently, whereas most scholars from the mid-twentieth century favored thought, one need only recall the 1960s mantra "If it feels good, do it" to realize that for many people during that period, feeling and sensation were the preferred currency.

Today members of religious communions partial to feeling sometimes consider thought suspect. Those still rooted in enlightenment thought, however, can seem nonplussed in the face of religious feeling. In addition, after the decades of attention feminist scholars have given to studying the body, sensation has gained currency in theological circles. At least in California, where I write this chapter, one often hears, "My body is telling me to . . ." In each era, it seems, we are tempted to make the same mistake—thinking that one way of knowing encompasses and speaks for them all.

Emotions Described and Expressed by Directees

Directees familiar with attending to their feelings typically report emotions they have experienced in the past that relate to events that have occurred in the past, which sometimes has the effect of bringing these emotions alive again in the present moment. Such directees also tend to experience new emotions during the course of a session, related to whatever is unfolding during the session.

Because reporting emotions from the past can feel safer than experiencing and expressing current emotion, directees less attuned to feeling sometimes prefer to remain in the realm of reporting past feelings, rather than risking entry into the realm of experiencing and expressing emotions in the present moment. When a session seems to go stale, such reporting may be the culprit. If so, it can be useful to invite directees into the present moment by asking them to notice what they feel *now* about what happened earlier. This invites them into their present experience, opens a new opportunity for experiencing God, and brings the session back to life. Sometimes directees respond to such a question not with a report of what they're currently feeling, but with tears, angry words, sighs of consolation, or other expressions of the emotion itself. Such expression opens them to new emotions, thoughts, and sensations, as well as a more pervasive sense of God's presence in the present moment.

Like sensations, however, emotions can generate confusion. One man I directed returned again and again to an abusive relationship because, he said, "It took me so many years to get out of my head that I promised myself I would always follow my heart." Was it truly thoughts that were the problem earlier in his life, or the fact that he believed his thoughts exclusively, ignoring other dimensions of his experience?

This directee reported to me that his body recoiled in pain when his partner assaulted him. His mind told him that continuing this relationship was a bad idea. This man's feelings hurt as well; even telling me what had happened brought tears to his eyes. In spite of what I perceived as overwhelming data that his body, mind, and emotions were giving him, the man continued to act *only* on his feelings of love for his partner. Only eventually did he realize that by choosing to dismiss the difficult sensations, thoughts, and feelings these encounters with his partner generated, he was repeating his earlier mistake, but with a twist. Now, instead of being ruled by the tyranny of thought, he had fallen prey to the tyranny of emotion—not all emotion, but the feelings of love and attachment he ascribed to his heart.

This man's story brings to mind the sentiment of Irenaeus of Lyon, who asserted in the second century that the glory of God is a human being fully alive. This directee truly came to life when he began to pay attention to the whole of his experience and use what he perceived to help him discern God's call. The story also provides a poignant illustration of the pitfalls of anointing emotions, or any other dimension of our experience, as the only path to truth, while excluding other possibilities for hearing God's invitation. More often than making a conscious choice to privilege emotion over thought and feeling, however, directees simply become overwhelmed, stuck in the realm of emotion.

From time to time, a director might encounter a directee who cries during a session almost to the exclusion of other forms of expression, leaving the director to discern whether to respond as if the directee is experiencing a catharsis, finally feeling free to express pent-up emotion, or is sinking into a mire. Some directors find themselves struggling in the face of a directee's tears. In such cases, a supervisor might suggest some strategies. For example, a director could start by sitting prayerfully and empathetically with the directee, open to God's promptings. Should the directee seem unable to stop crying, the director might acknowledge the tears aloud and respond appropriately to the directee's reaction to that acknowledgment. Perhaps the most effective strategy involves extending a gentle invitation to the directee to check in with another dimension of experience, such as expressing what he or she thinks about the emotion being felt or what sensations the emotion stirs in his or her body. Just as it is important to invite people lost in thought to an awareness of feeling, so it is important to invite people lost in feeling to consult their thought.

Emotions Experienced by Directors

Directors can learn much from their own emotions during sessions, for like their sensations, their emotions help them gauge what is happening not only within them, but also in the session itself. When emotions demand a director's attention, when they return again and again during a session, the director would do well to attempt to discern their relevance in light of a directee's story.

Perhaps a directee's grandfather has recently died, and he tells a story about walking as a boy with his grandfather on the banks of a river near his childhood home. During the story, the director feels a sense of poignancy, of sadness and loss. If these feelings accord with the story and pass rather quickly, it may be that the director is experiencing empathy because she, too, has lost her grandfather and has fond memories of times spent with him. If the narrative evokes in the director feelings that seem rather more intense than she would expect the story to elicit, she might discern that these feelings belong to her own life and realize, perhaps, that she has more mourning to do about the loss of her own grandfather. Finally, if the narrative stirs emotions that remain with the director, returning repeatedly during the session, they might prompt her to realize, for instance, that the directee has left his own feelings about his grandfather's death out of the conversation.

Emotions in Supervision

Like taking note of sensations, remembering the emotions experienced at particular points in sessions often assists spiritual directors in supervision. A director might notice that during the session under consideration, he experienced no feelings at all. Clearly, this bears examination. Or perhaps the director felt emotions toward the beginning of the session, but then something seemed to shut off their flow. Directors may even notice themselves censuring certain feelings that arise during a session; their supervisor can help them sort out why.

Supervision gives directors an opportunity to examine whether emotions they have experienced during a session relate to their own lives, to what was happening during the session, to their relationship with the directee, or to some combination of the three. Discerning this isn't always easy, but the attempt to do so can bear much fruit. Say that during the course of the supervision conversation, a director begins talking about a feeling of disgust that arises whenever he meets a certain directee. The director feels concerned about this reaction and has been trying to squelch it. Only recently has it come clearly into his view. As reluctant as he was to let himself acknowledge this feeling, he says he's even more reluctant to bring it to supervision, because he fears that he is disgusted by the person of the directee. Even admitting that fear to his supervisor appalls him.

During supervision, the disgust returns. The director starts to feel guilty, even ashamed of himself. But during the course of supervision, he may learn, for instance, that the directee reminds him of someone who has done something reprehensible to him, and that he is disgusted by that person's actions, not by the directee. In this way, supervision can help directors receive the healing they need in order to be able to listen freely and compassionately, not only to their directees, but also to themselves.

Thoughts

Sometimes directors who prize feeling as the dimension of human experience through which God is most likely to touch them believe that spiritual direction is meant to help directees move away from thought and into feeling. The model of relationship and spiritual direction explored here, however, assigns equal relevance to thought, feeling, and sensation, asserting that God communicates with us through all dimensions of human experience. The question becomes, then, how directors can make use of thought in spiritual direction in such a way as to minimize the likelihood of what concerns some directors: that directees will become "stuck in their heads."

Thoughts Expressed by the Directee

Karl Rahner's[4] theology suggests a helpful way of understanding thoughts as they relate to spiritual direction. His first point would surprise no spiritual director: There are things we human beings have experienced and can articulate. For example, directees might disclose information about their experiences in relationships clearly and effortlessly in spiritual direction.

Rahner also notes that there are things we have not experienced but can nevertheless articulate. An example of this would be information about spirituality learned through reading the spiritual classics. When directees focus in direction on things they can articulate but have not experienced—say, on a description of the seventh dwelling place in St. Teresa of Avila's *Interior Castle*—sessions tend to go dead as the conversation veers into abstraction.

There are also things, according to Rahner, that we have experienced and cannot articulate. When directees venture toward this territory, struggling to put such an experience into words, to describe what they have felt or sensed but have not yet made sense of, they begin moving into the realm of mystery and discovery. Surprise and awe often attend these moments in spiritual direction—surprise, awe, and a palpable experience of God's revelatory presence. More often than not, in such cases, the experience of God arrives specifically as directees begin to engage their thought processes in order to understand their experience.

I experienced the grace that comes with putting feelings and sensations into words while taking my first theology course, a course focused on Rahner's Christology and taught by the late William Dych. Dych had studied Rahner's work extensively and translated some of it into English. He was a gifted teacher, and throughout the term, I felt awestruck, thrilled by the experience of finally discovering, after several years of searching, ideas that fit what I had sensed and felt but never knew how to talk about. Christ's all-embracing presence consoled me, and as a directee in spiritual direction, I spoke not only of this consolation, but also of the ideas that occasioned it, helping the consolation expand and deepen. One of the most profound gifts that spiritual directors can share with their directees is to accompany them as they venture into this realm of what they have experienced but not yet articulated.

Thoughts Experienced by the Director

Most spiritual directors have vocations in addition to that of offering spiritual direction. We fill such roles as teacher, businessperson, religious sister, minister, doctor, theologian, and parent. What's more, we bring into our spiritual direction sessions the cognitive sets associated with each of our roles. This carries with it certain temptations. The teacher, for example, wants to instruct; the doctor finds advice about healing welling up within; the parent yearns to protect.

Regardless of the roles we play in life, most spiritual directors experience in direction, at one time or another, the temptation to engage their minds with theories, instructions, judgments, pontifications, corrections, and other thoughts that distract their attention.

Noticing their busy minds, beginning directors can experience a related temptation. Ensnared time after time by their many thoughts, some respond by attempting to banish most of their thoughts. Indeed, they work so hard at keeping their minds pristine during sessions that they lose the opportunity to make use of the myriad ideas that may arise in service to the directee. Rather than locking one's thoughts away during direction, the challenge becomes deciding which of the many thoughts might help the director notice and respond to the directee and to God, while at the same time letting go of thoughts that distract. This is one of the more difficult discernment skills for directors to learn, but one of the most necessary. Effective spiritual directors employ this skill time and again during their sessions, each time they think thoughts such as "Where is God moving in this story?" "Do I engage this part of it or that?" "Which aspects of the narrative shall I hold in my consciousness, and which shall I let go of?" "Shall I speak now or remain silent?" Each of these discernment questions stimulates relevant thought.

In addition, there are times during direction when the director feels invited to another type of thinking: interpretation. When directors interpret data during direction, they do not deliver rock-solid judgments about what something means. Rather, they report what they notice and respond according to those spiritual and psychological traditions with which they are most familiar: "Have you considered that you may be depressed?" or "You seem to be experiencing aridity in prayer."

Directors also make interpretations informed by their own sets of experiences. For example, as an educated Christian, I realize that Christian theologians have spilled much ink describing pride as a grave sin. Time and again, I have had the experience of wrestling with my own pride. But not only am I a Christian, I am a Christian who has at times experienced oppression. In addition, I have read the work of Christian theologians who have written that pride may not always be a sin for the oppressed; rather, pride may be the blessing that allows them to break free from their bonds.

As I read them, I experienced these words as good news, a gift from God that continues to give me a sense of hope and freedom. Since having this experience of freedom, I have been able to more accurately interpret the words of people speaking in direction about pride as a sin. Interpreting their words in light of my experience helps me know better how to respond to their concerns. In one case, I found myself hearing a call to leadership in the story of a directee who worried that she was being tempted by pride because she was giving serious thought to accepting an influential position in her parish.

Thoughts in Supervision

When directors bring to supervision a session primarily featuring the articulation of ideas, concepts, explanations, theories, rules, interpretations, doctrines, and the like, they often do so feeling frustrated that more didn't happen during the session. "It seems like a conversation I might have at the water cooler," they might say, "not like spiritual direction. I couldn't sense God's presence in this session, and I'm not sure what to do about it." In fact, such sessions can seem dry, and when they do, it's often because directees have moved away from discussing their concrete experiences and into the realm of abstraction.

In supervision, directors not only can examine their reactions to such sessions, but also can learn strategies for bringing the conversation back down to earth by relating it to a dimension of human experience other than thought. Here, it can help to role-play ways of breaking into a long excursus and relating it to a directee's experience, practicing responses such as "You sound really engaged by William Blake's poetry. Do poems ever come to you when you pray?" or "I can tell that you've thought a lot about the afterlife since your friend's death. Can you tell me a bit more about how it feels to have lost him?"

When directors bring to supervision sessions featuring numerous or heavy-handed interpretations, or interpretations that seem to miss the mark, supervisors can serve them well in a number of ways. If the accuracy of an interpretation raises questions in a supervisor's mind, he or she might inquire gently as to how the director arrived at it. If a session seems full of interpretations, a supervisor might assist the director by examining each one so that they can discern together which were truly essential. If the interpretations seem too heavy-handed or pat, supervisors might role-play with the directors. It can be helpful for them to practice the skill of arriving at provisional and open-ended interpretations, such as "I think the directee might be depressed; I'll keep that in mind as I continue to listen and inquire." It can also help to practice the skill of keeping an interpretation to oneself and allowing it to suggest responses, rather than voicing it aloud and closing prematurely the directee's investigation, or worse, inviting a compliant directee to agree with the director's interpretation rather than drawing his or her own conclusion.

Encompassing, Simultaneous Experiences

If it's true that opening ourselves to sensations, emotions, and thoughts helps us become more conscious of experiencing God, then it follows that types of experiences that encompass simultaneously more than one of these dimensions can quite powerfully communicate the holy to us. For example, as we struggle to understand some aspect of our lives, an image or metaphor might come to us that at once describes our situation, evokes our feeling, causes us to shiver with recognition, and thrusts us into the mystery of God.

A certain woman, during one period of her life, felt little freedom. Between loneliness, a lost job, and a troubled relationship, she felt frustrated and angry. She didn't know how to express what she felt; all she knew was that she seemed to live in unrelieved misery, and God seemed far away. During the course of spiritual direction, an image came to her of a lion in a too-small cage, pacing in front of the locked door. Immediately she felt moved and relieved by the image, her face became more relaxed, and she thought of a goal: locate the key. During the course of the session, this woman's challenges didn't change, but she changed: That image brought her freedom and aroused her desire for a key. Eventually, as it happened, she came to understand that desire *was* the key.

Images and metaphors often provide openings to the holy, and it is no accident that much of our religious language involves them. But they aren't the only types of encompassing, simultaneous experiences that quicken our sense of the divine by incorporating every dimension of human experience at once. The thrill of intuition, the "aha!" of insight or understanding, the roiling of desire—all of these, and others, too, seem to open us immediately to divine mystery.

Encompassing, Simultaneous Experiences of the Directee

It's not difficult to recognize when directees have encompassing, simultaneous experiences, as one or more of the following often attends them: visible (and invisible) changes in the body, a shift in mood or energy, sighs, tears, silence. Directors might find that the types of encompassing, simultaneous experiences that people have depend, at least in part, on their personalities. Images tend to arise for some people, others may be more likely to experience intuitions, and still others have flashes of insight or understanding.

Encompassing, Simultaneous Experiences of the Director

If a director has an encompassing, simultaneous experience while directing, he or she must discern whether to share it and, if so, how. When I have such an experience in the course of my daily life, I feel grateful for God's gift to me. When I have such an experience while I am directing someone else, however, my experience tells me that this grace usually comes for the benefit of my directee, rather than solely as a boon to my own faith. If sharing the insight or image, the desire or intuition, with the directee doesn't seem appropriate, I hold it within me and let it inform me as I consider my responses during the remainder of the session.

If the director decides that his or her own encompassing, simultaneous experience is meant to be shared with the directee, it's best to do so a bit tentatively and without shifting the energy in the room away from the directee and toward the director. If I receive an image that I think would be helpful for a directee to hear about, because it seems to pull together many strands that have come before it in the session or because I think it could help the directee articulate and better understand his or her experience, I might say something like this: "As you're describing your hopes for the future, I keep seeing an image of a bright valley blanketed by green grass." If the directee picks up on the image, we may sense God's presence together. If he or she doesn't, the conversation will simply move on, though I may continue to keep the image in mind in case it might be useful to me later in the session.

Encompassing, Simultaneous Experiences in Supervision

In supervision, supervisors can celebrate with directors the arrival of these grace-filled moments and commend them for what they've done to help the directee savor them. When such moments arise, directors might join directees in fruitful silence, highlight various aspects of the experience, or simply weave the experience back into the conversation when appropriate.

Supervisors also might role-play with directors certain skills meant to encourage encompassing, simultaneous experiences. For example, inquiring about a directee's desire at a particular moment can open that directee to such an experience by inviting him or her to engage thought, emotion, and sensation all at once, for desire tends to envelop all three. In addition, considering desire in the context of direction often elicits a directee's longing for God. A director might also welcome such experiences into a session by inviting the directee to engage his or her imagination. The directee might imagine what the topic at hand looks like, sounds like, feels like, tastes like, or smells like.

Meeting God in Our Relationships with the World

Becoming conscious of our own responses helps awaken us to our experiences of God. But what elicits these responses in the first place? It is our relationships with the world. In general, the notion that our relationships with the world reveal God's presence comes naturally to many spiritual directors. Sometimes it seems to me that it is only by virtue of the skin that delineates our own body from those of others, separating us physically from the rest of the world, that we can claim ourselves as individuals. We are conceived in relationship, grow through relationship with our mothers, and after our birth, we relate not simply with our families and neighborhoods but, in this era of increasing globalization, with the entire world. Indeed, technological advances even set us in relationship with the universe beyond.

Sadly, however, some directors hold fast to the notion that the material of spiritual direction should be limited to what directees report about their relationship with God specifically as that relationship unfolds during periods of formal prayer. Such directors tend to use the word God repeatedly during their sessions and listen for their directees to do the same. They habitually steer the spiritual direction conversation back to experiences of God in the context of formal prayer whenever possible, believing erroneously that when the conversation strays from the directee's prayer periods, it becomes irrelevant or even inappropriate to spiritual direction. In chapter 8, Elizabeth Liebert delineates various categories of human relationship with the world and the ways in which our relationships communicate God's presence to us. She also discusses the role of supervision in expanding the horizons of spiritual directors so that they can begin to notice that their experience of God imbues all categories of human relationship.

A model of spiritual direction that encompasses every dimension of human experience across all categories of human relationship can aid both directors and supervisors. Directors working from such a model listen not only to the specific experiences of their directees, but also for the categories into which these experiences fit. A director may note, for example, that a directee has spoken in depth about an experience of God she had in the mountains by herself, and then wait to hear whether and how that experience has affected relationships in other categories. Has the consolation she experienced in the mountains extended also to her marriage? Has it affected in any way the relationship she has with the parish council or her troublesome colleague? One assumption behind this model is that our experience of God in one relationship has the potential to transform not just that relationship, but all our other relationships as well. Though I would not advocate following up the woman's story about the mountains with a series of questions about her other relationships, I *would* suggest listening for the ways in which they have been affected, and directing her attention to these transformations if she seems unaware of them.

In addition, as directors working from this model listen to their directees' experiences of relationships, they also consider which human dimensions these experiences fall into. If, during a session, a directee mentions only one or two dimensions of experience, the director may give him or her a little nudge. The director may ask the directee how he or she feels about a thought just discussed or to elaborate on an offhand comment made about a sensation. Just as experiencing God in one relationship can transform other relationships, so we can take it on faith that experiencing God through thought can open into an experience of God in feeling and sensation as well. In addition, directors assess over time which dimensions of experience seem to show up only occasionally in directees' conversation, identifying those who love to conceptualize and seldom speak of feeling or those who lavishly feel but rarely mention sensation, and let that information influence their responses in direction.

In these ways, little by little, directors seek to assist directees as they attempt to "grasp fully, with all the holy ones, the breadth and length and height and depth of Christ's love" (Eph 3:18).[5] In supervision, we model our awareness that our relationship with God imbues all categories of our relationships and encourage directors to engage in this awareness when they meet their directees. We also collaborate with directors as they seek to become more conscious of the concrete ways in which their bodies, minds, and emotions resonate with the relational dynamics of their sessions. In this way, both the direction session and the supervision session serve as subtle training in the art of paying loving attention to the world and to oneself in relationship to the world, doing so in faith and with hope that God will meet us there.

Notes

1. Gerard Manley Hopkins, "God's Grandeur," in *Poems and Prose of Gerard Manley Hopkins*, ed. W. H. Gardner (Middlesex, England: Penguin, 1954), 27.

2. Karl Rahner, *Foundations of Christian Faith*, trans. William V. Dych (New York: Crossroad, 1984; English translation, 1978), 17–19, 24–23; and *Theological Investigations*, Vol. XVI, trans. David Morland, O.S.B., (New York: Seabury, 1979), 27–29.

3. Tania Singer et al., "Empathy for Pain Involves the Affective but not Sensory Components of Pain," *Science* 303 (2004): 1157–62.

4. Karl Rahner, *Theological Investigations*, Vol. XIII, trans. David Bourke (New York: Seabury, 1975), 122–32; *Theological Investigations*, Vol. XI, trans. David Bourke (New York: Seabury, 1974), 149–65; and *Theological Investigations*, Vol. XVI, trans. David Morland, O.S.B. (New York: Seabury, 1979), 227–43.

5. Paraphrase of biblical text by author.

CHAPTER SIX

The Given and the Gift:
Sexuality and God's Eros in Spiritual Direction and Supervision

Samuel Hamilton-Poore

T he details of what she talked about are hard for me to remember.[1] It has been more than a decade, after all, since this particular conversation took place. But even today my own interior and visceral responses are easy to recollect: attraction, confusion, fear.

As she unveiled her soul to me, I felt a flush of attraction. I was alert, very. The blood was rushing to my head, through my body. More than likely, my face was turning red. And almost as immediately as I noticed my attraction to her, I became confused. Why was I feeling this way—and why so strongly? To complicate matters, as soon as I noticed my confusion, I became frightened. I was frightened by my attraction. I was frightened by my confusion. I suppose I was even frightened by my fear.

On one level, my behavior with her that day was thoroughly professional and above reproach. Recognizing my discomfort, I somehow made it through our conversation without saying or doing anything inappropriate. On another level, however, I failed her, professionally and spiritually. She had come to me in trust, wanting to speak from the deepest part of her self, her soul. She had wanted me to help her hear God's heart. But I could "hear" neither her nor God, because I was overwhelmed by the clamor of my own thoughts and emotions. I was not free to be fully present to her or to God.

I recount this particular conversation for two reasons. First, it was one in an emerging pattern of encounters at that period in my ministry. People were coming to me in hope that I might assist them in deepening their relationship with God. I was (and am) an ordained minister, but these people were seeking more than just someone in my professional role. I began to recognize what they were recognizing in me: someone with a vocation, perhaps even a gift, for listening. As a result of such encounters, I eventually entered a program of training in spiritual direction.

But I also recount this conversation and my flush-faced response because it led me to ask questions about myself and God and listening that have everything to do with the subject of this chapter. Why did I feel such a flush of attraction when this woman began speaking from the deepest part of her soul? She was, in fact, an attractive young woman, but never before in any other setting with her had I felt overwhelmed the way I did that day. Why? Was there something wrong with me? Something amiss in my marriage?

Why was it that I became sexually confused and uncomfortable the moment she became spiritually intimate and vulnerable? Did it have anything to do with power and the fact that she was making herself vulnerable to me? What is the connection between sexuality and spiritual intimacy? Did this experience mean that there are some people I would not be able to listen to or areas of their lives that I would never be able to enter?

And where, by the way, was God? The God who had led her to seek me as a listener? The God who had led me to be open to her? The God who was present in her life and her speaking and who was supposed to be present in my listening?

Time, prayer, training, and experience in spiritual direction, collegial support and supervision have helped me to discover answers to some of these questions. These answers are, for the most part, provisional. I claim no authority beyond that of a spiritual director who is trying his best, with God's help, to grow in this ministry of holy listening. I am trying to pay attention.

Naming the Erotic

I now believe that there is something inherently sexual in any relationship in which human hearts or spirits are open and responsive to one another. I believe this is especially true in the intimacy of spiritual direction, in which our hearts are open and vulnerable to one another within the presence of the open and vulnerable heart of God. Gerald May assumes that a dynamic of sexual feelings exists, at least unconsciously, in "every spiritual relationship that has sufficient closeness to warrant the name of direction."[2]

As spiritual directors and supervisors, we must pay attention to this sexual dimension and dynamic. We need to acknowledge, honor, and respond to it in ways that are guided by God's grace rather than derailed by our own fears, compulsions, or confusion. Only so will we be prepared, when invited by our directees, to enter with them, safely and freely, the most intimate places of their hearts: the places where they, and we, often encounter the heart of God.

It has been helpful for me to find or give names to what I have experienced. My naming is more for the sake of my own self-awareness. Few things have caused as much damage as one person or group (usually male) exercising sexual or spiritual control over another person or group (usually female) by way of naming. This is not my intent. My purpose in naming is to find a place of interior and relational freedom where we can move together, safely, in intimacy and wholeness. What follows is my own personal "glossary-in-progress."

I have come to understand *spirituality* as the process of becoming fully human. I borrow this definition from the 1977 Scottish Council of Churches.[3] To become more fully human is to grow in compassion and sensitivity to one's own self, others, the nonhuman creation, and to God, who is within and beyond this totality. By this definition, then, spirituality is profoundly relational. *Christian* spirituality, in particular, is to become more fully human by being formed more and more in the image of Christ. We grow as Christians the more we are able to mirror or embody the Spirit of Christ in all the various ways we relate to ourselves, others, the creation, and God.

But why is our spirituality so profoundly relational? A simple answer is that this is the way God has made us. There is a God-given and, therefore, graced power that moves us to seek intimate communication and communion with others, with our own selves, with creation, and—in, through, under, and beyond all things—with God. I call this graced power *eros* or the *erotic*.[4] This power is what made Augustine "restless" until he found his rest in God. It is the foundation of our capacity for love, whether love is expressed in friendship, marriage, partnerships, family, prayer, a passion for justice, or a desire for God.[5]

Sexuality is our embodied, relational response to this erotic power.[6] Our sexuality is the particular context in which our erotic longings or desires are expressed or repressed. According to this understanding of sexuality, it may or may not involve the sharing of genital pleasure. It may be expressed by way of a deep and committed friendship (same or opposite sex), a passion to protect or preserve a wetland, a drive to paint or sculpt or dance, or the quiet thrill of our souls resting in God. To the degree that our sexuality is free from unjust or abusive power relations or expressions, it helps us grow in our relationships to self, others, the nonhuman creation, and God, who is within and beyond this totality. The God, that is, who urges, draws, and invites us.

Of all our possible responses to God's erotic pull or push, few have the capacity to change us as the experience of *intimacy* with another person or with God. Sheila Murphy describes intimacy as "the profound risk of vulnerability before another resulting from self-disclosure." Intimacy requires us to stand "in brutal honesty before the self and another, which allows nakedness before God."[7] No one can see God and live, Moses the prophet tells us. It is also true that no one can stand in intimate nakedness before God and not be changed. And no one can either touch or be touched by another person in intimacy without being somehow transformed.

When I am intimate with another, I make myself—my true or honest self—known to the other, and in a sense, I come to discover myself. I risk the other's acceptance or rejection. I risk losing myself to the other. When someone is intimate with me—whether my wife, my child, a friend—that person has rendered himself or herself vulnerable to my response. I am allowed to see, hear, or touch this person in the naked holiness of who he or she really is. If the intimacy between us is shared, mutually, then our relationship may expand to a deeper and broader level of trust and honesty. We both become new—new to ourselves and new to one another.

Finally, I understand *spiritual direction* as the art, discipline, and commitment of one person assisting another (or members of a group assisting each other) in listening to the ways God may be drawing, luring, or inviting the directee into deeper, truer, and more fully human relationships. In a sense, the director assists the directee in noticing and responding to the movement of God's eros, God's love, God's grace in his or her life, prayer, and relationships.

As in any other significant relationship, the foundation of spiritual direction is God's erotic love or power. When we do our ministry well, then we are able to work with God's Spirit in urging, drawing, and inviting our directees into a deeper, truer, and more intimate relationship with God. Much of our ability or skill in doing this, however, hinges on our capacity for intimacy, as well as our own comfort or discomfort, as individuals and spiritual directors, with our own sexuality. Murphy writes the following for a readership of Catholic and celibate ministers, but I believe it applies broadly to all of us who practice the ministry of spiritual direction: "[T]he relational nature of ministry places even greater demands on ministers to embrace and grow in their sexuality and intimacy because those constitute the foundation of their spirituality."[8]

Setting aside this "glossary," at least temporarily, let's look at how we, as spiritual directors and supervisors, may embrace our own sexuality and intimacy and thus find a place of interior freedom where we can allow our directees to embrace their own—safely and in wholeness before God. We begin by acknowledging and honoring sexuality as both a "given" and a "gift," taking into account both the biblical witness and our own experiences. After this, we will consider a few ways in which our sexuality may be misunderstood or misused within the context of spiritual direction. Again, what seems to matter most is paying attention, and this is where supervision becomes especially important to us all.

Paying Attention to Sexuality as a Given

There is always a sexual dimension or dynamic within the relationship of spiritual direction. This is true, first of all, because we who come together in spiritual direction are always, ourselves, sexual beings. What Ann and Barry Ulanov say of prayer may also be said of spiritual direction: "Young or old, celibate or active, married or single, with or without children, we live as men and women and we pray as men and women."[9]

There is the physiological "givenness" of our sexuality. We do not "have" bodies to which our minds or souls are loosely attached. In a very real sense, as Sallie McFague notes, "We *are* bodies, 'body and soul.'"[10] And our bodies are, with rare exceptions, either male or female. When given life, we are given bodies, and along with our bodies we receive other genetic "givens" that predispose us in biological directions that may bring us pleasure, delight, confusion, or suffering.

Although we are never less than our bodies, we are always more than our biology. We also carry within us and communicate the sociopolitical identity of what it "means" to be male or female. No one emerges from a mother's womb wearing either a pink or blue knitted cap, nor are we born with names printed on our bodies. And yet soon after birth, we receive names that, like our pink or blue caps, are social signals of our sexuality: Sam or Susan, Robert or Roberta. At the beginning, and for the rest of our lives, our names serve as a linguistic bridge into a life of everyday spiritual, social, political, and sexual relationships.

In addition to the biological messages we receive from our bodies—sometimes faint, sometimes urgent—we quickly learn from our parents and communities what a "man" or a "woman" is supposed to be, do, desire, aspire to, expect. Whether we accept, reject, or struggle with these messages, we bring them with our body-soul into spiritual direction.

The fact that we are sexual beings touches every aspect of our lives—physiological, interpersonal, social, political, emotional, economic, spiritual. Philip Sheldrake writes: "We can try to ignore sexuality and repress it, or we can seek to live positively and healthily within it. What is not open to us is to bypass it or to escape completely from it."[11]

Much of what we bring to spiritual direction may be seen as our search, longing, or frustration to uncover the positive, healthy, or even "holy" ways we may live within the given of our sexuality. The Ulanovs catalog many aspects of sexuality about which people might pray, from the depths of nearly every possible sexual or bodily dysfunction and disappointment to the heights of satisfaction and even ecstasy.[12] We may also find ourselves taking these concerns to spiritual direction—or having them brought to us as spiritual directors.

I would add to the Ulanovs' list the following: anger and continued suffering over childhood sexual abuse; a wish to reject or embrace one's sexual orientation; anger over the injustice of gender discrimination. With these added, I can say that as a spiritual director, I have heard each of these themes raised at least once within the context of direction. They were spoken by normal, ordinary men and women who were trying, with God's help, to pay attention—people created "male and female" in God's own image.

We are sexual beings; this is a given. In Appendix D, I suggest ways in which spiritual directors may better attend to their directees by paying attention to the "givenness" of their own sexuality. But more than a "given," our sexuality is also a "gift." Not only is there a sexual dimension within spiritual direction, but a spiritual dimension is also inherent in our sexuality.

Paying Attention to the Gift of Sexuality

I realize that it may be difficult, if not nearly impossible, for some readers to see or experience sexuality as gift. The statistics on the number of people who have endured sexual abuse, violation, and discrimination are truly staggering. Unless we find some way to affirm our sexuality as a divine gift, however, we may inadvertently compound the tragedy of sexual abuse and misconduct. Without affirmation, without seeing the gift, we allow our sexuality to be defined and demeaned by its misuse.

Within the Old Testament, the clearest and strongest affirmation of sexuality, desire, and the erotic is found in the Song of Songs. The Old Testament is filled with stories of desire: God for Israel, Israel for God, Jacob for Rebecca, Saul for the crown, David for Bathsheba, or the desire of the exiles to return home. What distinguishes the Song most sharply from the rest of the Old Testament scriptures is not that it takes desire or sexuality seriously, but rather "the exuberant, thoroughly erotic, and nonjudgmental manner in which it depicts the love between a man and a woman."[13] The Song depicts—even celebrates—the yearning that compels two lovers to seek one another repeatedly, relentlessly. It is as if the yearning itself is a main character in the poetry, a yearning that is, at times, like the woman or the man, lustful, desperate, playful, thrilling, stubborn, endearing, even maddening. It is, however, never boring. Listen to the woman of the Song:

> At night in bed, I want him—
> The one I love is not here.
>
> I'll rise and search the city,
> Through the streets and squares
>
> Until the city watchmen
> Find me wandering there
>
> And I ask them—have you seen him?
> The one I love is not here.
>
> When they have gone, I find him
> And I won't let him go
>
> Until he's in my mother's home,
> The room where I was born.
>
> O women of the city,
> Swear by the wild field doe

> Not to wake or rouse us
> Till we fulfill our love.[14]

As commentators note, there is a cyclical rhythm within the Song of seeking, finding, and losing. The lovers continually seek each other, sometimes connect, and begin their search again when circumstances pull them apart. "Absence" is as much a main theme of the Song, in a sense, as yearning—for it is the lovers' absence from each other that fuels their desire for one another. The love that is celebrated, then, within the Song is a human, sexual, erotic longing two people possess (or are possessed by) to connect with each other—body, soul, mind, lips, limbs, skin, breasts, feet, voices, hair.

In what way is erotic and sexual yearning—theirs, ours, or anyone's—a gift? And why would God give them or us such a gift—one that can transform us into creatures who are, at times, desperate, playful, stubborn, or flirtatious? This gift has sent many an adolescent to a school dance, like singer Don McLean, "with a pink carnation and a pickup truck"—and left poets such as Anne Sexton adrift before blank paper, daydreaming of "That Day":

> That was the day of your face,
> your face after love, close to the pillow, a lullaby . . .
> Yesterday I did not want to be borrowed
> but this is the typewriter that sits before me
> and love is where yesterday is at.[15]

Sexuality is a gift because it brings us enormous pleasure, as it does to the woman and the man of the Song, even if it also causes us frustration or heartache. Desire or eros is a gift to us, as it is to lovers of the Song, because it gives motion and passion to our living. It draws us out to seek and find companionship—intimate and life-infusing connections—with others. The love, the eros, that moves this man and this woman is much bigger than simply the two of them. Although the lovers' desire is focused and exquisite, it simultaneously appears to open them both to the beauty of all creation as they stretch for metaphor and means to communicate and connect. Desire awakens them to everyone and everything around them.

> Arise, my love, my fair one,
> and come away;
> for now the winter is past,
> the rain is over and gone.
> The flowers appear on the earth;
> the time of singing has come,
> and the voice of the turtledove
> is heard in our land.

> The fig tree puts forth its figs,
> and the vines are in blossom;
> they give forth fragrance.
> Arise, my love, my fair one,
> and come away. (2:10b–13)

The desire—the eros—that draws these two lovers together also urges, draws, and invites them out to embrace the larger creation that is also pulsing with love. Their senses and their experience of the world are enlarged by the gift of eros.

But there is still more. The name of God is not spoken in the Song, yet this poetry of erotic yearning and fulfillment is placed within the larger context of God's unfolding self-revelation. The inclusion of the Song within the sacred scriptures is both significant and wise. Read within the context of synagogue or church, there is a connection, the Song suggests, between the desire that drives these two human lovers and the desire that urges, draws, or invites us into intimate relationship with God.

This may explain why the Song has been held in such high regard through the centuries by Jewish and Christian interpreters of a mystical bent.[16] No matter the philosophical or hermeneutical presumptions of their reading—allegorical, typological, or literal—these interpreters all seem to affirm that "the love that forms human partnership and community, and that sustains the whole of creation, is a gift of God's own self."[17] Whether the woman of the Song is simply and wondrously just that or is seen to represent the people of Israel or the church or Mary or the individual soul, we can agree with Cary Ellen Walsh's recent comment: "The woman gives a demonstration of what loving heart, soul, and might would look like. And this could come in handy as wisdom when practicing the command to start loving God that way (Deut 5:5)."[18]

For Christians, an even more compelling demonstration of what loving "heart, soul, and might" looks like is found in Jesus of Nazareth. This brings us to the second great biblical affirmation of sexuality and eros: the *Incarnation*. The gospel proclamation is that in Jesus Christ, God's love "became flesh and lived among us" (John 1:14). God's purpose in coming to us in Jesus was "to reconcile to [God's] self all things" (Col 1:20)—to bring together, to reconnect, all that had become separated from God by sin. In a sense, Jesus is the humanly embodied expression of God's own erotic desire. Jesus was and is God's effort to urge, draw, and invite the world into deeper communion and intimacy with God's own self.

God affirms our sexuality by becoming a human being in Jesus, with all the physiological and sociological givens of sexuality and gender. Though the gospels are silent on whether Jesus married or experienced genital pleasure, they are very vocal in presenting Jesus as deeply, passionately engaged with the people he encounters—heart, mind, soul, body, and strength. He feeds the hungry, heals the sick, exorcises demons, confronts the oppressive powers of the religious and political elite, and constantly proclaims God's forgiveness. By his words and actions, Jesus communicates God's desire, stronger even than death, to reconcile and reunite.

If *intimacy* is understood as "the profound risk of vulnerability before another resulting from self-disclosure," then the Incarnation is the supreme example of such intimacy. God's own self is disclosed in Jesus, risking rejection and even death in order to bring God's relationship with us to a level that is deeper, truer, and more intimate. As the old hymn says, "What wondrous love is this, O my soul!" Jesus expresses his own sexuality—his own "embodied, relational response" to God's eros, God's love—by making himself completely available and vulnerable to himself, others, the nonhuman creation, and to his Father, who is within and beyond this totality.

By becoming incarnate, and therefore humanly and sexually relational, in Christ, God blesses and redeems our own humanly and sexually relational nature. We are able to become "one" with Christ and "one" with God not in spite of our sexuality, but precisely *because* we are sexual beings with a capacity, as Jesus both demonstrates and enables, to give an embodied, passionate response to the God who desires us. And we come to God not by way of some disembodied, disincarnate, desexualized, dispassionate discipline (if there can be such a thing), but by yielding ourselves to the power of God's desire for us, making ourselves vulnerable to the caresses of the Spirit, trusting that our bodies and souls will be loved by God.

Those who are followers of Jesus are invited into the community that is the "Body of Christ" to join with others who together incarnate the presence of Christ in the world. Nourished by the body and blood of Jesus, the Church engages the world with the depth and passion modeled by Jesus: feeding the hungry, healing the sick, confronting oppressive powers, offering a consistent message of forgiveness. The Church, as Christ's Body, continues to embody or incarnate God's desire to bring all things together in Christ.

From my own perspective as a Christian, the ministry of spiritual direction is itself a participation in the mystery of the Incarnation. Jesus promised that "wherever two or three are gathered in [his] name" (Matt 18:20), he would be with them. When two or more people come together to be present to God's presence through prayer and contemplative listening, God has a way of showing up, too, and often. And not only this, but the director very often embodies or mirrors for the directee the love, presence, and vulnerability that God has extended to us through Christ. We directors are not Christ, of course, but Christ can and does often work through us. He continues the mystery of his Incarnation as we, his followers, meet our directees as they are, and as who they are. And spiritual direction is one of the ways in which Christ continues to do his work of urging, drawing, and inviting people to a deeper, truer, more intimate relationship with God.

Paying Attention to the Gift of Sexuality within Spiritual Direction

The gift, as well as the given, of sexuality, desire, and the erotic makes an appearance every time we meet for spiritual direction. Not only do we always, inevitably come together as men and women, we also always come together as men and women whom God desires. In her recent and excellent reappraisal of the tradition of "love mysticism" within Christian spirituality and spiritual direction, Janet Ruffing writes: "All that we do in spiritual practice—either through scriptural contemplation of the mysteries of faith and the reality of Jesus or through centering prayer—leads us to the experience of God's desiring us. God's love moves us and moves toward us, enabling us to reciprocate that love."[19]

Like the young woman of the Song yearning for her absent lover, or like the Word becoming flesh and living among us, God loves us, wants us, longs for intimacy with us. Whether we realize it or not, it is fundamentally God's desire for us—more of us, more from us—that has somehow drawn us or our directees into spiritual direction.

Our directees may or may not be aware of how much God wants them—indeed, it may frighten them. But we, their directors, try to carry in our hearts and in our listening the urgent, gentle message that God is communicating to them in a thousand different ways: *I want you.* Yes, our directees are each a child of God—but they are also always, in the eyes of God, *desirable.* When we are able to hear this message from God being spoken to our directees through their life stories, we serve them well, as directors, to call their attention to it.

The gift of the erotic also appears in spiritual direction whenever we hear or sense in our directees their own yearning for God—more of God, more from God. One directee may say, "My prayer is so dry, so dead," which may be her way of expressing an experience similar to that of the psalmist: "My soul thirsts for God, for the living God. When shall I come and behold the face of God?" (Ps 42:2). Or like the young man felt for his lover in the Song, another directee may feel an urgent need to be touched and embraced by God.

I once asked a directee what it was he most wanted from God at that moment. During the longish silence that followed my question, his body clenched and released like a fist, and he began to cry. Finally, he spoke his heart: "I want God to hold me." I invited him to imagine himself, right then, being held by God—and I assumed, silently, that he wanted God to hold him as a father might a beloved child. My directee was willing, and let himself be held. After a time, when I asked him to talk about his experience of being held by God, I was surprised to learn that what he had wanted, and what he had received, was not at all the experience of a child being held by a father, but of one lover being tenderly embraced by another. His experience was a turning point in his path of intimacy with God—and also another great learning for me in the reciprocal movement of holy, erotic longing.

Once we hear in our directees some hint or declaration of their longing for God, we may begin to explore with them what move they wish to make next. How do they, in their own incarnation of God's desiring, wish now to pray, act, or love? As Margaret Guenther observes, "To inquire how people pray is *the* intimate question."[20] To ask directees how they may now wish to express their own longing for God invites directees into a deepening of their intimacy with God.

The gift of the erotic also appears in spiritual direction whenever our directees speak of relationships in any aspect of their lives: family, lovers, friends, work, the nonhuman environment, religious community, politics, and social structures. Our directees will speak to us of all these things, sharing their frustrations and joys, along with how well or how poorly they perceive themselves to be living as men, women, husbands, wives, lovers, friends, fathers, mothers, sons, daughters, priests, pastors, church members, citizens, and so on. Just as we carry in our hearts and in our listening the fundamental truth that each directee is desirable to God, we also pay attention to the ways in which God's erotic power may be inviting them into deeper, truer, and more fully human relationships with other people or the creation itself.

Ruffing states that in spiritual direction, "the clarification of feelings and especially desires is one of the most important things we can pursue."[21] Whenever a directee comes forward with any expression of longing or desire—however clear or confused, "spiritual" or carnal, realistic or unrealistic—it is an occasion for giving thanks: The directee or God has given us an entry into the intimate and holy places where the directee may potentially come face-to-face with who he or she really is and wishes to become, and what or who is actually pushing them or pulling them. Kathleen Fischer puts it succinctly: "Spiritual direction concerns the movement of our entire lives in and toward God."[22] Our movements in and toward God have everything to do with how we move in and toward all of the relationships that our living comprises.

Eros is God's own power or love that moves us to seek intimate communication and even communion with others, the nonhuman creation, and God, who is within and beyond all things. It is what pulls us to move beyond ourselves, to "cross over" and make connections with others. We all fall in love with other human beings, and we may express this love in the community and communion of physical, sexual intercourse. We all commit ourselves in friendship. Many of us bind ourselves heart, body, mind, and soul to our children—protecting, nurturing, cherishing them. We campaign for causes or candidates. We write sonnets or psalms or sonatas or blues ballads. We show up at dances "with a pink carnation and a pickup truck," or some equivalent. Any of these loves or friendships or commitments or campaigns or artistic expressions or apparently foolish acts is promising material for spiritual direction, which is itself a committed relationship:

Directors are committed to assisting their directees in listening to the ways God may be urging, drawing, or inviting directees into deeper, truer, and more fully human relationships.

Living in the Midwest but originally from the Southeast, I often find myself yearning for, even dreaming of, the ocean—the sand on my bare feet, the taste of salt on my tongue, the warmth of sun on my skin, the smell of low tide. This yearning is physical, emotional, spiritual, and sexual all at the same time. My own spiritual director is a blessing to me. When I share with her something like my desire for the ocean, she does not give it a label, such as "homesickness" or "displacement," nor does she treat it as "merely" indicative of something else. She takes my desire seriously—which I experience as taking *me* seriously—and gently encourages me in my speaking to give my desire its due. Somewhere, somehow, in the midst of my talking (this is her artfulness as a director), she helps me move in the direction God may be wanting to draw me: toward the God who made the ocean *and* me, the God who loves the ocean *and* me, the God who loves my love for the ocean. At some point, I begin to recognize that this longing I have for the ocean, so deep and so powerful, is connected to the longing, so deep and so powerful, that God and I have for one another.

In writing about the spirituality of Francis of Assisi, Leonardo Boff quotes an old legend about Francis that became a song:

One day Francis said to the Lord, weeping:

> I love the sun and the stars,
> I love Clare and her sisters,
> I love the human hearts
> And all beautiful things,
> Lord, forgive me
> For I should love only you.
> The Lord smiled and replied:
> I love the sun and the stars,
> I love Clare and her sisters,
> I love the human hearts
> And all beautiful things,
> My dear Francis
> You need not weep
> For I also love all this.[23]

In the ministry of spiritual direction, we invite our directees to both articulate and clarify their desires, whatever these desires may be. But we do so with the hope that God will move them to the experience of loving and desiring in concert with God's own love, desire, and delight.

As spiritual directors, God's erotic power or love also appears as gift in the responses our directees evoke in us, their directors. The sort of arousal I experienced when the young woman began to bare her soul has become, for me, one very important indicator that the person to whom I am listening may be moving in a direction of greater intimacy with God—that the directee is beginning to yield, not to me, but to the God who desires her; that the directee is becoming vulnerable to the caresses of the Spirit; that she is, within my hearing, entrusting her body and soul to God's love. I do not experience this sensation of erotic energy or power in every direction session with every directee, but I have come to realize that it may appear at any moment with any directee. So I try, again with God's help, to pay attention and be ready.

Something else very important may happen to us when our directees speak of their desires. Their longing for intimate communication and connection with God or another person may awaken our own longing for the same. A metaphor I find helpful is the way a piano string vibrates in sympathy and symphony whenever another nearby string has been struck. The strings of my heart, my desire, may begin to vibrate in sympathy to the strings that have been plucked within the heart of my directee. His experience of joy or ecstasy in the presence of God may cause my heart to vibrate, too—or I may become envious that my strings have not been so played of late. Her desire for a true friend with whom she may share her heart may cause me to thrill slightly with happiness that I myself have such a friend—or tremble in sympathy because I also seek such a friend.

It is not whether we experience these sympathetic vibrations that is most important, but how we respond to them as spiritual directors. One of the best ways we can respond to these erotic vibrations is to receive them simply as gifts— gifts that invite us to attend to our own yearnings at another time and another place. This is one reason why it is so important for spiritual directors to be in spiritual direction as well as supervision. Together with my own spiritual director, I may explore, for example, how parched I am for God—a thirst that I may have first recognized as my directee spoke of his own thirst or satisfaction. Or I may ask my director to celebrate with me before God the joy I am experiencing in my relationship with my wife—a joy that began vibrating in me as I heard my directee speak of her intimate relationship with her husband.

Receiving these erotic vibrations as gifts and remembering that I have a spiritual director or supervisor with whom I may revisit them later allows me more freedom to listen to the person who is presently before me. It is, after all, my directee's story that has set off the vibration within me, and it is his or her life with God—not my responses—that is the focus of our relationship.

It has taken me quite some time in my own life, prayer, and practice as a spiritual director to begin to understand as divine gift the power of eros and sexuality. And I readily admit that I still am often confused. But confusion about sexuality and desire is normal, I believe, both within ourselves and our directees.

After all, this gift is a force, an energy, that is powerful enough to move us beyond ourselves, to seek love and make commitments with other people, to pledge our allegiance to communities of faith or political causes, or to yield ourselves naked and vulnerable to the God who desires us. No wonder we are often confused.

If I had known earlier what I know now about the divine gift of eros and sexuality, I might have been a better listener to many of my former directees. I think of Greg, a young charismatic Christian from a fundamentalist background who experienced an emergence of a demonic force on an occasion of physical intimacy with his girlfriend. There was quite a lot going on here, of course, and on many levels. But I allowed my feelings of professional inadequacy ("I am not a therapist") and theological discomfort ("I'm not sure what I believe about demons") to keep me from asking what now seems a fairly obvious question: What were the deeper urges of his heart, soul, and body that were leading him toward intimacy with his girlfriend and with God—but at the same time driving him away from both?

Having a more positive and comprehensive framework for sexuality may have helped me listen more contemplatively when Susan began to express a new awareness of God that came to her in the wake of a powerful orgasm she had recently experienced with her partner. As it was, I immediately assumed that her "new awareness" was probably delusional or unfounded. I stopped listening to her, in other words, because I was not prepared to hear what she—or perhaps God—had to say.

It might have helped me in listening to Frank as he continued to mourn the death of his wife, now thirty years past. His loneliness had not diminished, nor had he yet received a satisfactory answer from God as to why his wife had died so young. Not that I would have tried to give Frank answers—but I might have been more brave to walk with him into his loneliness, trusting that God was in the midst of it as well as on the other side, drawing Frank closer.

I hope that today I am more free and faithful in my listening. I hope that my own "embodied, relational ways of responding" to the push and pull of God's eros within the lives of my directees serve God's purpose and desire for them. I hope that my own sexuality, my own response to God's eros, and my own capacity for intimacy are helps rather than hindrances to the love and communion that God is continuing to cultivate in my directees. I hope, but I cannot assume. The reason I cannot assume these things is because, at any given time, I am not always the same person at the same place in my life with God, my family, my friends, my community, or even my own body-self. My ability to respond calmly and contemplatively to what I am hearing may be overwhelmed by the sound of the chord that my directee's desire has touched, plucked, or struck in me.

There are still times when the movement of God's eros within my directees throws me off-balance and confuses me—and not only or even especially me. The men and women with whom I listen and pray are often confused by their own desires and longings as well. And when the relationship of spiritual direction is lost in erotic confusion, there is a great potential for misunderstanding, misdirection, misuse, or even abuse of our sexuality. Again, we need to pay attention.

Paying Attention to the Problems

My primary purpose in this essay has been to uncover the gift of sexuality and the erotic to our spirituality and spiritual direction. At this time, however, I wish to call attention to a few of the problems we may encounter in spiritual direction. Perhaps I should say more strongly that we *will* encounter these problems if, as Gerald May says, our relationships with our directees have "sufficient closeness to warrant the name of direction."[24] Again, it is not whether we have these problems (we all do or will), but the response we give, that is most important.

If we believe, and invite our directees to believe, that "God is the deepest dimension of all experience," and that spiritual direction concerns "the movement of our entire lives in and toward God,"[25] then we should be prepared to have our faith and our invitation taken seriously by our directees. A directee may bring into the conversation his frustration or puzzlement over why his penis no longer seems to "work," or she may express great pleasure in the sensations of her body during intercourse. If so, would he or she receive from us a contemplative hearing? It is a question of the quality of the hospitality we bring or provide for the relationship—a hospitality that is rooted in prayer and self-awareness.

Our directees are both alert and fragile, especially when they may be on the verge of risking themselves to us. And our directees also are often inclined, as we all are, to resist or avoid facing their deepest truths or fears. It only takes a second—with the twitch of an eyebrow, the crossing of a leg, or a nervous laugh from us—to confirm the rightness of their hesitancy to speak to us. They may know better than we do what we are able to hear. There is not necessarily anything wrong with this—we all have our limits to what we are able to hear at any given time—unless the issue the directee most needs his or her spiritual director to help "hear into speech" is the very thing he or she believes the director is unable to hear.

Our ability to be fully present and welcoming to our directees, regardless of the content of their speaking, may be compromised by any number of reasons, such as exhaustion, distress or distraction over something else, or timing. But if we add to this mix a personal ambivalence or discomfort with issues related to sexuality, desire, or the erotic, then we may be quite unprepared to hear our directees into speech.

I took the conversation with Susan, who wanted to share with me a "new awareness" she had received from God during the midst of sexual orgasm, and my inability to hear her, to my supervisor. After looking together at the ways in which I experienced my own anxiety and (none too subtly) redirected the conversation, my supervisor began to ask me some very good questions. What was my level of comfort with my own sexuality? Why? What were my feelings toward Susan? My supervisor's questions had the effect of doing what good supervision will do: They gently pushed me toward a greater self-awareness of my own openness and limitations. In Appendix D, I present a series of questions that I hope will serve the same purpose.

Along with issues related to the quality of our hospitality, we may experience problems related to the arousal of sexual feelings between ourselves and our directees. Though these feelings or vibrations may be received by us as a gift, we also need to be wise and cautious. In their discussions of transference and countertransference, Gerald May, William Barry and William Connolly, and Janet Ruffing underline some of the ways in which sexual feelings within direction can be misunderstood or misdirected.

As a matter of either projection or transference, a directee may "fall in love" with his or her director. After all, the directee is sharing the deepest longings of the heart, telling the director things that he or she has "never spoken about to anyone else," and no one seems to listen to him or her the way the director does. Gerald May believes that "since the level of intimacy and the degree of vulnerability required for spiritual direction is so great—in fact greater than that of any therapeutic relationship—and so many inner feelings are liberated and shared, it is not surprising that some sexual feelings emerge and find an object in the person of the director."[26]

If the directee is, in fact, being drawn closer to God by means of spiritual direction—if our directees begin to experience the power of God's erotic desire—then one of the first ways a directee may respond unconsciously to this love is to resist it, and one of the most common ways to offer resistance is to "distort the reality of the director" through transference.[27] The director becomes God's substitute, and the directee begins to transfer onto the director the erotic longing he or she may feel for God, whether the longing is for friendship, companionship, or union.

If something like this should happen, as Barry and Connolly recommend, we should not "waste time blaming" ourselves.[28] The ministry of spiritual direction is, after all, an expression of the mystery of Incarnation. The way in which we respond to our directees may represent for them how God or Jesus may be responding to them. And if we facilitate our directees in their desire for God—if we help them see themselves as *desirable* to God—then it should come as little surprise that they, on occasion, mistake us for the one who desires them most.

Rather than blame ourselves or the directee, the better response is to pay attention to what is happening, and then do what we normally would do if we found ourselves subject to transference. One way or another, we try to "help them shift their primary focus away from their relationship with us and toward their primary relationship with God."[29] As Ruffing explains, "Whenever possible, we should gently point the directee toward God, so that God can console, comfort, challenge, and love them in their prayer experience in a way similar to ours and, of course, better than ours."[30]

As an example of how this might be done, let's look at my directee who expressed a painful longing to be held by God. At the time he spoke and in the silence that followed, I experienced a very strong urge to leave my chair, step over, and embrace him. I knew that some of his strongest experiences of God had come from his participation in a men's spirituality group that incorporated physical, male-to-male bonding and embracing. Although I could imagine acting— even appropriately—as God's physical stand-in for my directee on another day at another time, I felt ambivalent on that day. I was not sure where the urge to embrace him was originating—in me, in him, in God. Not being sure, I remember deciding to let *God* deal with it. It was then that I invited the directee to imagine himself being held by God, encouraging him to direct his erotic longing toward the one who really did most want to embrace him.

It can be difficult for us to recognize transference when it is occurring. After all, sometimes our directees really do like *us*. Sometimes our directees appreciate the ways in which we embody God's grace for them, and they express gratitude and affection. Helping us learn to recognize transference—whatever its nature or intensity—as well as how we may best respond, is an excellent reason, in itself, to seek out and remain in regular supervision.

Countertransference usually occurs when we respond to transference unconsciously or unreflectively.[31] Within the relationship of spiritual direction, with its dynamics of sexuality and the divine erotic, countertransference may mean that I try to become the "friend" or "lover" for whom my directee longs—or that I become flushed with confusion or even anger that he or she has such feelings for me. Whether I unconsciously accept or reject the transference, I unwittingly allow *our* relationship (director-directee) to become the center of attention, rather than the relationship between God and the directee—the very thing to which I have promised to attend.

Every spiritual director I know has sooner or later become enmeshed in countertransference. The first step is to become aware and honest. Again, along with prayer, regular supervision is enormously helpful here. Once you are aware of countertransference, you can begin to explore what is going on *in you*. Why do you want to be her friend? Why are you so attracted to him? What frightens you about this? Where is the lack in you—in your relationship with God, others, your own self—that you feel such an excess of emotions? With God's help through prayer, and incarnate through our own supervisors and spiritual directors, most of us find the assistance we need to regain our balance and return such relationships to their true focus.

But sometimes we do not. Although eros and sexuality can play a positive role in spirituality and spiritual direction, it can be very damaging to all concerned when the gift is misused or abused. There may be situations where the director might appropriately "stand in" physically for God or Jesus, but under no circumstances would physical, sexual intimacy with a directee be a faithful, much less appropriate, incarnation of God's love. Aside from the interpersonal damage it may do to both parties' families and communities, engaging in intercourse may forever stunt or wreck the ability of both the director and the directee to give love or receive it from another—truly, honestly, intimately, faithfully.

Another possible misuse or abuse is for the director to become a sort of spiritual voyeur or manipulator. This happens when a director uses the direction relationship as a way of gratifying his or her own needs rather than assisting the directees. Instead of meeting the directees where they are in their life with God, the director urges or lures them to a place where *he or she* wants them to be—back to that place of desperate longing, ahead to the garden where God or some other love awaits them. Rather than being gently pulled or pushed by God's desire, the directees may feel pulled or pushed by the director. One of the refrains throughout the Song of Songs is a warning not to "rouse" love before it is time. Directors need to heed this and be reverent, sensitive, and discerning.

Directors also must be discerning about whether, when, or how to make physical contact of any kind with their directees. The messages we give with our bodies are both more potent and more ambiguous than the messages we give with our words, especially if we are dealing with a directee who has been a victim of physical or sexual abuse. Again, I find Janet Ruffing eminently wise, helpful, and to the point: "Whenever an emotionally vulnerable person entrusts him- or herself to an identified ministerial person, the latter is ethically responsible for maintaining appropriate boundaries and for preventing harm to the more vulnerable person."[32]

Paying Attention in Supervision

Supervision can be particularly important in regard to issues of sexuality and eros. Supervisors can help directors come to a greater self-awareness concerning their own comfort or discomfort with both the "given" and the "gift" of sexuality. Supervisors may help directors begin to discover their own place of interior freedom in which they may embrace and grow in their sexuality and intimacy. Supervisors can help directors recognize transference or countertransference and start to form appropriate responses. As important and invaluable as these insights are for directors, supervisors have an even more important role to play in the ministry of spiritual directors.

The men and women who practice the ministry of spiritual direction do so, for the most part, because they believe God *wants* them for this ministry. It is a holy desire, and their ministry is itself a response to God's erotic longing to draw us—directors, directees, everyone—into deeper, truer, and fuller relationships.

Whatever their foibles, frailties, or seeming lack of expertise, when spiritual directors come for supervision, they are trying to give a true and faithful response to this longing they have experienced from God. Perhaps the most profound assistance a supervisor may give to a spiritual director, then, is to help the director remain aware, attentive, and faithful to the holy desire that has urged, drawn, or invited the director into this ministry.

Several years ago, I was in a room with about twenty-five people, all of us either instructors or spiritual-directors-in-training. It was our third and final year together, and the directors-in-training (myself included) had come a long way. Three years of course work, lectures, papers, and verbatims; two or more years of receiving direction and supervision as we made our first attempts to offer direction to others; three years of personal and professional challenges as we each experienced the various birth pangs that accompanied our transition into the people, the directors, that we believed God was calling us to be.

One of our instructors that day, Mary Rose Bumpus (one of the editors of this book), invited us each to recall, silently, how far we had traveled in this journey over the preceding three years. After several minutes, she then invited us to remember the "desire" that had first led each of us to begin this journey. In the silence that followed, it was as if the floor of the room opened and dropped: a profound, communal, and palpable experience of the presence of God as we each reconnected with the graced power of God's eros.

I confess that floors rarely "drop open" for me today in supervision. And yet I am continually graced by those occasions when my supervisors recall me to the original desire that first drew me into this ministry. God's desire, that is—a desire that I attempt to embody in this ministry of spiritual direction by helping others pay attention to how and how much God wants them and loves them.

It is also a graced occasion whenever my supervisors invite me to *trust* this desire, which is, at the same time, God's desire for me and my desire for God. The more I am able to trust this desire, the more open and eager I am to supervision—to face my own resistances to God, my own interior compulsions or confusions; to savor the ways in which God is clearly working through me and in the lives of my directees; to embrace all the gifts and the givens of my own life in all of my relationships. I want my colleagues' assistance because I want to become the person, the spiritual director, that I trust God wants me to become. They help me see myself not simply as someone whose ministry is useful to God, but as someone who is God's desire—body, mind, soul, and strength. Supervision helps me pay attention.

Continuing to Pay Attention

More could, and probably should, be said on this subject of eros, sexuality, spiritual direction, and supervision. I hope my reflections, provisional as they are, encourage my colleagues to talk to each other, their supervisors, and me about their own experiences as directors in responding to the erotic and sexual dimensions that are present within this ministry. God's desire for us, our desire for God, our longings for community and communion with others and with creation itself—this is all very sacred ground in spiritual direction. It deserves our ongoing attention.

Notes

1. With two exceptions, all directees cited have given permission to use their stories. The first exception involves a former directee who is now deceased with no surviving relatives; the second is from a directee who cannot be located. In every case, the names and sometimes the genders have been changed to protect anonymity.

2. Gerald G. May, *Care of Mind, Care of Spirit: A Psychiatrist Explores Spiritual Direction* (New York: HarperCollins, 1982), 135.

3. Quoted in Sallie McFague, *Super, Natural Christians: How We Should Love Nature* (Minneapolis: Fortress, 1997), 10.

4. I have found the following description of sexuality and eros most helpful. It is by James B. Nelson and Sandra P. Longfellow in their introduction to *Sexuality and the Sacred: Sources for Theological Reflection* (Louisville: Westminster-John Knox, 1994), xiv: "Theologically, we believe that human sexuality, while including God's gift of the procreative capacity, is most fundamentally the divine invitation to find our destinies not in loneliness but in deep connection. To the degree that it is free from distortions of unjust and abusive power relations, we experience our sexuality as the basic eros of our humanness that urges, invites, and lures us out of our loneliness into intimate communication and communion with God and the world."

5. There is, of course, a long tradition within Christian theology and spirituality that distinguishes different kinds or degrees of love. The usual language is that of *eros, philia*, and *agape*—with agape presented as the "highest" or "purest" form. Although helpful to some extent, I do not find these distinctions true to my own experience or very clearly delineated in scripture. My presupposition in this essay is that eros may underlie and thus lead to all forms of love, including agape.

6. Carter Heyward, *Touching Our Strength: The Erotic as Power and the Love of God* (San Francisco: Harper & Row, 1989), 193–94.

7. Sheila Murphy, "Spirituality, Sexuality, Intimacy, and Ministry," in *Handbook of Spirituality for Ministers*, ed. Robert J. Wicks (New York: Paulist, 1995), 412.

8. Ibid., 413.

9. Ann and Barry Ulanov, *Primary Speech: A Psychology of Prayer* (Atlanta: John Knox, 1982), 74.

10. Sallie McFague, *The Body of God: An Ecological Theology* (Minneapolis: Fortress, 1993), 16.

11. Philip Sheldrake, S.J., *Befriending Our Desires* (Notre Dame, IN: Ave Maria, 1994), 67.

12. Ann and Barry Ulanov, *Primary Speech*, 76–77.

13. Roland E. Murphy, O.Carm., *The Song of Songs* (Minneapolis: Fortress, 1990), 97.

14. Marcia Falk, *The Song of Songs: A New Translation* (New York: HarperCollins, 1993), Section 13.

15. Anne Sexton, "That Day," from *Love Poems* (Boston: Houghton Mifflin, 1969) 11.

16. Cf. Ann Matter, *The Voice of My Beloved: The Song of Songs in Western Medieval Christianity* (Philadelphia: University of Pennsylvania, 1990), 6: ". . . [T]he Song of Songs is a book of the Bible that does not particularly appeal to modern theological exegesis, since it offers no divine law,

moral precepts, or sacred history. This last observation makes it all the more intriguing that the Song of Songs was the most frequently interpreted book of medieval Christianity."

17. Murphy, *Song of Songs*, 105.

18. Cary Ellen Walsh, *Exquisite Desire: Religion, the Erotic, and the Song of Songs* (Minneapolis: Fortress, 2000), 212.

19. Janet K. Ruffing, R.S.M., *Spiritual Direction: Beyond the Beginnings* (New York: Paulist, 2000), 111.

20. Margaret Guenther, *Holy Listening: The Art of Spiritual Direction* (Cambridge, MA: Cowley, 1992), 20.

21. Ruffing, *Spiritual Direction*, 24.

22. Kathleen Fischer, *Women at the Well: Feminist Perspectives on Spiritual Direction* (New York: Paulist, 1988), 3.

23. Leonardo Boff, *Cry of the Earth, Cry of the Poor*, trans. Phillip Berryman (Maryknoll, NY: Orbis, 1997), 214–15.

24. May, *Care of Mind*, 135.

25. Fischer, *Women at the Well*, 3.

26. May, *Care of Mind*, 135.

27. William A. Barry and William J. Connolly, *The Practice of Spiritual Direction* (New York: HarperSanFrancisco, 1986), 157.

28. Ibid., 165.

29. Ruffing, *Spiritual Direction*, 172.

30. Ibid., 174.

31. There are ways in which a director may choose, consciously, to make use of a directee's transference for the sake of the directee's own growth or self-awareness. Technically this is not countertransference, since countertransference is, by definition, unconscious. Those who choose to make use of their directees' transference are ordinarily directors who are also trained as psychotherapists. I am not trained as a psychotherapist and have never, therefore, chosen to make use of a directee's transference. In addition, the conscious use of transference in spiritual direction seems to shift the focus, however temporarily, onto *our* relationship rather than keeping the focus on the relationship between the directee and God.

32. Ruffing, *Spiritual Direction*, 164.

CHAPTER SEVEN

Preventing Common Quagmires with Ethical Forethought

Joseph D. Driskill

Are you tempted to skip this chapter on ethical dilemmas and move along to something that seems more interesting? As supervisors, we listen in the presence of God as directors bring to supervision not only their own hopes, struggles, fears, inadequacies, breakthroughs, and resistances, but also those of their directees. We pray for our supervisees before and between supervision sessions and consider it both a privilege and a duty to hold our supervisees in the light of God's presence. In the midst of this graced work, worrying about ethical dilemmas seems largely unnecessary, and reading codes of ethics, even those designed for spiritual directors, mundane and dry! How could participation in such sacred work lead to an unanticipated ethical quagmire?

As supervisors, we assume that those who come to our supervisees for spiritual direction are people with good intentions who are seeking a "guide" for their faith journey. We also assume that the directors we supervise are people of good intentions who would not knowingly harm those seeking guidance. Yet we must ask ourselves some important questions: Is it true that everyone who seeks spiritual guidance has good intentions and transparent motives? Is it also true that the directors we supervise are able to keep their personal agendas and unconscious intentions in the service of an altruistic concern for those they direct? In spite of the best intentions of our supervisees and our greatest hopes for those seeking direction, we know the answer to both questions is no. And even if the answer could be yes to both questions, would that nullify the need to give careful consideration to ethical dilemmas that surface in the routine practice of doing spiritual direction? If we are to be faithful in our work as supervisors, we need to give careful thought to ethical practices, as well as to prioritizing the study of ethical issues that emerge in the process of supervising spiritual direction.

In the contemporary postmodern context, numerous people seeking spiritual direction are not deeply steeped in religious traditions and do not belong to religious communities. Many seeking an experiential relationship with the divine no longer easily entrust their spirits to religious institutions or religious professionals. Even before the now ubiquitous newspaper and television stories about the abuse of children by religious leaders, there was a cultural undercurrent of skepticism toward institutional religion. It is most often expressed in the phrase "I am spiritual, but I am not religious." Recent revelations have reinforced this anti-institutional trend by sensitizing the general population to the need to hold religious leaders accountable for ethical behavior. Those of us who supervise spiritual directors are aware that we must not, knowingly or unknowingly, betray the sacred trust that our directors place in us. We need to be vigilant in supervising spiritual direction in conformity with ethical codes and widely agreed upon standards.

Helping relationships that are subject to federal regulations are currently being redefined by the Health Insurance Portability and Accountability Act (HIPAA).[1] The passage of this law has set more stringent boundaries on confidentiality and patients' rights in institutions that receive federal support. Though spiritual directors are not subject to HIPAA regulations, this bill is strongly influencing the culture of helping professions.

This chapter looks at six common ethical dilemmas that spiritual directors might bring to supervision. Each is introduced with a brief vignette, which is followed by a discussion of selected key points. Some contemporary resources for those seeking additional information are provided at the end.

Dynamics and Boundaries

For two years Sister Anne O'Malley has been directing Rev. John Lee, pastor of a rapidly growing Korean United Methodist Church. John, a second-generation Korean American, sought spiritual direction when he found that the demands of his parish were leaving him little time for personal prayer. As John's relationship with God has grown and deepened, he has felt increased gratitude for his time in spiritual direction. In their last session, Anne noticed that John is complimenting her repeatedly for her compassionate and attentive spirit. Anne recalls that during John's first year of direction, he seemed more reserved. She is pleased that John finds the direction sessions meaningful and recalls that he gave her a lovely devotional book for Christmas and a small candle at Easter. Anne is wondering whether she should give John a small present to express her appreciation to him. After thinking of two or three things she could give him, she wonders if there are guidelines for gift giving in a direction relationship. She decides to take her quandary about gift giving to supervision.

Psychological Dynamics

Sister Anne's supervisor will encourage her to explore her thoughts and feelings about giving John a gift, including her reaction to the positive attention she has received from him. He is complimenting her on her "compassionate and attentive spirit" and on the way in which she contributes to his deepening sense of God's presence in his life. As she thinks in supervision about the positive affirmation she has received from John and about giving him a gift, she recalls her feelings of being underappreciated. In the conversation, she might discover that her relationship with her father, who was emotionally remote, left her seeking positive affirmation from male authority figures. Or she may recognize that her need for affirmation is an issue she has dealt with in the past, and it is not motivating her desire to give John a small gift. After engaging in the introspection and dialogue necessary to gain insights into her motivations, Anne may then return to the issue of gift giving. Does she still think it is appropriate to give John a gift? Is the thought of giving a gift done out of freedom, or does she sense that her motives are mixed?

The supervisor will also ask her to reflect on the recent changes in John's behavior and consider the dynamics of transference, including both its "positive" and "negative" characteristics. For example, when John speaks of Anne's "compassionate and attentive spirit," she notices an intensity that is out of proportion to his previous behavior. As a result, she needs to consider whether his sense of gratitude comes from a place of freedom as a genuine response to what is happening in his relationship with God or from other motivations. The supervisor will ask whether John is responding to her as he has to other caring, thoughtful women who are in positions of power or authority. For example, if his mother was a deeply caring person who also expected frequent affirmation from her children, he may feel he must repeat the pattern with Anne. Another possibility is that Anne's compassion may be arousing feelings of sexual attraction in John. Actions are often complex and multidetermined. One aim in supervision is to help the director be self-reflective in a context where grace and trust foster the understanding necessary to maintain appropriate boundaries and avoid ethical quagmires. As Sister Anne sorts through these possibilities, she may decide from her vantage point that giving John a gift might stir within him feelings focused on her instead of his relationship with God.

In contrast to therapy, where working with the transference between the counselee and counselor is often a source of healing, in spiritual direction the transference is focused on God. Spiritual directors frequently invite their directees to take their concerns, emotions, and expectations to God with the gentle question,

"Have you taken this to prayer?" Here it is the directee's experiential relationship with the Divine, rather than the transference with the director, that is the primary avenue for healing and faithfulness.

Supervisors need to be especially sensitive to problematic transference and countertransference dynamics of which the supervisee is unaware. In the spiritual direction relationship, it is the director who is responsible for identifying and, when necessary, managing the transference and countertransference issues. Ethical violations can occur when transference and countertransference issues are unrecognized and when the dynamic is problematic.

Supervisors need to be able to help directors gain insights into their own blind spots. They can invite their supervisees to reflect on content that either the supervisee or supervisor is noticing about the supervisee's direction relationship. Insights gained from typical questions such as "I wonder what you are feeling when your directee says that?" or "Notice how you are feeling when you said . . ." help supervisees identify dynamics associated with transference and countertransference. Most often, maintaining clear and appropriate boundaries between the directors and directees is the healthiest way to deal with these concerns.

Intercultural Realities and Systems Thinking

Before deciding whether it is ethical to give John a gift, Anne's supervisor will also encourage her to explore the intercultural realities and institutional systems that shape their realities. Sister Anne O'Malley, a Caucasian, is doing spiritual direction with Rev. John Lee, a Korean American. Honoring the intercultural reality of their relationship requires sensitivity from both of them. Pastor Lee is no doubt acutely aware of this dynamic, because as a Korean serving in the United States, he has experienced being an "outsider" to the dominant culture. He will also be aware that he is an outsider to vowed religious life in a community. Anne, because she is a member of the dominant culture, may be less aware of issues raised by intercultural realities. Yet the contrast between her lifestyle in a religious community and more common living patterns, such as the nuclear family, may have increased her sensitivity to her own "otherness," as well as to issues raised by intercultural realities.

To explore these issues, a number of questions can be explored in supervision. What does giving small gifts mean in the Korean community? Is it expected or customary to give small gifts to those with whom you have a professional relationship? If a gift is given, is there an expectation that one will be returned? Is the gift understood as an important expression of gratitude or an act of hospitality? What are the expectations of the Korean community in regard to their pastor? Is it customary for parishioners to give the pastor a gift? If so, does John believe that a small gift would be expected by Anne? Anne also wonders how much John knows about gift giving in a religious community. How are her expectations shaped by her life in the community? Though Sister Anne's supervisor would not be expected to know the specific implications of the diversity present in this case, he or she would need to be aware of and sensitive to the presence of intercultural realities and systems issues in order to pose appropriate questions.

Guidelines

Small gifts of appreciation may be appropriate in a direction relationship if both the giver and receiver are clear about their meaning. Such gifts could be given at an appropriate time, such as Christmas or Easter in Christian contexts or at the termination of a direction relationship. Gifts are normally kept small and serve to honor and celebrate the spiritual direction process and relationship per se. Gifts become inappropriate if they are too frequent and begin to honor the director rather than the direction relationship. In most instances, the director does not initiate gift giving. In cases where the director does give a small gift, such as at Christmas, it should be made clear that all of the director's directees are receiving a gift. In this way, the director avoids fostering a special relationship with any of her or his directees. Though these suggestions may serve as general guidelines for gift giving, this supervision session has demonstrated the reflection necessary to explore the dynamics that may be involved in the act of gift giving in the context of spiritual direction.

Sexuality and Boundaries

Ruth Jarvis, a middle-aged lay person, has been an active member of First Presbyterian Church for a number of years. Recently Ruth asked Rev. Louise Wyatt, the minister for pastoral care of a neighboring Presbyterian church, if she would serve as her spiritual director. Louise is delighted with Ruth's request and readily agrees to meet.

At the end of their second session together, Ruth is feeling happy about her new spiritual director. As she is leaving, she reaches out to give Louise a hug. There is an awkward moment when Louise takes Ruth's hands and gently explains that for the good of directees, giving hugs is discouraged. Ruth appears surprised because she and Louise have hugged and kissed each other on the cheek at numerous times when "passing the peace" at Presbytery events. Louise also feels ambivalent. She has hugged directees for a number of years and has only recently stopped this practice. Louise continues to wonder whether it is necessary to be so cautious. She decides to take her ambivalence to supervision.

In supervision, Louise raises her ambivalence about not giving a hug to directees who initiate this contact at the end of a spiritual direction session. Louise has been a pastor for a number of years and has always enjoyed her closeness with those she serves. She believes in embodied spirituality and now finds a conflict between her theological commitments and the contemporary climate in which helping professionals are trained to avoid touch. Louise admits that she sometimes ignores the admonitions and gives a quick hug to a directee. In this session, however, Louise observed the rules, but she felt embarrassed by the awkward moment she created when she deflected Ruth's gesture of gratitude.

Theological and Psychological Concerns

The supervisor will explore three major issues with Louise: her beliefs and feelings about touch, the social factors that influence decision making, and the specific ethical guidelines developed for spiritual directors. Louise's theological commitments include a feminist understanding of the importance of the body. A holistic approach to faith includes celebrating the role of the body in human life. The supervisor will invite Louise to explore ways that this theological affirmation can be honored in a direction session. Attention to the physical surroundings, including art and music, as well as bodily comfort will likely be discussed.

The supervisor will also ask Louise about whose needs are being met when directors and directees embrace. Does Louise need this contact to feel affirmed by the directee? Does the directee seek physical contact as a ritual for saying goodbye, or does the embrace meet other needs for acceptance? Since Ruth initiated the physical contact, it would appear that she does not have a problem with a hug. But is that necessarily so? Ruth might think that she is expected to end a session with an embrace. The supervisor may ask Louise if there are other ways for Ruth to express her affection and appreciation. After reflecting on these questions, it is important for the supervisor to raise another set of questions.

Institutional and Social Context

In our institutional and social contexts, the messages we find in regard to touch are often ambiguous. On the one hand, practices that involve touching are commonplace in many of our congregations and parishes, such as greeting one another with hugs and "passing the peace" with loving embraces. Those who have grown up attending and leading church camp programs will recognize how much physical contact is involved in supervising and teaching children who are away from home for a week. Many vowed religious and members of parish communities recognize that our theological commitments to healing and wholeness and our reclaiming of the body may include not only public displays of affection, but also the ministries associated with healing touch, such as anointing and massage.

On the other hand, we are appalled by the frequency with which clergy and religious leaders perpetrate sexual violations, primarily against women and children. Religious institutions attempt to prevent unqualified people from being trained as spiritual directors or, if trained, from serving. Anyone with a pattern of acting out his or her sexual needs on persons coming for guidance should be barred from doing direction with potential victims. There is community consensus that such persons need treatment themselves and must not be in positions where they can exploit the vulnerability of others.

The issues associated with touch raise further complexities when we observe how touch is understood in various racial and ethnic communities. Do blacks, whites, and Asians hold the same attitudes toward touch? If not, how do they differ? A woman from the Philippines shared in one of my seminary classes her experience of inviting her supervising pastor, from a predominantly Caucasian church, to her largely Filipino home church. When her supervising pastor rose to address the congregation and express his appreciation for her work, he put his arm around the back of her shoulders. She said you could hear the quiet gasps from attendees, who felt it was entirely inappropriate to touch a woman in public this way. Fortunately, her supervisor was sensitive to such issues and realized that although his behavior had been motivated by a desire to affirm her gifts, in that context he had demeaned her as a leader. When supervising someone from a culture or racial or ethnic background that differs from your own, mutual learning will be fostered by creating a climate where issues associated with difference can be freely discussed.

Another institutional factor that informs social norms related to touch involves the customs of particular religious communities or parishes. Those within religious congregations often have unexpressed social conventions that guide their behavior. When members of a religious community are supervising those outside the community, the social norms may vary. The interpretation and meaning of physical contact are in part determined by these institutional factors.

Geographic context also exerts an influence on the approach to touch. When I was leading a workshop on ethics and spiritual direction recently, it became clear to participants that the cultural and community standards in Hawaii and California regarding physical boundaries were more flexible than in some other parts of the United States. A supervisor from Hawaii spoke of the expectation that safe touch would be incorporated into holistic healing. Attendees from the South and Midwest observed that in their regions, such touch could be suspect.

How do we hold with integrity our concern for the numerous people who have been harmed by inappropriate touch without renouncing our commitments to safe touch? Being sensitive to the personal, social, institutional, and interracial contexts in which we do supervision will serve us well. The guidelines that follow have been developed with an awareness of many of these concerns.

Ethical Guidelines

The *Guidelines for Ethical Conduct* of Spiritual Directors International say, "Spiritual directors honor the dignity of the directee by . . . establishing and maintaining appropriate physical and psychological boundaries with the directee . . . [and by] refraining from sexualized behavior, including, but not limited to manipulative, abusive, or coercive words or actions toward a directee."[2]

A Code of Ethics for Spiritual Directors (1992), from the Center for Sacred Psychology, has three paragraphs on physical boundaries. After speaking of the need to avoid "any sexual intimacy with directees," it encourages directors "to be aware of their own motives for touching," as well as the cultural attitudes toward touch. "Holding hands to pray, healing touch, and amiable embraces are all acceptable and natural, and can be most helpful in the spiritual direction partnership. Directors, however, should consciously—not accidentally—participate in such actions. . . . Neither does the wise director automatically consent to physical contact initiated by a directee without evaluating its benefit or detriment to their joint goal."[3]

Many training programs in spiritual direction discourage directors from touching their directees. Verbal affirmations are encouraged as appropriate, but physical boundaries should not be crossed. As we have learned more about the possibility of retraumatizing victims of physical and sexual abuse with what may seem like safe touch, such as a pat on the arm or shoulder, and as we know that both directors and directees can have mixed motives regarding touch, it seems safer in the contemporary environment to generally avoid touch. Until our society comes to terms with the widespread phenomenon of physical and sexual abuse perpetrated largely, though not exclusively, by men against women and children, touch must be used with great caution in one-on-one settings, where the opportunity for misunderstanding exists. The evolving cultural attitudes toward touch were captured by a friend who said to me a few years ago: "I did not feel comfortable hugging people during the 'passing of the peace' until the late seventies. Now here it is the late nineties, and I am told it isn't wise to assume that everyone wants a hug."

In this vignette, Louise can briefly explain to Ruth the changed social climate in secular and religious helping professions toward exchanging an embrace. She can also affirm her willingness to share the peace with Ruth in their traditional way when they are in the public space of worship.

Confidentiality and Anonymity

Mary Bradley, a religious education director, was asked by John Cleaves, an active layperson in the nearby parish, to serve as his spiritual director. After their initial session, Mary establishes a covenant with John explaining the nature of confidentiality and anonymity. Mary explains that a responsible spiritual director receives regular supervision, during which some details of her direction sessions are shared. The attention in supervision, she says, is on her work as a director, and the anonymity of the directees is preserved by using pseudonyms or initials.

Sister Teresa is Mary's supervisor. She has noticed that though Mary is careful to use initials in verbatims, she occasionally lets slip the names of her directees as she talks about them. Teresa intends to remind Mary to be more careful about preserving anonymity, but she has not been overly concerned about these slips, since she keeps everything in confidence and is careful to destroy any written materials used in the supervision sessions.

Some months earlier, Sister Teresa and John were both asked by their respective faith communities to serve on a local citywide committee dealing with homelessness. They have since been working on a subcommittee together and are becoming friends. As Teresa's friendship with John develops, he shares with her his anxiety about his impulsive younger brother, who mistreats their father. Teresa realizes that this situation sounds remarkably similar to that of one of Mary's directees. She decides to tell neither John nor Mary that she suspects Mary is John's director. But one day when John drops off committee material at Teresa's office, he meets Mary arriving for supervision. Mary tells Teresa what just happened. Teresa is concerned. She wonders if John will be upset now that he knows Teresa is Mary's supervisor. She also wonders if she should have done something earlier, when she suspected John might be Mary's directee. Sister Teresa decides to raise this concern with the sister who supervises her supervision.

Establishing a Covenant

Mary carefully established a covenant with John that included policies informing him of the nature of confidentiality and the ways in which the director's supervision maintained anonymity. Such covenants may be put in writing. I have found that persons who are new to direction often appreciate having written ground rules.

While it is the obligation of the director to hold in confidence that which the directee shares, I know some directors who ask directees also to hold in confidence personal experiences shared by the director. Self-disclosure by the director can be helpful on some occasions, and asking a directee to also maintain confidentiality can reinforce the sacred nature of the direction session. Such self-disclosure by the director must be in the best interests of the directee, however, and not done because of an unmet or unconscious need on the part of the director. If directors covenant for mutual confidentiality, they need to be clear with their directees that such covenants are not intended for the protection of the director. Directors should not share with directees things that they would not submit to their own supervision.

Cascading Decisions and Unanticipated Results

Ethical quagmires sometimes emerge from a series of small judgments that at some point have unanticipated consequences. The first small mistake occurs when Sister Teresa does not remind Mary to use initials or pseudonyms while they are discussing Mary's work with her directees. This is a simple slip. The next problematic point emerges when Teresa realizes that her new friend John's situation sounds similar to a case she supervises. Teresa realizes that John's anonymity has been compromised both because of the unique circumstances of his situation and because she has heard Mary refer to her directee in a similar circumstance as "John."

Now Teresa has several choices. She can tell Mary that she has inadvertently come to know one of Mary's directees, and that Mary should find another supervisor for her supervision of John. Teresa might also decide that because her friendship with John is in its initial stages, she can limit her association with him to committee meetings. If Teresa's friendship with John continues, and she also continues to supervise Mary's direction of John, Teresa will be learning information about John both through the friendship and from Mary. Teresa makes the mistake of deciding that if she says nothing, John and Mary will not realize she knows both of them. By continuing to develop her friendship with John while supervising Mary, she opens herself to the problematic situation that emerges when Mary and John meet at her office and discover she knows both of them. The unanticipated circumstances that arise from this series of mistakes creates a situation in which confidentiality and anonymity are both inappropriately compromised.

The chance encounter between Mary and John at Teresa's office does not in itself constitute an ethical breach. It is problematic because of decisions Teresa has made prior to the encounter. Maintaining total anonymity insofar as it relates to one's meeting space is not required. In many geographic areas, a limited number of people do supervision or direction. Some supervisors have waiting rooms where supervisees and directees may meet as they arrive and depart from sessions. Such chance meetings do not suggest that the director is in any way negligent. If I think two of my directees know or work with one another, however, I try not to schedule back-to-back appointments. When such scheduling is unavoidable, I inform the directee that he or she may know the person I am seeing next (without giving the name of the next directee) and offer him or her the option of leaving a few minutes early.

Informed Consent

Spiritual directors are ethically bound to respect their directees' right to privacy. Notes, files, and verbal comments must not be shared with others, including lawyers, doctors, professional therapists, and counselors, without written permission from the directee designating specific recipients of such communications. Though in the past, verbal authorization was generally considered acceptable, in the contemporary litigious context in the United States, it is recommended that consent be in writing.

Directees' right to privacy includes not sharing the names of people one is seeing in direction without their permission. If someone asks a director if he or she is seeing someone, and the director does not have permission to share that information, the director should say somethinglike this: "I assume you mean no harm by asking. But in order to respect my directees' right to privacy, I do not share with others the names of people I see for spiritual direction. This also means that I cannot say whether I see the person about whom you are asking." For people living in religious communities or in other small communities where such information might be general knowledge, this may seem extreme. Nevertheless, it is generally safer to err on the side of protecting a person's right to privacy.

Mandatory Reporting

Pam Fields, an elementary school teacher, approaches Lynn Hollis, a Roman Catholic layperson, for spiritual direction. In the first session, as they are getting to know one another, Pam describes her family. Suddenly Pam tears up and says that her husband is a very strict disciplinarian who believes in the dictum "spare the rod, spoil the child." On some occasions, he has hit their children so hard it left bruises. Lynn listens empathically. Pam wants to deepen her relationship with God, and she hopes that she will be able to do this through spiritual direction.

Lynn normally introduces the notion of a covenant in the second session, after she and her directee have prayed about working together. An important aspect of the covenant is making clear to the directee that confidentiality must be broken if the director has a reasonable suspicion that child or elder abuse is occurring. If the director fears abuse, the law requires reporting the suspicions to child protective services or the police. Unfortunately, Pam brought this issue forward before Lynn had an opportunity to inform her of the legal requirements to notify the authorities. Lynn decides she will take this issue to supervision before she speaks again with Pam. She also wants to clarify with her supervisor whether she must make a report based on what Pam has already said.

Informing the Directee

Lynn has a sound protocol for her initial sessions with a directee. After getting acquainted and sharing mutual goals and expectations in the first session, she introduces the notion of a covenant in the second session. Among the materials shared in the covenant, covering such things as frequency and time of meeting and the general structure of the sessions, is information about mandatory reporting of child or elder abuse. Lynn does this in her early encounters with a directee in order to avoid the kind of situation in which she now finds herself.

Legal Obligations

In supervision, Lynn wants to clarify the laws regarding mandatory reporting. This is a complex area requiring knowledge of statutes applicable in individual states. A number of states have statutes requiring mandatory reporting of child and elder abuse by any person who suspects it. Statutory laws vary from state to state, however, and supervisors need to keep up-to-date on these regulations. Because such statutes are amended from time to time, supervisors in the United States should check with the National Clearing House on Child Abuse and Neglect Information website at nccanch.acf.hhs.gov/general/statespecific/index.cfm for current information on each state. This information is provided by the U.S. Department of Health and Human Services.

Lynn has to determine to the best of her ability whether Pam's husband is engaging in physical abuse, and if she decides there is a reasonable suspicion, she must find out whether she is legally obligated to report. Lynn's supervisor will invite her to reflect on the comments Pam made about strict discipline. Does spanking constitute abuse? How mild or severe is punishment that constitutes abuse? Is this reportable behavior or borderline behavior?

An important factor in this instance is the secondhand nature of the information. Since Lynn does not suspect Pam herself of abusing the children, must she report? Eighteen states require any person who suspects child abuse to notify the police or child protective services, but in the states that have mandatory reporting, traditionally one reports if one is seeing the victim of abuse or the person thought to be the abuser. In most jurisdictions, reporting secondhand information has not been required; however, a recent court case has made such information reportable in California.

Moral Issues and Community Standards

The supervisor may encourage Lynn to invite Pam to reflect on the moral issues raised by her concerns. Is Pam feeling a sense of needing to take action to ensure the safety of her child? What other interventions might Pam feel led to consider? How does Pam understand her husband's behavior? Does Pam's training as an elementary school teacher contribute to her understanding of physical and sexual abuse? Does this training help Pam evaluate her husband's behavior, or does she fail to realistically appraise what she sees because she loves or fears him? If Pam says that her parents were strongly opposed to any form of corporal punishment, Lynn should invite Pam to consider how this influences her values. Is Pam's class or background different from her husband's? Does this difference influence child-rearing practices? Should Pam generalize her standards to others? Pam may conclude that she is overreacting to her husband's behavior, or she may decide that she needs God's support to do what she believes is right and report her husband. She may have come to direction seeking the courage and divine support needed to cope with unknown consequences.

If Lynn concludes that abuse did occur, she must decide whether she will report if Pam refuses. In this case, the issues are ambiguous enough that Lynn probably would not report. If, however, it was clear that Lynn was seeing someone who was abusing others, would she report? Many directors might be reluctant to report for fear of losing the directee. In such cases, the supervisor will want to be certain the decision is reached in freedom. This requires considering the best interests of those who are vulnerable and generally lack power, as well as the circumstances of the directee. In some cases, the loss of a spiritual direction relationship may be required if justice and compassion for the vulnerable is an important moral value. Failure to report a blatant case of abuse in a state with mandatory reporting also compromises the director.

Case Law

A court ruling in *Tarasoff v. The Regents of the State of California* in 1976 established a legal obligation in California for those in helping professions to break a confidence in order to warn someone of an immediate threat. This requires notifying the police as well as the intended victim. This "duty to warn" or "duty to protect" is subject to case law and thus varies from state to state. Although lawyers and helping professionals in all states learn the guidelines of the *Tarasoff* case, some states, such as Texas, have ruled in specific cases that *Tarasoff* is not applicable. Any time a directee is serious about homicide or suicide, a director has a moral obligation to notify the police and any potential victims. No court has held a professional negligent for breaking a confidence when public protection from impending violence is a reasonable threat.

Assessment and Referral

Todd Arnold is the pastor of a Lutheran Church in a large urban area. Sarah Wilson, the pastor of the nearby United Church of Christ, started coming to Todd for spiritual direction six weeks ago. During their second meeting, Sarah said that for the last couple months, her energy has been low. She feels down, and out of touch with God. She says that her work for social justice as a highly visible lesbian has come out of a deep sense of call, which has until now sustained her. This is the first time she has sought spiritual direction, and she hopes that by focusing on her spiritual life, she can get out of this "dark night of the soul."

Through gentle questioning, Todd discovers that Sarah's partner, Fern, thinks Sarah is depressed and needs therapy. Sarah shares with Todd her belief that even though her mother was depressed, she has never had "that" problem. She believes her failure to pray on a daily basis has contributed to her dryness. When Todd explains that he usually meets with people at four- to six-week intervals Sarah says she was hoping he might meet with her every other week at the beginning. Todd has seen a lot of depressed parishioners during his years in ministry and thinks he should refer Sarah to therapy. He decides he would like to discuss the possibility of referral with his supervisor.

Psychological Concerns

In supervision, Todd will be asked to reflect on both the elements of Sarah's life supporting her desire to enter spiritual direction and the aspects that suggest a psychological evaluation is appropriate. Todd notes that Sarah's commitment to social justice for gay and lesbian people grows out of her faith commitments. She identifies a deep sense of call that has given direction to her vocation as a United Church of Christ pastor. Sarah's description of her prayer life points to its dryness. She identifies this lack of spiritual discipline as contributing to her "dark night of the soul." Todd senses that this "dark night" language does not reflect a deep understanding of its use in mystical forms of prayer, but instead the popular usage to identify any troubled period in a person's life. Sarah's awareness that her relationship with God is dry right now may suggest that formerly she had a more robust experiential relationship with the divine. On the other hand, it could also indicate that the energy she receives from her social justice ministry itself has sustained her to this point.

Several indications suggest that Todd could refer Sarah for counseling. In the conversations in both the first and second sessions, Sarah is problem focused. Although Todd has shared with her that spiritual direction focuses primarily on the spiritual life rather than on problem solving per se, Sarah keeps returning to her symptoms. She reports several things that may be associated with depression, including a lack of energy, a change in her level of functioning, and the presence of these changes for at least two months. Todd also notes that when he suggested the three- to six-week intervals for meeting, Sarah's immediate response was to want more frequent appointments. This is often a sign that the person would benefit from therapy, where more frequent meetings allow the relationship between the counselor and the counselee to be the focus of healing. Input from immediate family members can also be helpful in assessing a person's needs, and it is helpful to know that Sarah's partner, Fern, has recognized changes in Sarah's behavior and thinks Sarah needs counseling. Also, Sarah's mother was clinically depressed, and it is well established that hereditary links exist for clinical depression.

Todd will share with Sarah his belief that even though this may be a "dark night of the soul" in a spiritual sense, she should still see a qualified counselor to rule out psychological issues. Given his established presence as a clergyman in the community, Todd likely will be able to recommend professional therapists who not only can evaluate Sarah, but also value the ministry of spiritual direction.

Selecting Healing Modalities

Todd's supervisor will also question whether he will continue to see Sarah for spiritual direction at this time. Several possibilities present themselves. If the counselor decides that Sarah is not suffering from depression (unlikely given the number of symptoms she reports), she would pursue her original plan and see Todd for spiritual direction. If the counselor determines that she is suffering from clinical depression, she may decide to receive therapy from a psychologist or pastoral counselor. She might also have the option of seeing a psychiatrist for medication. Sarah might decide to see Todd for spiritual direction in addition to her treatment interventions for depression. Many therapists, doctors, and counselors are quite willing to have a person continue in spiritual direction while working on other issues in therapy. In some instances, these professionals may think this is contraindicated, and in those cases, the spiritual director normally will want to comply with the request and agree to continue seeing the directee once other therapeutic work has been completed. Since Sarah has never had spiritual direction, she may decide she would rather not begin both counseling and direction at the same time, given the commitment of time and energy each requires. Todd could offer to see her at a later time, after she has grown comfortable with the counseling process or has completed it.

Todd's attention here to the ministry of assessment and referral prevents him from finding himself in the ethical quagmire of working outside his training. Ethically, the spiritual director must practice within the boundaries of her or his expertise. As training programs continue to produce directors who are formally educated and receive certificates or degrees in the field of spiritual direction and spirituality, it will be necessary to be clear about the guidelines and boundaries that guide one's practice. Increasing numbers of trained directors who offer their services for a fee, even if it is modest and on a sliding scale, must recognize that the payment of a fee for service brings with it ethical and legal responsibilities. Some insurance companies now offer liability insurance for a wide variety of one-on-one structured conversations that deal with a person's mental health. For example, the American Professional Agency says that "a 'mental health professional' means any natural person in his or her capacity as a mental health counselor, social worker, pastoral counselor, hypnotist, psychoanalyst, psychotherapist, life coach, marriage and family counselor, or any individual practicing other mental health disciplines approved by us."[4] Given the litigiousness of our society, I think it is only a matter of time until someone is sued for "malpractice" in matters spiritual. Making appropriate referrals when persons need additional assistance is important for both the directee and the director.

Dual Relationships

Alice Ward has been a directee of Father Tom Martin's for almost six years. Tom is a seminary professor who enjoys doing spiritual direction. Some years ago, Tom was assigned to Alice's parish, St. Mark's, for six months to support the resident priest, who needed to be relieved of some duties because of a lingering illness. During this time, Alice continued to see Tom for direction. Tom's retirement from the seminary happened within weeks of Alice being hired by St. Mark's to coordinate its educational programs. Now the bishop has asked Father Tom to assume the duties of rector at St. Mark's for an unspecified term. Alice is upset when Tom raises with her the possibility that he should no longer serve as her spiritual director. She reminds him that he remained her director while he was working in her parish some years ago. She assures him that even though they will now be working together for the first time, it will not influence their spiritual direction relationship. Tom decides he will consult with his supervisor before his next direction session with Alice.

Interpersonal Dynamics

Father Tom's decision to speak with Alice about the way their new roles as staff members of the parish will make it difficult for them to continue in a spiritual direction relationship indicates his awareness that dual relationships can create confusing interpersonal dynamics. Dual relationships are "situations in which a director and directee regularly have other dealings or connections with each other outside their spiritual direction meetings."[5] In *A Code of Ethics for Spiritual Directors*, the Center for Sacred Psychology describes some of the potential dual relationships:

> Types of dual relationships include socializing or business dealings with directees, direction relationships which flower into two-way friendships, bartering or exchanges of services, spiritual direction with one's friends, family members, students or supervisees, and directing close friends or more than one person from the same family. . . . Prohibited, of course, is any covert or overt sexual intimacy or involvement between the two parties, or between the director and a directee's spouse or partner.[6]

Though other helping professions have clear prohibitions against dual relationships, spiritual directors often find the issue more complex. For example, directors and directees may be members of the same religious congregation or parish faith community. Whether these dual relationships are problematic depends on a number of community and personal factors.

In this case, Father Tom was not concerned about the dual relationship he had with Alice when he served in a leadership position in her parish for a brief time. When Alice reminds him that they continued in direction in the past when he was working in her parish, he points out a number of factors that influenced that decision. First, his work in the parish was brief and circumscribed. He did not think that the dynamics created briefly by his changed role constituted a problem for the direction relationship. Second, Alice was not in a parish leadership position under direct supervision from Tom. Third, in Roman Catholic parishes and congregations—in contrast to Protestant settings—the religious community recognizes that priests frequently serve as spiritual directors.

Role Changes and Conflicting Expectations

Once Alice is supervised by Father Tom, another set of dynamics can emerge. For example, if they are serving on a committee together, will Alice be able to freely express her opinions, or will she feel she must support the ideas put forward by Tom? Conversely, will Tom feel he must support those presented by Alice? If they hold conflicting views on a given concern, will their disagreement influence their relationship in direction? When Tom evaluates Alice's work, will she feel resentful if the support she has felt in direction now has a tone of critique? Either the director or the directee may feel uncomfortable if they sense that their bond in spiritual direction will somehow be compromised by these other roles. Given the complexity of human interactions, it is also important to note that though consciously such dual relationships might seem "clean," either the director or the directee may have unconscious issues that only with time will come to light in situations confounded by dual relationships.

The dynamics of the spiritual direction relationship and the atmosphere of the session are crucial to the experience itself. The director is present with the directee and God as a listener whose love of God and the directee contributes to the presence of the sacred in the room. Directees come to associate these grace-filled times with both the presence of God and the presence of the director. In the role of director, a sacred ministry is being exercised. What can potentially happen if a directee must now deal with a director when the director is in another role or, as we often find in religious organizations, is "wearing another hat"?

Institutional Context

Again, the institutional context must be given consideration in deciding what dual relationships are acceptable and which are especially problematic. In Protestant churches, pastors would not normally do one-on-one spiritual direction with parishioners, because it could easily be construed as favoritism toward selected members. Since Protestants do not have a sacrament of reconciliation per se, pastors do not routinely offer structured guidance to parishioners. Pastors who are trained to offer spiritual direction normally do not see members of their own parish congregations precisely to avoid the problematic dynamics of dual relationships.

In the context of Roman Catholic congregations, sisters, brothers, and monks have a considerable amount of experience in changing roles with their peers. Here, one's superior may become one's subordinate in the roles outside the spiritual direction relationship. In these contexts, it is essential to maintain clear contracts to keep the relationship as free as possible from the dynamics of other settings. Even with such care, it is necessary to remember that when relationships involve evaluation, supervision, or any form of accountability, the potential exists for dysfunctional patterns of communication at a conscious or unconscious level.

Ethics Resources

There are three resources on ethics designed specifically for spiritual directors that I think all directors and supervisors should read. The first two are codes of ethics, and the third is a new book devoted to the topic.

Guidelines for Ethical Conduct, a pamphlet from Spiritual Directors International available at www.sdiworld.org; e-mail info@sdiworld.org for information.

A Code of Ethics for Spiritual Directors, by Thomas M. Hedberg, Betsy Caprio, and the Staff of the Center for Sacred Psychology, Dove Publications, Pecos, NM 87552, (505) 757-6597.

Trustworthy Connections: Interpersonal Issues in Spiritual Direction, by Anne Winchell Silver, (Cambridge, MA: Cowley Publications, 2003).

Notes

1. Although this act was passed in 1996, it did not require compliance until 2003. Counselors (e.g., psychiatrists, psychologists, licensed social workers, marriage and family counselors) working in health care facilities are now required to adhere to its privacy and confidentiality provisions.

2. *Guidelines for Ethical Conduct* (Bellevue, WA: Spiritual Directors International, 1999), 4–5.

3. Thomas M. Hedburg, Betsy Caprio, and the Staff of The Center for Sacred Psychology, *A Code of Ethics for Spiritual Directors*, rev. ed. (Pecos, NM: Dove Publications, 1992), 9.

4. American Professional Agency, Inc., Amityville, NY, for D33543 (April 2004).

5. Anne Winchell Silver, *Trustworthy Connections: Interpersonal Issues in Spiritual Direction* (Cambridge, MA: Cowley Publications, 2003), 38.

6. Hedberg and Caprio, 8.

PART THREE

Worldview and Supervision

CHAPTER EIGHT

Supervision as Widening the Horizons

Elizabeth Liebert

"We see what we can see," says one member of a supervision group.
"No, we see what we want to see," responds another.

Each of these statements could provoke a heated discussion on its meaning and validity. I will not try to unpack these sentences. Instead, I simply wish to use them as pointers to my thesis: There is so much more we could "see" in spiritual direction than we often recognize. There are so many levels and complexities, so much richness in the ways God's own self is revealed to us. How can we widen the horizons of our spiritual direction? How can we teach to these new horizons? How can we nurture growth in this ability to see past the obvious?

And whose horizons are at issue? Those seekers who come for spiritual direction, certainly. How we see God, where we perceive God to be present and active, absent or silent, limits our horizons. They are limited by our internalized images of holiness, a weak connection between our prayer and our action, limited conceptions of prayer, or an inability to move from an injunction to pray to the actual practice of prayer. I am always saddened when a directee says: "I didn't realize that (walking in nature, getting swept up in beautiful music or art, attending lovingly to a dying relative or helpless infant, trying to reach each child in a crowded classroom, struggling to change discriminatory laws, and on and on) could be part of my prayer! I've been doing that all my life, and I always thought I was not a prayerful person." Or a student, after learning some of the richness of the Christian tradition, says, sometimes angrily and sometimes wistfully: "How come I never heard this before? I was raised in the church, and this is the first time

I have heard it!" Or an adult exclaims (as a woman in a class for catechists once did): "Oh, there *is* something important going on in the Bible. I can't just leave it sit on the coffee table, can I?"

Whose horizons? The directors who serve as companions to seekers, certainly. Directors have frequently been schooled to see God in the "spiritual" things of formal prayer, be it private or corporate, and in the silence of our inner "closets." We may secretly believe that real contemplatives march through the rooms of Teresa's interior castle and the stages of John's dark night. They usually live in cloisters or monasteries, or at least they are ordained. The rest of us, we may believe, just dabble in holiness or play at sanctity, because we are too busy earning a living to afford the leisure of contemplative silence.

Whose horizons? Those who accompany spiritual directors in their ministry—supervisors—yes, us, too. Our horizons may also be too small, captured as they may have been by psychological assumptions and the clinical origin of our supervisory model. We look for slips and resistances, we seek to set directors free of their inner blocks to hearing their directees—good work, certainly—but in the process, we may still miss the breadth and depth of the Mystery of God in encounters between the director and the directee or in the directee's own encounter with God. If we really were to experience the Mystery of God, Annie Dillard warns us to be prepared:

> On the whole, I do not find Christians, outside of the catacombs, suffi-
> ciently sensible of conditions. Does anyone have the foggiest idea what
> sort of power we so blithely invoke? Or, as I suspect, does no one believe
> a word of it? The churches are children playing on the floor with their
> chemistry sets, mixing up a batch of TNT to kill a Sunday morning. It
> is madness to wear ladies' straw hats and velvet hats to church; we should
> all be wearing crash helmets. Ushers should issue life preservers and sig-
> nal flares; they should lash us to our pews. For the sleeping god may
> wake someday and take offense, or the waking god may draw us out to
> where we can never return.[1]

Seekers, directors, and supervisors all suffer from limited vision, and we all too frequently fail to recognize that we are on holy ground, all the time. Poet Rainer Maria Rilke voices our dilemma as he addresses "neighbor God":

> . . .
> Between us there is but a narrow wall,
> and by sheer chance; for it would take
> merely a call from your lips or from mine
> to break it down,
> and that without a sound.

> The wall is builded of your images.
> They stand before you hiding you like names . . .[2]

We hold so many deeply held, often unexamined assumptions building images that surround us like names:

- Spiritual life is interior life.
- One's spiritual life is private and personal.
- Psychology can free us from narrow and dogmatic views of God and the spiritual life.
- Moral life is about sexuality, not about economics or politics.
- Prayer is talking to God.
- My church is the true church.
- Body is opposed to spirit; body holds our spirits captive.
- Heaven is "up" and "after we die."
- God is in heaven.
- God is Father.
- Human nature must be tamed to be spiritual.
- God's will is ultimately inscrutable.
- Theology and science talk about mutually exclusive worlds.
- Church is for spiritual life and the world is for everything else.

This list could go on and on. We came by such assumptions quite innocently and "naturally." We grew up in the assumptive worlds that made one or several of our beliefs self-evident. We all have sets of such assumptions that simultaneously free us and continue to limit how we expect to experience God. Our ongoing challenge, whether as seekers, directors of seekers, or companions to directors, is twofold: to recognize the kernel of truth in each of these assumptions, but also to become free of the limits to imagination that they set for us, usually unconsciously. Our task in widening our horizons is to clear out some of the debris of unexamined assumptions and put on crash helmets.

Two Invitations to Expand Our Horizons

If we are helped to see the problem by poets, we are helped to see the solution by a spiritual master, Ignatius of Loyola, and a theologian, Karl Rahner. In the Contemplation to Attain Love at the conclusion of the *Spiritual Exercises*, Ignatius invites the loved sinner, who has accompanied Jesus through death and into resurrection, to a life of gratitude and to labor as God labors. For this person, the Mystery of God suffuses all:

I will ponder with deep affection how much God Our Lord has done for me, and how much [God] has given me of what [God] possesses, and consequently how [God], the same Lord, desires to give me even [God's] very self, in accordance with [God's] divine design. . . .

I will consider how God labors and works for me in all the creatures on the face of the earth, that is, acts as one who is laboring. For example, [God] is working in the heavens, elements, plants, fruits, cattle, and all the rest. . . .

I will ask for what I desire, for interior knowledge of all the great good I have received, in order that, stirred to profound gratitude, I may become able to love and serve [t]his Divine Majesty in all things.[3]

Simply put, our call is to experience God's presence in and through God's work, to give thanks, and to join God in the completion of this work. Since all of creation is God's work, it is possible to meet God in any part of creation: in the natural world, in our neighbor, in culture, in the depths of our own hearts.

Karl Rahner clothed this profoundly world-oriented and life-affirming spirituality with theological and philosophical language for today.[4] Echoing Ignatius, Rahner spoke of God as the one who continually gives of God's own self, so much so that we exist in a world of grace.[5] We are "surrounded by a God who, like a horizon is ever receding and therefore Absolute Mystery, but, as revealed by Jesus, is ever drawing near to us in gracious self-giving."[6] The experience of God, therefore, is not just one experience among many; it is the radical essence of every spiritual and personal experience. In fact, there exists an element of the ineffable in the concrete experience of our everyday life.[7] For our part, human beings are uniquely transcendent, that is to say, spiritual, beings. We are aware of more than the time and space that limit us; we reach out for the truth of ourselves and of God. Whether or not we have the language for our quest, all humans are characterized by this pull toward understanding ourselves in the light of the divine. And our uniquely human response is to freely love another person. Rahner was so convinced of this dynamic exchange between divine creator and human creature that he insisted that the love of God and the love of neighbor are but two names for the same reality. That is, the experience of God is simultaneously the experience of the depths of oneself and of the radical otherness of one's neighbor. This "simultaneity" provides directors and supervisors with one of their most useful insights, as we shall see.

Rahner also pondered the notion of human experiencing. He noted that our experience of God is primary and universal, and prior to any subsequent attempt to conceptualize it, it is frequently diffuse and unthematic. Yet we humans can reflect on our experience, stand back and look at it, think about it, categorize it, make decisions about it. Based upon this Rahnerian insight, we could say that we become aware of our experience through several degrees of explicitness, from the vague, almost somatic awareness (nonthematic), to more reflective, affective-laden, and imaginative awareness, to logically explicit interpretive awareness. Our consciousness of what is happening to us at a given moment may be very diffuse and inarticulate (nonthematic); it may be captured in an emotionally powerful dream or an image (affective-imaginative); or, upon attending to it, we may describe it logically, develop propositions, and make some decisions with respect to it (interpretive). These variations in the explicitness in our attending to experience flow into each other organically and in no particular order, and they may even exist simultaneously—a proposition may also contain an image that arouses strong feelings and register in one's body with a certain felt sense. This description of our awareness of our experience offers spiritual directors and supervisors another key insight.

The Role of Supervision

In light of these realities, we can now frame an understanding of supervision that takes them into account. Supervision is a ministry in which a relatively more experienced spiritual director assists another spiritual director to grow in self-awareness, inner freedom, and the ability to help others enter into the experience of God's presence and to respond in gratitude to the call that arises from that encounter.[8] Chief among the goals of supervision, however, is attending to the experience of the mystery of God, as God chooses to reveal God's own self, in three theaters: the conversation between the supervisor and director, the conversation between the director and directee, and the directee's life. The primary goal of both spiritual direction and supervision is the awareness of and reflection on Holy Mystery. William Creed asserts: "[S]piritual direction involves skills, but all the effort of listening and responding, noticing the verbal and non-verbal movements of the directee, do not make a good spiritual director. Directors need to know those skills, but the key is the Mystery where the divine and the human kiss."[9]

Supervision, then, though it may (and frequently does) touch on matters of skill, or the directors' own hidden blocks, does so primarily in service to this primary end, recognizing and responding to the Holy Mystery we Christians call God.

So far, so good. The problem, however, is in attending to the experience of God. Too little of our experience appears to be of God, and therefore "spiritual"; too much of it not of God, and therefore "nonspiritual." The Center for Spirituality and Justice in the Bronx offers a case in point. Over and over again, the staff found their commitment to social spirituality and the social dimension of sin getting lost as their interns slipped into their "spiritual director personas." Could this seemingly intractable dichotomy be bridged? In a now-classic essay, Elinor Shea describes their tentative steps to construct a more adequate model for integrating the classical teaching on prayer and spiritual direction with their commitment to social justice.[10]

Meanwhile, in Washington, D.C., the Center of Concern had begun to study the relationship between "social consciousness" and Ignatian spirituality. The work of Peter Henriot and Thomas Clarke, grounded in Karl Rahner's theological anthropology, gave the staff at the Center for Spirituality and Justice the clue they were searching for:

> [I]t is only possible to speak of the reality of the human person today by taking into full account the three dimensions of human existence: the *individual*, the *interpersonal* and the *public*. These are not three separate and distinct dimensions so much as three moments in our perception of a single reality, or three interrelated interpenetrated aspects. Thus the identity of the human person is inadequately situated outside a consideration of all three dimensions simultaneously.[11]

Every human person experiences himself or herself in this multidimensioned way, but it is the nature of human consciousness to attend to only one at a time, letting the others recede from attention. Thus it is possible to be unaware of or inattentive to whole aspects of one's experience. The staff at the Center of Concern began to wonder whether the problem of the division between the "spiritual" and the "secular" was at least partly due to the fact that the spiritual director's perspective was confined largely to one *arena* of human experience, namely, intrapersonal. When the notion of religious experience is broadened to include the interpersonal and the social and structural, and all arenas are seen as the theater of the experience of the mystery of God, the spiritual director's task is immensely widened.

The Experience Circle as a Tool for Widening Our Horizons

Thus began a theoretical perspective expressed in a tool we have come to call the Experience Circle. Rather soon, in several parts of the country, a fourth arena was added to the conception of human experience, called, variously, Nature, Environment, and Eco-environment.[12] The rectangular chart developed by the Center for Spirituality and Justice gave way to a circle, which provided a more adequate symbol of the unity of experience and also more readily suggested the fluidity, interconnectivity, and simultaneity than did blocked-off columns and rows.

The Experience Circle[13] attempts to overlay two theoretical foci in one visual: (1) an understanding of the *quadratic* nature of human experience (experience is simultaneously interior/intrapersonal, interpersonal, systemic/structural, and environmental/natural) with (2) the varying degrees of explicitness in

The Experience Circle

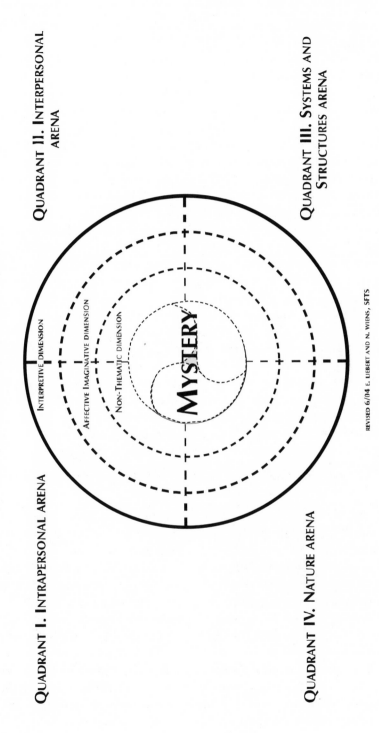

REVISED 6/04 E. LIEBERT AND N. WIENS, SFTS

Quadrants represent: 1. Literal Arenas of Human Experience of God; 2. Angles of Vision, Moments in Perception. Rings represent dimensions of human awareness: Non-Thematic, Affective Imaginative, and Interpretive. Center Circle represents Mystery: Ineffable Touch of the Holy, Experienced in Encounters with God, Self, Nature.

the perception of that experience (we attend affectively, interpretively, and/or nonthematically to our experience). The linchpin is *simultaneity*. All of the arenas of experience occur simultaneously, though our reflection process on our experience develops (or becomes more faint) through the various dimensions over time. Furthermore, the simultaneity in human experiencing is set against the primary notion of simultaneity between the creator and creature as Rahner understood it: An experience of depth of self or the radical otherness of one's neighbor is simultaneously an experience of God. We now have the core of a theory of the human experience of the divine that can be operationalized by spiritual directors and their supervisors.

The shaded area at the center of the diagram,[14] labeled "Mystery," is meant to suggest the unitive experience between the creator and creation that occurs at the moment of knowing oneself, one's God, and one's entire life context in a mysteriously profound, more enlarged way. It is divided into three mutually interlocking sections representing God, Self, and Nature.[15] The dashed lines indicate that these three actors influence one another. But they do not "capture" each other, and none is collapsed into another. Rather, they engage in a trinitarian dance of mutual interdependence and influence. Placing the Mystery at the center graphically represents the "location" of Holy Mystery in the depth of reality, at the center of our being, and as the "ground" of our experience. Expressing the Holy Mystery as three mutually interdependent actors, God, self, and nature, illustrates Rahner's insight that the experience of God is simultaneously the experience of self and the experience of neighbor—which now includes all of nature.

The fourfold dimensionality of human experience is expressed by the four quadrants of the circle, which focus on the various aspects of experience:

- The intrapersonal arena (top left) focuses on the experience of self as distinguished from other people. It attends primarily to interior dynamics.

- The interpersonal arena (moving clockwise) focuses on the experience of self with other people as individuals. It focuses on the relationships between and among people in face-to-face groups.

- The systems and structures arena focuses on the self-in-systems. It deals with those formal sets of rules, regulations, and relationships (systems or structures) that exist consciously and unconsciously and serve to partially constrain the individual actors. The focus of that arena rests more on the roles themselves and relationships among roles than on the individuals who fill the roles.

- The arena of nature focuses upon the self as continuous with and discontinuous from the whole universe. It draws attention to the interdependence among all the creatures in the universe and to the reciprocal influence between the natural world and the individual person.

Several caveats and illustrations are in order. First, the arenas are not hard and fast realities into which we fix our experiences. Rather, they are simply heuristic devices that depend on perspective and emphasis. For example, you are a director for Peter. He talks lately about being extremely worried about his spouse, Marta, who seems more and more depressed as winter comes on. They struggle to communicate. Their oldest child, Toby, is having more trouble than usual in school, and his teacher has called several times asking for a conference, adding to your directee's anxiety. You and Peter could begin to "open up" Peter's experience via a number of avenues. You could approach it primarily as a largely intrapersonal experience, attending to the worry that Peter has for Marta and his concern for Toby. By association, other sources of anxiety could flow naturally from this discussion, and you invite God to be with Peter in this time of anxiety. Or you could just as easily attend to the interpersonal dimension, focusing on the change in the relationship between Peter and Marta, holding this relationship before the light of God's love. Or the main attention could center on the family as a system of spouses and children—that is, the roles that the individuals play in a particular family structure. Your conversation could, quite plausibly, move toward how God might be calling Peter to respond in his role as husband and father. You could begin by noticing that the season of the year is weighing heavily on the situation. You might wonder about its role in the heaviness in the directee (intrapersonal), in the communication problem between the spouses (interpersonal), or on the family structure (the kids bickering and fighting during long afternoons cooped up indoors during inclement weather). Perhaps the leaden skies of December serve as a metaphor; perhaps the season is literally a "player" in this drama (nature). No avenue is "correct" to the exclusion of the others. The four arenas are potentially present in this single narration; Peter narrates a rich multidimensional experience.

Second, the boundaries among the quadrants are not to be seen as clear and distinct. It is quite possible, following the above example, to look at Peter and Marta as persons who are in an intimate relationship of marriage (interpersonal dimension), or to focus on Peter and Marta primarily in their roles as husband, wife, and parent (structural dimension). Both are valid, and either might be appropriate.

Third, and providing a corrector to its absence in so much spiritual literature, the body can be understood as present in all arenas, depending upon which aspect one desires to focus. The body is the ground and medium of our inner movements and affections (intrapersonal), we relate to other persons as body-selves (interpersonal), the body is a system itself and represents other systems (such as the Body of Christ), and the body and all that it is made of is shared with the rest of the universe (nature).

Fourth, language and imagery are often arena-specific. In our culture, what we think of as "spiritual" language is typically language of the intrapersonal or interpersonal arenas. Language that describes the structural arena doesn't appear or feel spiritual; hence we have to learn to "hear" it as such, just as we have to learn to "see" the action of God, not merely in the persons within a structure, but in the structure itself. Language that describes experiences in nature is more readily perceived as spiritual, but the experience is often ruled "out of bounds" as somehow not Christian.

Finally, and of great significance for spiritual direction, the notion of simultaneity suggests that an experience of the Holy in one arena will "overflow" or "bleed into" all the other arenas of a single life. A new experience of freedom in one arena will have a reverberation in the other arenas, though it may be so subtle and nonthematic that it goes unnoticed. Spiritual directors who are aware of the notion of simultaneity are more apt to notice these "echoes," help bring them to light, and invite directees to deepen them through attending, naming, and responding.

In this light, we can understand spiritual direction to be a privileged relationship in which director and directee together "live into" the expectation that God is working in all arenas of the directee's life. Similarly, supervision is the ministry of assisting directors in this multifaceted attending to Holy Mystery as it appears both in their directees' lives and in their work as spiritual directors.

The concentric rings represent different degrees of explicitness in our receiving and processing experience. The ring immediately surrounding Mystery represents nonthematic awareness: Something registers somatically but is not yet specifically named, categorized as a certain kind of experience, or attended to in such a way that it reveals its richness. This immediate experience is as yet virtually unformulated and directed by our cognitive processes. Often these experiences are so subtle as to be barely evident to our consciousness, yet nonetheless they are truly present. Our deepest touches of the Holy often register nonthematically, as "sighs too deep for words," a "flood of newness," spontaneous upwellings of tears, or inexpressible attraction. Nonthematic experiences often invite a simple contemplative presence and awareness.

The second dimension, termed affective-imaginative, represents all the nonlinear and often nonverbal ways we experience and process: felt senses, intuitions, metaphors and images, colors, odors, fantasies, dreams, fables and myths, stories. The kinds of processing that flow from and nourish this dimension include art, music, dance, poetry, and other sorts of creative and evocative ways of opening up the multilayered possibilities inherent in affective, imaginative, largely nondiscursive awareness.

The third dimension represents our conscious reflection and interpretation. It is the province of the rational and the logical, of ideas, definitions, conceptual insights, and analysis. Because it depends heavily on the verbal, it can be relatively more communicable through shared language. Theological reflection and discursive meditation reside in this dimension.

How are these dimensions related to each other? The nonthematic dimension, whether or not attended to, underlies all experience. In a sense, it is the foundation on which the other two dimensions are built. Likewise, the affective-imaginative dimension underlies the interpretive dimension, because thoughts have an affective component that may or may not be in the thinker's awareness but that provides the impetus to act.

Because of the propensity to focus our attention on one dimension at a time, it is relatively easy to overlook or undervalue the other two. A person on a "head trip" processes in the interpretive dimension without much attention to the affective or nonthematic aspects of the experience, but we want to encourage just such integration. "Impractical visionaries" or persons of "artistic temperament" can be invited to ground their heavily affective-imaginative experiences in a bit of logic and analysis. Persons who remain largely in the nonthematic dimension will be left without much language with which to assess and communicate their experiences, to relate them to the wider Christian story, or to engage in discernment about their demands, and directors will help the affective and interpretive dimensions to mature. To attend to our experience fully, in this view, is to range through all the dimensions of awareness, savoring and plumbing each.

It is not possible to portray everything we might want to say on a single graphic. For example, placing Mystery in the center could leave the impression that only the nonthematic dimension "drops into" the direct touch of God, and that the other two dimensions are only preparations for the real work of spiritual direction—which we then assume to be arriving at nonthematic direct presence to God. A direction session in which the directee "stays in her head" can be judged as somehow not as good as it should be, because the directee did not "drop down" into the direct experience of the Holy. Of course, we want to encourage just such immediate presence to Mystery (which is always God's gift, and does not appear through our direction skill or the directee's generosity!). But we should just as faithfully encourage theological reflection so that directees can connect their experience to the larger tradition and grow in their understanding of God. And both the person prone to live in the interpretive dimension and the person prone to desire the quiet, nonthematic resting of the first dimension can enrich their experiences by tapping into the huge store of energy held in the affective-reflective dimension.

Keeping this graphic in mind adds a second facet to the spiritual director's task—and, by extension, that of the supervisor: The spiritual director invites and assists the directee in moving through all dimensions of the experience, attending and relishing the fruit of each.

Spiritual Direction and Supervision in Light of the Experience Circle

With this background, the movement of the spiritual direction session can be seen as something like this:

- Director and directee together ask for the grace to attend to the Mystery of God and to respond to it.

- The directee narrates a portion of his or her experience, something that caught his or her attention in daily life, something that seemed significant in the directee's relationship with God.

- The director discerns where there seems to be the most potential for noticing the "trace of the finger of God" in the directee's narration and begins responding around this aspect of the directee's experience. Alternatively, the directee directs the conversation by asking to talk about something specific. In either case, the experience usually "shows up" clearly in one arena.

- The director, using first- and second-level contemplative listening,[16] helps the directee expand the experience through the interpretive, affective, and nonthematic dimensions, moving back and forth as the conversation opens up. If God so chooses, the directee may enter again into a moment in which God touches the directee directly and immediately; if so, director and directee linger and relish this contemplative moment.

- They also attend to other arenas, wondering how God's life will show up there, believing that because of simultaneity, it will. (This portion may extend over several sessions.)

- As director and directee follow the thread of simultaneity leading to another arena of the directee's experience, they attend to all the dimensions of the directee's experience as manifested in this new arena.

- The director summarizes and invites the directee to respond to God's initiative. (Again, this process may extend over several sessions.)

- Director and directee celebrate God's grace, mercy, and presence during the direction session.

The supervision relationship, using this model, proceeds somewhat like this:

- Director and supervisor ask for the grace to attend to the Mystery of God and to respond to it.

- The director narrates a portion of his or her experience of direction, something that seemed significant in his or her relationship with the directee, a slip, a momentary inattention, a sense that there was something more that was missed, a moment of breakthrough for the directee or for the director, and so on.

- The supervisor may discern where there seems to be the most potential for noticing the "trace of the finger of God" in the director's narration. But more typically, the one coming for supervision directs the conversation's early stages by bringing a specific question and accompanying illustration from a particular spiritual direction session.

- Director and supervisor proceed, using first- and second-level contemplative listening, to expand the experience that the director wishes to unpack. They are looking for the finger of God in three theaters: in the life of the directee, in God's work in the director as director, and in the present conversation between director and supervisor. Simultaneity suggests that the work of God in all three will be connected.

- Together, supervisor and spiritual director follow the thread of this first topic through the interpretive, affective, and nonthematic dimensions, moving back and forth as the conversation opens up. If God so chooses, the director may enter again into a moment in which God touches him or her directly and immediately; if so, supervisor and director linger and relish this contemplative moment just as the director and directee would relish a contemplative moment during the spiritual direction session.

- Director and supervisor attend to other arenas of the director's life as they enter into the practice of spiritual direction, wondering how God's life will show up there, believing, because of their trust in simultaneity, that it will. Supervision ranges far beyond the intrapsychic dynamics of the director and the interpersonal relationships of director-directee and director-supervisor. It can attend to the various roles being enacted (structural), to the setting and environment in which the direction or supervision takes place, to the influence of the natural world on the attentiveness of the director, to the director's own prayer as a font for the spiritual direction relationship, and so on.

- As they discover the thread of simultaneity leading them to another arena, they repeat their attending to foster all the dimensions in the director's reflection.

- They notice how this new insight carries over into this director's work with other directees.

- The supervisor summarizes and invites a response to God's invitation. They may "practice" how this new experience of freedom will show up in the director's work with this directee and with others.

- They celebrate God's grace, mercy, and presence during the supervision session.

The Model in Action

This section examines a critical incident in supervision.[17] It begins with the spiritual direction session that the director is bringing to supervision and follows the example from the direction session into the supervision session. The goal is both to illumine the model and to clarify how it functions, as revealed through supervision of a spiritual direction session. The directee is Andrea; the director, Mary; and the supervisor, Art.

Andrea is a Presbyterian clergywoman who has been seeing her director, Mary, for about two years, since she graduated from seminary and moved to the area to become Associate Pastor for Christian Education and Spiritual Formation of a medium-size church. She felt welcomed by the church and loves the area, with its many options for outdoor activities and its culture. She is single and tends to spend a good deal of time engaged in ministry. She is slowly building a support system among other pastors, especially women in the interfaith clergy group. She is also beginning to build nonclergy friendships through her love of bicycling, which she does regularly on her days off.

The senior pastor was installed in her church eighteen years earlier and is well loved and respected by the entire congregation. The congregation has been unfailingly gracious, as has the senior pastor—indeed, this is one of the qualities that drew her to this church. Consequently, it took more than a year for Andrea to notice that whenever she talked over her ideas and plans with the pastor, though they were met with characteristic graciousness, nothing ever seemed to come of them. Lately she has noticed a similar dynamic in her work with the Education Commission: Her ideas seem to go nowhere unless the commission members receive a nod from the senior pastor. In her last several spiritual direction sessions, Andrea has pinpointed and named her feelings of disappointment and frustration, as well as her annoyance that it took her so long to notice the pattern, covered as it is by graciousness on the part of the pastor and loyalty to the senior pastor on the part of the members of the Education Commission. She is aware that she will probably have to take more direct action but dreads "upsetting the apple cart."

In her most recent session, Andrea begins by relaying the results of her prayer around the situation with her pastor, which has been a topic of conversation for the past several sessions. She reports that the overriding feeling that has emerged from her prayer is irritation that God has not softened the pastor's gracious snowballing technique. "I think I'm going to have to bring it up directly, and I am afraid that when I do, the graciousness toward me will end. I think I've gotten a bit dependent on that graciousness," she concludes. "That's the main thing going on in my prayer, but I also want to tell you about a show I saw last night, because it really touched me and has stayed with me all day. It was one of the National Geographic programs, set in Africa. The photographer was following the migration of the wildebeests. The image that has stayed with me is of a cow and her calf. They are moving along at a pace that the calf can manage, heading from where the water holes are drying up to new grazing ground where there is more water and grass. As they are crossing a mostly dry riverbed, the calf gets stuck in some mud. As it struggles, it sinks deeper. You see the cow calling to her calf to get it to come along. The next scene, though, is the one that really got to me. The camera looked past the struggling calf to the herd moving slowly out of sight in the distance, leaving the calf trapped in the mud. The photographer went back the next day to show the outcome. The calf was totally encased in hardened mud, dead. When I saw that, I burst into tears. I'm not sure exactly why, but it really got to me." (Tears well up, and one or two roll silently down her cheek.) "I don't know why I'm crying. It was just a show on TV. I didn't actually see it happen."

Mary remains quiet for a few moments, letting Andrea sit with her tears and feelings. "It just seems so incredibly sad," Andrea says after a few moments.

"You seem very sad even now as you remember."

"Yes, I am . . ." (pause)

"Is there another feeling under that one?" (pause)

"I don't know. The sadness is so strong." (pause)

"Maybe the calf represents something to you that you feel very strongly, very sad about." (pause)

"I think I am like the calf. I am sad that things with the church and Tom [the pastor] have turned out like this. So I am sad . . . and irritated. Yeah. Sad and mad together."

Mary and Andrea continue to attend to the feelings, trying to notice and bring to light all the different ones that are actually present in the moment. The list grows to include "boxed in," "ineffective," and "resistant."

Mary picks up on the last one, and Andrea responds. "Resistant. That doesn't seem quite like the other feelings. It's connected in my mind because I know I have to talk to Tom about the way things are going, and I really don't want to. I really have a hard time moving outside my 'nice girl' image. If I talk to Tom, I won't be a 'nice girl' Associate any longer. I think I am sad because I had secretly hoped for the perfect church. I am mad because it turned out not to be the perfect church. And I have this sinking feeling because I don't want to do what I suspect I am going to have to do if I want to move ahead."

"You really don't want to move outside of your 'nice girl' image? Talking to Tom means you are not a nice girl any longer?"

"Yeah. I have this thing. I hated being nagged by my mom to be perfect and nice all the time. I never did *anything* because I knew I would disappoint her. I learned how to be a nice girl. I've been doing it all my life."

"So you learned it early and practiced it often."

"Uh-huh."

"Sounds like this might be an area where you are not as free as you would like to be. Not as free as God wants you to be."

"Well, yeah. In my *head* I realize that the world won't end if I bring all this up with Tom, but somehow I don't believe it deep down."

"Let's just stop there for a minute. Sit for a minute and see if you can notice your deepest desire about this need to be good . . ." (pause)

After a couple minutes, Andrea starts to tear up again. "I think I was so sad because just like the calf, I am caught. But needing to be nice traps me. Just as stuck. I don't want to be just as dead."

"Maybe you could say that to God, what you want, right now." (pause)

After a couple more minutes, Andrea lets out a little chuckle. "I just got it! Wildebeest. Wild beast. There is a part of me that is like a wild beast trapped in this huge mud hole. So I want to break out of the mud and be more myself than I let myself be."

"That seems like a great grace to pray for this week!"

Mary recalls that Psalm 69 speaks about getting stuck in the mire and invites Andrea to pray that psalm, a few verses at a time, every day over the next week or two, trying to notice her desire for freedom and asking God for it at the beginning of her prayer.

The conversation then turns to other matters. One that Mary notes is that Andrea comments that she hasn't been riding her bike this week because it is in the shop. She is looking forward to getting it back and getting out in the hills again next week. As they close the session, Mary prays a few verses from Psalm 69.

This session is essentially what Mary presents to her supervisor, Art. She is interested primarily in the story of the wildebeest calf and the insights that Andrea received from it, which is why she has selected this portion of the conversation. Mary is not certain that she and Andrea have mined the possibilities. What is there still to be revealed? What has Mary missed? A portion of her session with Art follows.

Art: Let's begin today by reading this dialogue. You be Andrea, and I will read your part. (They read the dialogue parts aloud.)

Mary: The first thing that strikes me as I read Andrea's part is that I have a lot more energy around "boxed in" than "resistant," but "resistant" is what I picked up on with Andrea. It did go somewhere, though— back to the interpersonal arena, her relationship with her mother. It's the first time we've really gone there, although I have been aware, at some level, that Andrea needs to be nice. [Mary thus begins in the intrapersonal arena, affective dimension, noticing that she has more energy inside her around the term "boxed in." But she quickly moves to the interpretive dimension to assess the effectiveness of her move with Andrea.]

Art: And the image of "wild beast" has now given you a way to open up this area in the future. She may very well return with more associations. Notice, however, your energy around "boxed in" and her "trapped" at the point where she recognized the pun in the image. You had energy around the same sense that she brought up again. [Art starts in the interpretive dimension, where Mary is, but he underlines the nature arena as the locus of Andrea's experience and notices that the image has a lot of potential for future unpacking. He then invites Mary to go back to the affective-imaginative dimension of her own experience to see what else is there for her.]

Mary: That suggests that the trapped feeling is probably present in other areas of her life besides the obvious one of the situation with the pastor. [Mary responds quickly with another connection in the interpretive dimension.]

Art: You will want to be on the alert, but don't assume that you know. Wait for her to "tell" you in some way. Any data in the conversation? [Wanting Mary's interpretation not to get too far from Andrea's experience, he sends her back there for testing.]

Mary: Well, the obvious is the way she gets boxed in by both the pastor and the Education Commission . . . And there is also the matter of the bike being in the shop. She couldn't ride this week, leaving her "boxed in" from her usual exercise. And her regular time outdoors, come to think of it, is where she is not boxed in at all, but goes as far as her legs can carry her. [Mary notices another experience of being boxed in in another arena of Andrea's narration, though neither of them had made the connection at the time.]

Art: Uh-huh. And it came to Andrea in the reflection time that she is like the trapped calf. Did you notice what you did with that noticing? (pause)

Mary: Oh, I turned it to asking for freedom.

Art: Without pausing to open up "trapped." You moved very quickly to the antidote. [Art encourages Mary to slow down to more fully unpack the multiple dimensions of an important image.]

Mary: (thoughtfully) Oh yeah, I did, didn't I? And the word that had energy when I read Andrea's part was "boxed in." Maybe it is a word for me. [Mary assumes some simultaneity between her and her directee as indicated by energy on similar words.]

Art: Let's ask it. Go to the word and see if it has something to say to you: another word, an image, a memory, a present situation, whatever. (They slip into silence. Mary closes her eyes and sits quietly). [Art thus invites a noninterpretive and potentially contemplative moment to be part of the revelation.]

Mary: Odd, but what comes to me is the words from Psalm 139, the part about "You hem me in." How does it go? Something like "Behind me and before me you hem me in, you lay your hand upon me." But I don't feel trapped at all, though I know some people do by this psalm because it seems that they are hemmed in by an all-seeing God from whom they can't escape. For me, this psalm is always a comfort (it is today, too). Because I know that I am known, and it's okay and comforting. [Mary starts nonthematically from the felt sense, then moves quickly from the words to a rather wordy interpretive aside and back to the nonthematic sense of being known and taking comfort.]

Art: Stay with it a little longer; be in the words of the psalm. Let the psalmist pray them through you. (Silence for several minutes.) [Art recognizes Mary's penchant for intellectualizing and helps her experience through more dimensions.]

Mary: (sighing and opening her eyes) That was so sweet. It's as if, because I am known, I can do anything I want and need to. I know it will be okay. (pauses, savoring)

Art: Here's a way to pray for Andrea, too: that the trapped feeling could dissolve into being held by God in complete transparency and love. [Art expects that the experience Mary has just had has some connection to the work she is doing with Andrea.]

Mary: Oh yeah!

Art: So, at least today, the word "trapped" has led you to your own way to pray in support of Andrea's desire for freedom. Kind of nice of God, isn't it?

Mary: (smiling) Uh-huh. (They savor the graciousness of God for a few moments.)

Art: I also notice that you didn't do anything with Andrea's sense that she was irritated with God. Your suggestions are usually fruitful; Andrea takes them and does something with them. She's a "good directee" in that way. It's how fast . . . [Art starts to move from the present verbatim to other times when Mary has moved too quickly.]

Mary: (interrupting) Oh my gosh! I wonder how nice Andrea needs to be with *me*? [Mary, relying on simultaneity, makes a new connection that could have major implications for her work with Andrea, and beyond.]

Art: Good question. What made you ask it?

Mary: Because I can't think of even one time when Andrea hasn't done exactly what I suggested. If there was a time, I don't remember it.

Art: Whether or not you are correct Andrea will eventually confirm. But it is clear that she is struggling with expressing her irritation with her pastor, and she probably isn't good at doing it with God, either. [Art notes the possible negative simultaneity between Andrea's lack of freedom in the interpersonal and structural arenas.]

Mary: Yes, I see . . .

Art: If she needs another place and relationship in which to practice being free, you could suggest yours.

Mary: Oh, right! (She makes a wry face.)

Art: No, seriously. Would you be free enough to let Andrea quit being a "good directee" for her own growth?

Mary: Now there's a question! I really don't know. I do know I have liked working with Andrea, and I do suspect that it has helped that she is always so compliant and complimentary.

(Mary and Art continue looking at Mary's other directees. They notice that she does favor those who are compliant. They begin to explore Mary's need to "keep" directees "good" by her own lack of freedom to let directees struggle, not only in her presence, but directly with her.)

A single instance of supervision over a single direction session can only suggest the richness of the model. Its primary virtues, I believe, are that it invites us to a very wide understanding of God's activity and encourages multivalent reflection on the multidimensional experience of Mystery. It invites us not only to see more adequately, but also to bring this richness into our direction and supervision. It invites us to live consciously the vision of another poet, Gerard Manley Hopkins: "The world is charged with the grandeur of God"[18] and "For Christ plays in ten thousand places, / Lovely in limbs, and lovely in eyes not his / To the Father through the features of men's faces."[19]

Notes

1. Annie Dillard, *Teaching a Stone to Talk: Expeditions and Encounters* (New York: Harper and Row, 1982), 40–41.

2. Rainer Maria Rilke, "You, neighbor God" ("Du Nachbar Gott, wenn ich dich manches-mal"), *Poems from the Book of Hours*, trans. Babette Deutsch (New York: New Directions Publishing Corporation, 1941), reprinted in *A Christian's Prayer Book: Psalms and Prayers for the Church's Year*, ed. Peter Coughlin, Ronald C. D. Jasper, and Teresa Rodrigues (Chicago: Franciscan Herald, n.d.), 124. The metaphor of the wall built of images that surround God like names is principally a function of the particular translation.

3. Ignatius of Loyola, *Spiritual Exercises*, in *Ignatius of Loyola: Spiritual Exercises and Selected Works*, ed. George Ganss, S.J. (New York: Paulist, 1991), #234, #235, #233.

4. Rahner's key essays include: "The Experience of God Today," *Theological Investigations* XI (New York: Seabury, 1974), 149–65; "Experience of Self and Experience of God," *Theological Investigations* XIII (New York: Seabury, 1975), 122–32; and "Institution and Freedom," *Theological Investigations* XIII (New York: Seabury, 1975), 105–21. See also *Foundations of Christian Faith* (New York: Seabury, 1978), Introduction and chapters 1–4; and *The Practice of Faith* (New York: Crossroad, 1983), chapters 10–11.

5. Rahner was primarily concerned to illumine God's self-communication—God with us; upon this concern he built a theological anthropology that accounts for how this communication occurs. Catherine LaCugna rightly reminds us that this discussion needs to be balanced by the other term of the Trinitarian paradox: that "God freely, utterly and completely bestows God's very self in the encounter with human persons, yet God remains ineffable because the creature is incapable of fully receiving or understanding the One who is imparted." See *God For Us: The Trinity and Christian Life* (San Francisco: HarperCollins, 1993), 231.

6. Ron Modras, *Ignatian Humanism: A Dynamic Spirituality for the 21st Century* (Chicago: Loyola University Press, 2004), 223. See pp. 218–30 for a brief yet clear summary of Rahner's under-standing of God's graciousness and human freedom.

7. Declan Marmion, *A Spirituality of Everyday Faith: A Theological Investigation of the Notion of Spiritual-ity in Karl Rahner* (Louvain, Belgium: Peeters Press, 1998), 119.

8. Maureen Conroy, R.S.M., "The Ministry of Supervision: Call, Competency, Commit-ment," *Presence* I (September 1995): 13.

9. William Creed, S.J., "Supervision Plus Reflection: A Way to Form Spiritual Directors," *Presence* 4 (January 1998): 37.

10. Elinor Shea, "Spiritual Direction and Social Consciousness," *The Way Supplement* 54 (autumn 1985): 30–42.

11. Peter Henriot, "The Public Dimension of the Spiritual Life: The Problem of Simultane-ity," *Soundings* (Washington, D.C.: Center of Concern, 1974): 13–14, quote from p. 13.

12. Various versions of the Experience Circle exist. Nancy Wiens has surveyed the history of the development of the Experience Circle, under its various names; see "The Definition and Role of the Environment in Christian Spiritual Discernment," unpublished paper, Graduate Theological Union, December 14, 1998. She has also done sustained philosophical and theological reflection, in dialogue with the theology and natural sciences literature, on the meaning of nature and environ-ment as it impacts the Experience Circle. Wiens may be reached at nswsj@aol.com.

13. Original graphic courtesy of Lorraine Nelsen.

14. This diagram is adapted from several versions of the Experience Circle in use in the Diploma in the Art of Spiritual Direction at San Francisco Theological Seminary. Nancy Wiens has made significant contributions to this particular version.

15. Clearly humans are both a part of nature and also distinguishable from the rest of the created order in their ability to reflect and act on their reflection. It is impossible to develop such nuances in the context of this essay, though they will eventually be available through the work of Wiens (see note 12). For our purposes in this essay, I will use "nature" in its common-sense meaning, namely as the created but non-human order.

16. Helping skills are based in contemplative awareness and taught and practiced throughout our training modules. Beginning contemplative listening contains the skills that receive and expand the experience; while advanced contemplative listening adds probes and challenges.

17. My thanks to Rev. Catharine Collette for several discussions of this case, which she uses to present the Experience Circle in the Diploma in the Art of Spiritual Direction at San Francisco Theological Seminary. The elaborations for purposes of this essay are my own.

18. Gerard Manley Hopkins, "God's Grandeur," in *Gerard Manley Hopkins*, ed. Catherine Phillips (Oxford and New York: Oxford University Press, 1986), 128.

19. Hopkins, "As kingfishers catch fire," in *Gerard Manley Hopkins*, ed. Catherine Phillips (Oxford and New York: Oxford University Press, 1986), 129.

CHAPTER NINE

Using the Concept of "Co-cultures" in Supervision

Cleo Molina and Hutch Haney

T hat we live in a diverse society of many cultures is not news. The United States has always included diverse cultures with a variety of values and both distinct and subtle behaviors. We have always had differences in language, religion, politics, dress, food, lifestyles, feelings and emotions, thoughts and ideas. What *is* new is the celebration of the richness that comes from diversity. At the professional level, there is an emphasis on how to prepare people to work effectively and compassionately with those who do not share, or do not appear to share, many commonalities. This relatively new emphasis on diversity may come from both the media and the cumulative effects of various civil rights efforts over the past thirty years; we are more aware of the diversity around us and among us.

In the fall of 2000, we were asked to launch a special "multicultural" section of the supervision course for students in master's programs in theology and ministry at a Catholic university. Both of us were graduates of the program: Cleo was a diversity educator and consultant, and Hutch was director of the counseling program in a university college of education. Together we had many years of teaching and supervising students. We were asked to teach this course because of what we shared in common regarding our knowledge and experience, and, significantly, because of our perceived differences. Cleo is a Latina (third-generation Mexican American) raised in Southern California, and Hutch is a white male raised in Colorado. We would not have been asked to teach the course together if we had both been the same gender or ethnicity.

We did not know each other until a few weeks before the course began. To our great surprise and delight, we discovered that despite the perceived differences, we shared many *co-cultures*: We were born the same year and therefore raised in a common era; both of us had a passion for and had worked in the area of peace and justice; we had master's degrees in counseling; we had children the same age; we had spent considerable time in the U.S. Southwest; and we both loved cars, especially those designed and built in the United States in the 1950s. We were so delighted that we had so much in common that we were concerned for a moment that we might have to make up some differences in order to model dealing with conflict for the students.

A tool that helped us discover our commonalities even more quickly than perhaps a long lunch or a couple afternoons at Starbucks was the concept of *co-cultures*. Cleo had successfully used this concept for several years when working with people to facilitate their awareness and understanding of their own cultures. This was a new concept for Hutch, but one that had an immediate impact. As we became more and more comfortable using this tool in tandem to help students understand areas of potential conflict, as well as areas that can help mediate it, we knew we were on to something—a powerful concept that helped individuals develop greater self-awareness in terms of their own cultural identities and helped teams build trust and more effective relationships. In the years that have passed since we first taught that supervision course, we have continued to use this concept in teaching, consulting, counseling, diversity training, and our own personal lives. Thus this idea is not limited to supervision. We believe, however, that it is a simple concept that can add an important dimension to the supervision of spiritual directors.

Spiritual direction requires that the director engage the directee in a process that leads to a deeper relationship with God. Susan Rakoczy states that "[t]o meet and be present to the uniqueness of each person in the spiritual direction relationship is an immense challenge, especially as one begins to understand how culture shapes each of us."[1] She suggests the use of Augsburger's concept of interpathy (different from empathy and sympathy) to help directors understand the type of presence required to be effective. Interpathy is described as "an intentional cognitive envisioning and affective experiencing of another's thoughts and feelings, even though the thoughts rise from another process of knowing, the values grow from another frame of moral reasoning, and the feelings spring from another basis of assumptions."[2]

In order for spiritual directors to truly access empathy, sympathy, and interpathy—particularly when directing someone from a culture quite different than their own—it is essential that directors become deeply aware of the cultural lenses that they use in the process. The concept of co-cultures and the practice of co-cultural mapping and analysis are useful tools for identifying those cultural lenses. As Margaret Guenther observes, however, becoming self-aware requires some help.[3] This is where the role of the supervisor is essential. William A. Barry and William

J. Connolly write, "Just as the relationship of director to directee is one of the best means for facilitating the directee's growth in the relationship with God, so too the relationship of supervisor to spiritual director is one of the best means of facilitating the director's growth as a director."[4] Therefore, supervisor and director (as well as directee) benefit by understanding and using the co-culture tool.

Identifying and Using the Concept of Co-cultures

The steps as outlined in this chapter will facilitate the understanding of the concept of co-cultures, provide examples and directions for how to implement this tool, and offer suggestions specifically for supervisors of spiritual directors. Our hypothesis is that we all share diverse cultural richness through a variety of co-cultures. The first step is to define our co-cultures. By doing so, we increase our self-understanding, understanding of others, and professional competence. To understand our co-cultures, the second step is to explore the values and behaviors embedded in them. The third step is to address the issues of privilege and oppression, because people in particular co-cultures experience both in varying degrees. The fourth step focuses on cultural identity development within the co-cultures. In the final step, supervisees address questions related to an integration and reflection process.

We recommend starting with step I, but the other steps may flow in different ways, depending on the group. There is no set way to begin, but the mapping of co-cultures included in the first step is a good place to start.

Before starting step I, however, ask each student or participant to introduce himself or herself and state how he or she is different from everyone else in the room. No one may use the same answer that another has given. Someone might say, "I am the only African American," only to have someone else say, "No you are not. I am, too; I am just not as visible as you are!" Or someone might say, "I am the only person here that is wearing a red shirt," to be followed by the response, "Yes, but I could be the same as you if I had worn my red shirt!" This exercise increases awareness both of differences and of common connections. Another step in the process is to ask, "How are all of you the same?" The first time we asked this question, we expected to immediately hear what we thought was the obvious answer: "We are all in this class." Curiously, however, most groups have taken about ten minutes to reach a consensus, possibly because their minds have been set on how they are different. This exercise leads to naming the many examples of co-cultures in the room, which may include women, men, visible ethnicities, nonvisible identities, particular styles, neighborhoods or geographic areas of origin or current residence, hobbies, and many others.

We use a variety of examples in this chapter to illustrate particular points. In these examples, we have changed the names, ethnic or geographic origins, genders, or other co-cultures of the people involved to make them less identifiable.

Step I: Defining Our Co-cultures

Culture is not typically a word we spend much time thinking about unless we are involved in some aspect of *high culture*, such as the ballet, opera, or symphony. High culture, however, is only a tiny part of what the term *culture* includes. Culture can be defined as the way of life among a group of people. Selma Myers and Barbara Filner define culture as "a learned set of rules, written and unwritten, that instruct individuals on how to operate effectively with one another and with their environment. It not only defines ways to act, but also ways to react, and, therefore, is an essential component of our capacity to live as human beings in a social context. In other words, 'It's the way we do things around here.'"[5] Culture informs all that people *do* as well as all that they *are*. The culture in which we were raised instructed us on how to eat, dress, wash, play, speak, and touch, and it affected the way we are in every role we play.

Culture is visible and invisible. Though we can see the clothes we wear, how we hold our eating utensils, the food we eat, and all our various behaviors, we cannot see the values that drive our behaviors, the religious faiths we hold, the traditions that are important to us, or the experiences that have shaped our lives. Edward T. Hall states that "there is not one aspect of human life that is not touched and altered by culture."[6] Yet for all its importance, culture is amazingly taken for granted. In a group, before an exercise that defines co-cultures, there often are people who do not consider themselves as even having a culture. Diversity trainers often hear: "You are so lucky. At least you have a culture. I don't have a clue about mine." This is a common reaction of people raised in the "dominant" culture, where their language, values, dress, and food were similar to those around them. They were not distinct; their culture was not distinct and therefore they were not aware it existed. By identifying co-cultures, people can understand distinct patterns of co-cultures, and more significantly, they can understand that they do have cultural identities that are typically multilayered, each with its own set of rules, values, and norms that drive their behavior.

Larry Samovar and Richard Porter explain the concept of *co-culture* in the following:

> The key to co-cultures is two fold. First, it should be obvious that people often hold dual or multiple memberships, and that these affiliations have behaviors and perceptions that are learned. For a number of years, the social scientific literature employed the word *subculture* when referring to individuals and groups of people who, while living in the dominant culture, had membership in another culture. In recent years, however, the term has been replaced and the concept itself reformulated. The term *co-culture* is now used because the prefix *sub* implies that members of the non-dominant group are deficient and inadequate. . . . Therefore, we use

the word **co-culture** *when talking about groups or social communities exhibiting communication characteristics, perceptions, values, beliefs, and practices that are significantly different enough to distinguish them from the other groups, communities, and the dominant culture.*[7]

Ethnicity, then, is only one category of co-cultures. Other categories could include geographic region, profession, socioeconomic class, hobby or special interest, political party, union, club or organization, generation, school, and neighborhood, to name a few. Gender is increasingly considered a culture. Tayler Cox includes gender as a cultural identity group, saying that "[e]vidence indicates that the socialization of people in most societies of the world is greatly influenced by gender, so that women, as a group, hold a distinctly different world view from men."[8] Weiss observes, "In a sense, gender groups have their own cultures and mixed interaction within a national culture is already cross-cultural."[9]

Explaining the concepts of *culture* and *co-culture* is only the starting point in grasping the depth of their meaning. An important exercise that helps in identifying and naming individual co-cultures includes the use of mapping to visually capture the categories. In the chart on page 150, Cleo's co-cultures are in circles, Hutch's in squares. After this initial step, you could add additional co-cultures or begin to provide more specific information regarding each co-culture identified. For instance, *university* might lead to education, then to degrees attained, and to sororities/fraternities or other organizations joined. Another important step is for each person to identify the top four or five core co-cultures, and then list the core values and behaviors for each (step 2).

When this exercise is done in a group, it is very helpful to ask people to work in pairs and identify similarities and differences, potential areas of conflict, and co-cultural similarities that can help mediate the conflict. When we did this exercise, we found so many similarities (see the *overlap* in the co-cultural map diagram below) that we could almost finish each other's sentences. We also identified key areas of potential conflict. One, in particular, was the value and concept of *time*. Hutch was raised with the notion that to *"be on time"* meant that you not only arrived by the appointed time, but even a little early. Cleo's core notion of time is *mas o menos quince minutos*—fifteen minutes, more or less—for her, *time* is a more fluid concept. This difference could have led to major conflict, or at least to irritation, misunderstanding, and lack of respect, if we had failed to identify the difference, the core values that led to the behavior, and the co-cultures from which they came. After a lively conversation, we came to the agreement that Cleo would be considered *on time* if within fifteen minutes of the appointed time, but she would be *late* if arriving after that and, in that case, obliged to call. We both gained a greater understanding of our co-cultural values.

Another story illustrates co-cultural differences regarding the value for timeliness. We asked a guest who is from China to come to a class to talk about the experience of being an immigrant. He was two hours late and did not apologize or give an excuse. When he left, there were questions about what co-culture he may have been acting out of both by being late and by not being apologetic. A student from Vietnam said that he could not possibly be acting out of *any* Asian co-culture, because not only would he never be late, but if he was, he would be *very* apologetic. This led to a discussion about values, judgments, the danger of assuming what someone's co-culture may be, and the implications of acting out of a particular co-culture: The student from Vietnam was acting out of her Asian co-culture; the guest from China may not have been.

An important next step in increasing cultural awareness is to identify overlapping co-cultures in the individual co-cultural maps. This process was helpful in identifying areas of internal conflict. One student expressed the inherent contradictions *intraculturally* (within a culture) and *interculturally* (between co-cultures) of her gay, Roman Catholic, Latina, and female co-cultures. She could represent these concretely on her map and wrote an insightful and moving description of the significance on her developing identity. Identifying their own co-cultures was helpful to many students in examining and understanding areas of internal conflict. We could then begin to talk about values and behavior.

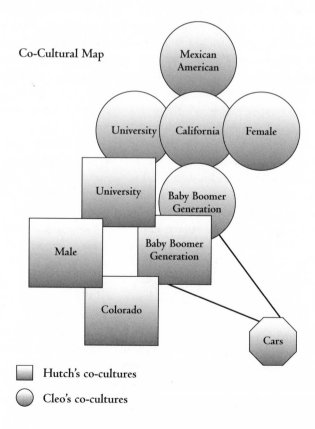

Co-Cultural Map

Hutch's co-cultures
Cleo's co-cultures

After we identified the co-cultures that overlapped in our maps and described areas of potential conflict as well as areas that could help mediate conflict, students worked in pairs and then in small groups and did the same.

Application for Supervisors of Spiritual Directors

The individual co-cultural map exercise can be an effective tool for supervisors to use with spiritual directors. Under a supervisor's guidance, directors can identify all their co-cultures and pay special attention to how each affects spiritual development. It should also be helpful to spend some time describing the spiritual director co-culture. For example, what are core values and behaviors of spiritual directors? What is the typical language used by spiritual directors—code words and phrases, terminology, and so on.

Reference to co-cultures can be an ongoing element of supervision. This tool might be especially helpful when a director is reflecting on particular issues raised in himself or herself through an interaction with a directee, particularly if that directee is from different ethnic and other co-cultures than the director.

Step 2: Exploring the Values and Behaviors of Our Co-cultures

As we worked with students in group supervision, we became aware that though we came from different cultural heritages, we shared many of the same values. Our experience told us that social injustice is often the result of a conflict of values, or perceived values, and an imbalance of power. Not unexpectedly, as we shared our values through our stories, and as students did likewise, the commonalities emerged, conflicts melted, empathy increased, and dialogue then began about how we as teachers and ministers could create communities where there is less oppression and greater equity.

A major lesson learned from our experience of teaching the multicultural supervision course was the importance of having the students identify their co-cultural core values and then share them with each other, emphasizing the areas of similarities and differences. When students began to list core values and behaviors for each of their most influential co-cultures, it was not uncommon to find that some of these values and behaviors clashed. One student said, "My culture values the independent career woman, yet at the same time women are expected to be meek and submissive." The cultural map can help identify key values and their consequential behaviors.

In his classic book, *Values Shift*, Brian Hall writes that "[p]ersonal transformation is intricately connected to organizational transformation, because people are able to change when they get positive reinforcement from the primary institutions in their lives—their families, their schools, and their work environments."[10] These primary institutions were usually identified by students as being among their most influential co-cultures, in addition to gender, ethnicity, and religion. Hall sees these institutions, or co-cultures, as setting boundaries or limiting personal freedom. But he does not see them as driving a person's behavior all the time, because people typically balance about ten core values at any given time. The direct correlation between values and behavior may be difficult to make, but this is all the more reason why "mapping" possible connections can result in both greater insight and potential behavior change. Hall further states:

> It is important to know what your values are, and what values you have as a man or a woman. It is important to know how your job, your religion, and your culture place certain value expectations on you. If you do not do this then you may well become what others want you to become rather than choosing life for yourself. To choose life, we need to do two things:
>
> 1. Become conscious of the values influences in our lives.
> 2. Ask: What does it mean to be an excellent human being? What values do I need to be the best person I can possibly be in spite of all the influences in my life?[11]

We like the following definition of *values* by Milton Rokeach, as William Huitt cites in "Values" on the Valdosta State University Educational Psychology interactive website, because it mentions that values guide behavior but do not necessarily require it. According to Rokeach: "Values are defined in literature as everything from eternal ideas to behavioral actions. As used here values refer to criteria for determining levels of goodness, worth or beauty. Values are affectively-laden [*sic*] thoughts about objects, ideas, behavior, etc. that guide behavior, but do not necessarily require it."[12] Huitt defines the term *value* as a verb: "The act of valuing is considered an act of making value judgments, an expression of feeling, or the acquisition of and adherence to a set of principles."[13]

Thus we believe that values and behaviors must be named. We pushed our students for very concrete definitions and specific behaviors. Then we asked what they thought it would take to change each of them. One student described a value as the "crunch that is uniquely American: that being the need to be busy, and the stress related to a faster pace" (that is often distinct from other cultures' paces). We asked her to name the values that are related to the busyness, the rush, and the stress. After some discussion, she said: "I value productiveness and I have equated busy with being productive. But my 'busy behavior'—working sixty hours a week—is not productive, it's tiring." Another student shared her experience of values and behaviors relative to co-cultures: "I believe in human equity, but I have a strong cultural value not to be demonstrative. Thus I am criticized for not fighting—speaking up and writing letters—for my values. There is a conflict between the values of my Chinese culture and the expected behavior of my American friends."

We used L. Robert Kohls's *Survival Kit for Overseas Living: For Americans Planning to Live and Work Abroad*[14] to discuss differences in values. We asked students to do these three things:

1. Define a behavior for each value. (Example: I value my individualism and privacy and therefore want my own room.)
2. Select values from Kohls's list that may be different from those of people you work with. (Example: individualism and privacy versus group membership and shared space.)
3. Describe a behavior that may result from understanding your different values. (Example: We may avoid placing a client with "group" values in a private room.)

We visited an elderly relative from Mexico who shares a room with five others in a nursing home. We said, "Isn't it too bad that she can't have a private room?" She said, "Que milagro que no estoy en un cuarto solita." ("Isn't it wonderful that I am not in a room by myself.")

A core "American" value is that people have choices. But many of the people we see in our classes and as clients do not believe that they really do have choices. It is not a primary core value for them and does not match their experience. Other "American" values that Kohls defines can be challenged. For example, *equality* is often an asserted value, but behaviors do not always reflect this value.

The value of *trust* is an important variable in relationships. People fear that their values will not be accepted, and this fear influences what and with whom they choose to share. As people start to trust, and as they learn that at least some of their values are shared across co-cultures, bias and prejudice seem to diminish. One young woman shared in class that her primary co-culture dictated that she be beautiful, not too smart, and associate with others like herself. She also shared her angst over revealing this co-culture to the class, because she was sure that others in the group would judge her negatively. Several people let her know that they appreciated her willingness to share (a shared value) and that they did not see her as "not too smart." They also noted that they were "not like her," so she was now violating two of her co-cultural norms. She not only had an affirming experience, but she also was able to trust others not like herself and was able to further explore whether she wanted to continue to follow the dictates of this particular co-culture.

Application for Supervisors of Spiritual Directors

Identifying core values for at least three or four primary co-cultures would be a very helpful exercise for supervisors to use with directors. This process would provide the opportunity for directors to further understand possible internal conflicts as well as insight into how their spirituality has been shaped. Part of the exercise could include discovering how and when certain values are prioritized. This exercise could also provide insights into times when directors felt that communication during a session with a directee was not completely satisfactory. This might be a good opportunity to suggest to the director that he or she teach this tool to directees.

Step 3: Understanding Issues of Oppression and Privilege in Our Co-cultures

> Hardly any of us have as white children in the USA avoided situations similar to this: we were on the bus in early childhood when a black guy of a certain type stepped inside the bus. Unconsciously our mother pulled us a little closer to herself. Since we were incapable of understanding why this signal was given, it helped—along with many other similar early messages about blacks—to cripple us with a paralyzing fear of blacks the rest of our lives.[15]

What Holdt describes is the genesis of oppression. In this case, it was transmitted through a subtle movement by a caring, protective mother toward her children. Although this may be hard to hear, note the phrase "paralyzing fear . . . the rest of our lives." The mother was the oppressor, the children were oppressed, and the "black guy of a certain type" was also oppressed. Our hypothesis is that we are all oppressed and oppressor in some way. Understanding this point unites us; it can no longer be *"me versus you."* Each of us has been the oppressor (most often from lack of awareness) and has been oppressed in some way.

Both oppression and privilege exist in all co-cultures. To understand your co-cultures is to understand how you have been oppressed and privileged; to understand *yourself*, you must understand how you have been an oppressor and how you have used or abused your privilege. Our students read and discussed Peggy McIntosh's "White Privilege: Unpacking the Invisible Knapsack." McIntosh states that "[w]hites are carefully taught not to recognize white privilege, as males are taught not to recognize male privilege."[16] Our experience, using the questions below, is that whites—and, in particular, white males—have not recognized their privilege, but they can when "nudged." Usually women of all co-cultures and individuals from nonmajority co-cultures are very familiar with white privilege, and they can also identify privilege within their own co-cultures. The same is true for oppression. We have not seen evidence, as McIntosh asserts, that whites and males have been "carefully taught." Rather, we have found that white males especially are shocked and embarrassed when they identify themselves as privileged and as oppressors, and they usually have problems identifying the co-cultural source. This shock is not true of people who have experienced overt oppression. Our students struggled with these issues, often experiencing guilt and shame.

We in no way want to evaluate the quantity and quality of oppression and privilege; it could be easy to dismiss six years in the army as nothing compared with a lifetime in slavery. Our belief is that these concepts cannot be compared; they can only be appreciated within one's own experience. That appreciation, however, can lead to an identification and understanding of the oppression and privilege of others. In this work with students, it is imperative to give them sufficient time and space to process the questions.

With caution, we asked students to describe how they had been oppressed. Some of their answers included the following:

- "I was oppressed for six years in the army."
- "My father sexually abused me."
- "I cannot be married in the Catholic Church."
- "People stare at me because they see me as this obese, lazy person."
- "My parents won't meet my partner or see our children."

Elizabeth Kubler-Ross tells of wandering through postwar Europe, starving. She saw a small child with a loaf of bread and knew she could kill the child for the bread. She understood then that she had met her Hitler. We asked students to "meet their Hitler," or consider how they had been an oppressor. They did not like to answer this question, but invariably they could.

- "I haven't talked to my sister for five years."
- "I didn't object when a coworker was treated unfairly."
- "I assume all obese people have no self-control."
- "I expect my children to be perfect."
- "I told a blond joke just to be accepted as one of the guys."

We also asked: "How have you been privileged?" Here are some of the answers we received:

- "As a light-skinned African American, I am treated better."
- "As a Japanese male, I was more privileged than Japanese females."
- "Men hold doors for me."
- "I can live, eat, travel anywhere I want."
- "I can share pictures of my husband and children anywhere and not worry."
- "Because I fit a certain standard of beauty, I am invited places, waited on in stores and restaurants, and given a lot more attention than some others."
- "I can rent an apartment just about anywhere I want without a lot of questions."

When we asked, "How have you abused your privilege?" we heard, with some resistance, statements such as the following:

- "I have used my looks to manipulate men."
- "I used my 'minority status' to get a scholarship even though I didn't need it."
- "I pulled rank."
- "I cheated on my income tax, with the help of a tax lawyer."
- "I flaunt my new car."
- "I allow the women in my extended family to serve me first because I'm a man."

We also asked students to identify the co-cultures that generated their oppression and privilege. After the discussion of these questions, which was very difficult for many, a student said, "Being white has given me the advantage *and* the disadvantage of not having to explore oppression and privilege . . . until now."

Application for Supervisors of Spiritual Directors

The topic of oppression and privilege may not be an easy one for supervisors to raise with spiritual directors. We recommend going back to the co-cultural map and asking which of the co-cultures have experienced oppression and which have experienced privilege. Follow-up questions could include: How do you know? How does it feel to be aware of your privilege as a member of this co-culture? How has your oppression affected you? This topic lends itself to theological reflection. Supervisors could suggest a theological reflection process as "homework" for the next session.

Step 4: Cultural Identity Development

Once students have defined their co-cultures, identified their values and behaviors, and discussed oppression and privilege, the next step is to consider the process of identity development. Issues of identity are complex, and being aware of our own identity development through the understanding of our participation in our various co-cultures leads to greater awareness and compassion for others. Some questions we asked students are as follows:

- When were you first aware that you were part of a culture? What are your memories regarding that culture? In what way do you still participate in that co-culture?
- How do each of your co-cultures affect the way you view the world?

- What is one "rule" that is part of each of your co-cultures' written or unwritten codes of conduct?
- What aspects, both values and behavior, of any of your co-cultures do you want to change?
- How might other people view any or all of your co-cultures?
- What are some stereotypes others might hold of any of your co-cultures?
- Whom do you know that share few or many of your co-cultures?
- How do you think shared or lack of shared co-cultures affects your relationships?
- What are your *prevailing* co-cultures, and what dynamics make them prevailing?
- Where did you learn about the values and behaviors of your co-cultures?

We presented various cultural identity development models (such as that of Atkinson, Morten, and Sue[17]) in an effort to help students understand how the development of individual cultural identity both differs and shares some similar characteristics among majority and minority groups.

We asked students to pick a developmental model and trace at least two of their co-cultural identities. In the discussion of the exercise, we emphasized the encounter, conflict, or dissonance aspect of the cultural identity development process, because this is often the stage that leads to an awareness of identity. For example, a student shared that her encounter, or conflict, with her mother (or her mother's co-culture) over the fact that she was a girl (in a family of brothers) came to a climax when her mother made her wear a shirt in the summertime. It was then that she knew for certain that she was a girl and started developing an awareness of all the related implications.

Another example involves a friend of Cleo's whose primary co-cultural identification was as a Hispanic male from the Southwest. He was living in another region of the country when he came out as a gay male. For a while, he immersed himself in the local gay cultural scene and dressed and behaved according to the prevalent norms of that particular co-culture. After a period of time, however, he decided that the gay co-culture (at least in that particular area) was not who he really was, so he returned to his hometown and became involved in the study of Hispanic art, music, folk practices, and religion from that region. Thus he chose one particular co-culture over another. He had experienced significant internal conflict over core values related to these two co-cultures and decided to resolve the conflict by moving home. He did not *reject* one co-culture and judge others who held it; instead, he chose to focus on the other because he felt more "at home."

The issue of rejecting a co-culture because of internal values conflicts often surfaced when students talked about being raised in a racist family or community or shared that they came from backgrounds of poverty. It was not unusual to hear comments such as "That's not me anymore." Helping students understand the process of identity development was useful in resolving feelings of guilt or shame over what they had seen as rejection of a whole culture, often including people they had known and cared about who were part of it. Once values were identified, it became easier to see that one can change certain values and behaviors without rejecting a whole culture.

Application for Supervisors of Spiritual Directors

We believe that the questions listed earlier in this section are important ones for supervisors to raise with spiritual directors. These questions do not necessarily need to be asked all at one time; they can be presented over a period of several sessions. These questions can also relate to the development of spirituality. When was the director first aware of God's presence? Was this awareness related to a particular co-culture? How have any or all co-cultures affected his or her knowledge and understanding of the divine?

If the spiritual director is a member of a minority group, the supervisor may want to ask questions related to the Atkinson et al. cultural identity model, especially in terms of "attitudes toward self."[18] Did the director experience the stages between "self-depreciating" and "self-appreciating?" How did this image of self relate to his or her image of God?

There are numerous ways that supervisors can use the material in this section with directors. A first step for supervisors, however, is to go through this material themselves before using it.

Step 5: Integration and Reflection

After creating co-cultural maps, identifying values and behavior, looking at privilege and oppression, and examining identity development, the final step is to take time to reflect on this experience. The first reflection question that we asked our students acknowledged that we all have more to learn, and that this process is just jump-starting a lifelong learning experience. The following are some of the questions we posed for reflection and journaling:

- Reflect on what you still need to know, what you want to change, and what gaps still exist in your knowledge or experience regarding co-cultures.
- How has a better understanding of your co-cultures changed how you deal with other people?
- What has not changed about how you deal with others?
- What actions will you take based on what you have learned about yourself and your co-cultures?

- How will you evaluate your actions?

In addition, we developed a process to use for theological reflection over a particular incident or issue. This process included some additional questions:

- What do I know about my own co-cultures that might serve as a help or hindrance to my understanding of this experience?
- What do I know/understand about the other's co-cultures? How do I know these things? What would I like to know?
- What kinds of assumptions am I making based on any one or more of my co-cultures?
- What are the co-cultures I can identify in this situation? How are they a blessing? A challenge?
- Where is God in this experience, and how is God calling me to grow?
- What can I do to help this situation?
- How will I be different as a result?

Other activities that we felt helped the students better integrate insights and led to new behaviors included the following:

- Making collages that symbolically represented their co-cultures.
- Conducting interviews of family members, friends, and others, focusing on cultural identity.
- Participating in cultural immersions.

We also asked for action and learning plans, and we expected students to evaluate their plans. These activities helped students reach different levels of awareness.

Application for Supervisors of Spiritual Directors

Theological reflection is a central part of a spiritual director's discipline. Supervisors could share the theological reflection process described in this section as a means of continually keeping the cultural aspect of the experience of God present. Activities could be suggested as homework between sessions as well.

Because many people are not used to considering culture as an important part of their decision making, behaviors, attitudes, beliefs, rituals, and thoughts, directors may be resistant to this process. Engaging with this topic, however, will lead to greater depths of self-understanding and awareness, as well as a deeper knowledge of God.

The Value of Using the Co-cultural Concept

Through the process delineated in this chapter, students who believed they had no cultures identified their co-cultures and, in so doing, enriched their lives and affected the way they interact with others. By identifying their co-cultures and reflecting on the significance of their identity, the students gained insights into their own behaviors and attitudes toward themselves and others. They also gained another tool for dealing with differences that could empower them in their relationships. The "us versus them" paradigm was diminished as students understood the dynamics of oppression and privilege. Through reflection and action, students integrated new knowledge, awareness, and understanding that led to changed attitudes, beliefs, and behaviors. If students were able to accomplish this level of change and transformation, then the possibilities should be limitless for spiritual directees, directors, and supervisors.

Barry and Connolly state that "[t]he primary purpose of supervision is the personal growth of the spiritual director as spiritual director," and that when directors seek supervision, they are asking for help in becoming someone.[19] If supervisors are able to guide directors in understanding how they experience and come to know God through their co-cultural lenses, directors will reach a new level of compassion and understanding for themselves and for others on their journey to becoming someone.

It takes courage to be willing to explore one's co-cultures and their related values and behaviors. When one undertakes this journey of exploration, one can discover all manner of beliefs, attitudes, and values. We are proud to claim some of these, because they help keep us on the road to "becoming someone" and to developing a closer relationship to God. But typically there are other beliefs, attitudes, and values in one or more of our co-cultures that can make us feel uncomfortable and ashamed—and yet also feel closer to God if we but dare to understand and make peace with where they came from. This is why supervisors can play an essential role in helping directors look more closely at their co-cultural "shadow" sides. Barry and Connolly state:

> We do well to recall that individuals grow and change as persons through relationships with others and that the amount of growth depends on the quality and depth of the relationship involved. Growth as a spiritual director cannot be superficial, it must take root in the core of the person, in the heart, in that center where directors meet God and other people most intimately. They must develop as persons whose hearts are open and discerning, whose faith, hope and love are almost tangible. To develop in this way, they have to relate to God and also to their supervisor in depth. They must risk exposure of the strengths and

limitations of their hearts, their minds, their faith, their hope, and their love to the supervisor.[20]

We hope that the concepts and tools we have provided in this chapter will assist directors and supervisors in this process.

Notes

1. Susan Rakoczy, "Unity, Diversity, and Uniqueness: Foundations of Cross Cultural Spiritual Direction," in *Common Journey, Different Paths: Spiritual Direction in Cross-Cultural Perspective*, edited by Susan Rakoczy, IHM (Maryknoll, NY: Oribis, 1992), 21.

2. Ibid., 18.

3. Margaret Guenther, *Holy Listening: The Art of Spiritual Direction* (Boston: Cowley, 1992), 11.

4. William A. Barry and William J. Connolly, *The Practice of Spiritual Direction* (New York: HarperSanFrancisco, 1986), 176.

5. Selma Myers and Barbara Filner, *Mediation Across Cultures: A Handbook About Conflict & Culture* (Amherst, MA: Amherst Educational Publishing, 1994), 21.

6. Edward T. Hall, *The Silent Language* (New York: Doubleday, 1959), 169.

7. Larry A. Samovar and Richard E. Porter, *Communication Between Cultures, Fourth Edition* (Belmont, CA: Wadsworth/Thomson Learning, 2001), 47.

8. Tayler Cox Jr., *Cultural Diversity In Organizations: Theory, Research & Practice* (San Francisco: Berrett-Koehler, 1994), 106.

9. S. E. Weiss, "Negotiating with 'Romans' part 2," in *Sloan Management Review*, 35, no. 3 (1994): 85–99.

10. Brian Hall, *Values Shift: A Guide to Personal and Organizational Transformation* (Rockport, MA: Twin Lights, 1994).

11. Ibid., 74.

12. Milton Rokeach, quoted in William Huitt, *Values: Educational Psychology Interactive website* (Valdosta, GA: Valdosta State University, accessed December 8, 2004); available from http://www.chiron.valdosta.edu/whuitt/col/affsys/values.html.

13. Ibid.

14. L. Robert Kohls, *Survival Kit for Overseas Living: For Americans Planning to Live and Work Abroad* (Yarmouth, MA: Nicholas Brealey Intercultural, 2001).

15. Jacob Holdt, *Frequent Questions on Oppression—With Answers From Jacob Holdt*, American Pictures website (1997).

16. Peggy MacIntosh, "White Privilege: Unpacking the Invisible Knapsack," *Peace and Freedom* (July/August, 1989): 10–12.

17. Donald R. Atkinson, George Morten, and Derald Wing Sue, *Counseling American Minorities: A Cross-Cultural Perspective*, 3rd ed. (Dubuque, IA: Wm. C. Brown Publishers, 1989).

18. Ibid.

19. Barry and Connolly, *Practice of Spiritual Direction*, 177, 178.

20. Ibid., 179.

CHAPTER TEN

Regarding the Spiritual Direction of Disabled Persons

Susan S. Phillips

If you love to listen you will gain knowledge, and if you pay attention you will become wise.
(Sir 6:33)

Spiritual directors are attentive companions to those striving to "comprehend, with all the saints, what is the breadth and length and height and depth of Christ's love, that [we] may be filled with the fullness of God" (Eph 3:18–19).[1] As spiritual directors, we accompany others as they explore dimensions of God's wide world, and this often places us in unfamiliar locations. Each person who is accompanied is unique and enjoys a relationship with God, and it is this relationship that spiritual directors hope to know and honor.

The role of the supervisor of spiritual directors is to care, with skill, compassion, and prayer, for the supervisee's formation as a spiritual director and, in so doing, for the companioning relationship of director and directees. It is a role that profoundly shapes us as we learn increasingly more about hearts, minds, spirits, and bodies. As a Jungian analyst states, "I acknowledge that as supervisor I am learning from the relationship with the supervisee, and from their [*sic*] relationship with their patient."[2] In turn, the supervisee learns from the relationship with the directee, as well as from that with the supervisor. Each of these relationships may bridge great distances between persons, lengthening our strides as we work together.

The Christian religion is distinctive in its commitment to those the world considers other-than-normal: the poor, bereft, sick, aged, marginalized, foreign, and afflicted. Jesus turned his attention to individuals in all these categories, engaging them in conversations and elevating them to historical prominence.

From Scripture, we hear more from Bartimaeus and the Samaritan woman at the well than we do from Herod. Not only are the blind man and the marginalized foreign woman the subject of compassionate attention, they are full moral and spiritual agents. Jesus asks them what they want and responds accordingly. Christianity insists that the love of God in its broad, long, high, and deep capaciousness envelops all of these, without regard to human evaluations of "most," "least," or "normal." As historic figures, the woman at the well and Bartimaeus stand as our teachers no less than the disciples do.

People in these other-than-normal categories were not accorded full personhood in ancient times and classical literature. Jesus' stance toward them was revolutionary. This chapter considers that stance toward people who are different specifically in terms of their physical abilities and reflects on what that stance looks like in spiritual direction. In doing so, it considers how a spiritual director is shaped and taught by working with people with different capabilities, a formative process crucial to supervisory work. How do we regard and recognize the caring stance of a spiritual director, especially as it manifests in Christian love toward a physically other-than-normal directee?

"Normal" is a social construct. In earlier times, people encountered the normal realities of fate, death, pain, and harm without benefit of modern technologies of care and cure. Some encountered fates, congenital or circumstantial, that rendered them other-than-normal: the deaf, lame, blind, mute, and halt. To our ears, the monosyllabic list rings harsh, immutable, and socially isolating, as were the conditions the afflicted people experienced. Today we speak of "challenge" rather than affliction and prefer the optimistically erasable "dis-," a prefix we assume only temporarily mars the achievable states of ease, function, and ability.

The Contemporary Social Landscape

We in the Western world are heirs of Enlightenment rationality and anthropocentrism. Our inclination to make questions about abnormality and suffering abstract and theoretical has been exacerbated by our continuing successes in and reliance on technological solutions to all kinds of unwanted conditions. Many afflictions described in the Bible may be averted or remedied today through advances in sanitation, nutrition, medicine, technology, education, and human rights implementation.

We have developed tremendous powers for understanding the world; created rational systems of government, commerce, and social life; and harnessed nature for our own well-being. It is no wonder that we are especially distressed by the inexplicable and uncontrollable, viewing disease, disaster, disability, and death as aberrations that are, in large part, subject to our control. Similarly, we see success, health, and longevity as personal achievements.

The development of cures for various afflictions has been of great benefit to our society. Systems, however imperfect, have been developed to cure the sick and aid the disabled, and increasingly, rights to services have been established and extended to them. This contrasts with conditions in other societies where the weak and disabled are expelled or quarantined for life in their homes. Linguistically, we also have attempted to enfranchise the disabled, moving from words like "crippled" and "handicapped" to "disabled," somehow "impaired," "differently abled," and "physically challenged." My mother is in this category and likes to enumerate the changing labels she's borne throughout her life. Awkward as the words may be, they demonstrate an increasing commitment to emphasize the personhood of those who bear some mark of difference.

While reason, science, and democratic legislation have carried us far in addressing differences, an orientation toward cure has eclipsed the place of care. The practice of spiritual direction lies in the domain of care. It is a practice that involves creative, imaginative skill guided by ethical and theological consideration within a community of discourse, discipline, and discernment. It is an art of serving, not one of fixing, classifying, objectifying, managing, commodifying, or standardizing. It is a particular way of serving people by entering their worlds while holding faith in God's kingdom.

A mark of postmodernity is that we have learned to value people's firsthand knowledge. We want to hear personally what people from other cultures tell us about their cultures, rather than learning only from ethnographers sent from our culture to study theirs. We have learned to treasure the knowledge inherent in narrative and hold that knowledge as equal to, if not more precious than, the knowledge gained from detached theorizing and analysis. Knowledge is understood to be perspectival. We want to hear from the other, as Jesus did when he asked the blind man, "What do you want me to do for you?" allowing the other full stature and voice, not presuming to articulate the other's desire.

I have been taught by disabled persons I have known through relationships and reading. Though I am not disabled, the experience of aging brings increasing understanding of diminished eyesight, hearing, and mobility. I am the daughter of a disabled mother and the mother of a deaf son. They have taught me more than I can put into words. I also have been taught by writers, including Nancy Mairs, Andre Dubus, Harriet McBryde Johnson, Reynolds Price, Christopher Reeve, Jean-Dominique Bauby, and many others who have opened their lives so that we can learn what it means to be a person in other-than-normal physical circumstances.

These people have enlarged my sense of the breadth, length, height, and depth of God's love, stretched my heart, and shed light on my own humanity. They have also benefited my work as a spiritual director with people who are different from me, some of them disabled, some physically constrained by age or illness. The contemporary valuation of the other's distinctive voice guides my work as a supervisor of others who listen.

Looking through the Window

Caring of all kinds involves reaching out to something or someone other than oneself. In the case of spiritual direction, we care about the directee and the directee's spiritual health and flourishing. We do so in light of the Christian story, allowing the living Word to shape us and our relationships. We behold the other before the face of God, as revealed through Jesus Christ and illuminated by the Holy Spirit. The motivating force behind our caring disposition and comportment is our spirituality. We express that spirituality in every relationship.

Caring is relational. A caring act is one that not only is intended as such, but also is so experienced by the care receiver. Therefore, the quality of care is dependent on how well the caregiver is attuned to the receiver. Attuning across differences is a challenge. As we know from telescopes and radios, the greater the distance between viewer and the viewed, the more interference there is, and the more frequently we must fine-tune our reception. Therein lies the call for the spiritual director working with a directee who, unlike the director, is ill, paralyzed, dying, marginalized, grief-stricken, despairing, impoverished, or in some other way afflicted. The call of the supervisor is to attend to and encourage that attunement.

The supervisory relationship is itself relational, caring, and unique. It is akin to the direction relationship but exists for the sake of the supervisee's caregiving and formation as a director. To that end, the supervision space includes a window into the supervisee's work.

Imagine with me the following scenario: The supervisee/director enters the world of the directee and creates in it a sheltered listening space in which the directee can experience the director's care. Later, the director comes to me for supervision in the sheltered listening space I offer, and together we look through a window at that spiritual direction space from which the director has come. As much as possible, I try to comprehend that world and the directee who inhabits it, but I can do so only by looking through the window constructed and held by the director before me, noticing how it is constructed and held, and how the director relates to it. I trust the light of God's love and truth to shine on us and through that window as together we lean toward it, trying to see all we can see. The director helps me by pointing out significant features and moments. The experience I bring to the conversation, as well as my observations through the window and of the director beside me, help clarify the director's impressions, memories, and hopes.

I think back to a time my supervisor looked through that window with me. My first experience of a certain directee was hearing a (to my ears) distorted voice on my message machine inquiring about spiritual direction. My mind full of experiences I had had with people with similar speech as a result of strokes or cerebral palsy, I felt challenged and prayed to be of service. Months later, with my supervisor, I looked at the development and direction of the relationship. I remembered my early struggle to understand the speech and how embarrassed I had felt at not understanding words. I remembered mistakes I had made out of ignorance: times I forgot the disability and neglected to offer needed help; times I was overly helpful and got in the way of the other's action. The existential distance between the directee and me was great, shaped by the differences in life experiences created by our different physical capacities, and I had much to learn.

Gradually I was able to focus and make distinctions in this unfamiliar landscape. As my supervisor and I regarded my work with the directee, she helped me see how I had approached and entered the other's world, what gifts and baggage I carried with me, when I moved ahead in conscious reliance on God and when not, with what acuity and agility I perceived and traversed variations in the terrain. My supervisor smiled as I told of the relief I had felt when I began to relax, listen, and be myself. This had enabled the directee to tell me what was and was not helpful, thus enabling me to offer true hospitality.

Elements of Care in Spiritual Direction with the Disabled

Desire, courage, and hope mingle in helping us to the threshold of the other's world. Once we arrive there, we pray to assume the stance of Christian love as we practice the art of spiritual direction. As with other caring practices, the stance comprises certain elements. These are elements the supervisor looks for as the supervisee talks about the direction relationship.

Attention

A fundamental element in the stance of care toward another is that of attentiveness. The philosopher Simone Weil believed that the capacity for attention was crucial for human interaction, its absence a moral failing. Appalled by the brutality of Nazi Germany, she argued for the cultivation of attention in young people, writing:

> Attention consists in suspending our thought, leaving it detached, empty, and ready to be penetrated by the object; it means holding in our minds, within reach of this thought, but on a lower level and not in contact with it, the diverse knowledge we have acquired which we are forced to make use of. . . . Above all our thought should be empty, waiting, not seeking anything, but ready to receive in its naked truth the object that is about to penetrate it. . . . Not only does the love of God have attention

for its substance; the love of our neighbor, which we know to be the same love, is made of this same substance.[3]

In spiritual direction, we speak of openness to the Holy Spirit's presence. In attentiveness to the other, we wait in trust for what will come. There is a willingness to receive. We bring our full selves with all our "diverse knowledge" to the encounter, having made space to take in the fullness of the other. We are able to be with the other, putting aside our need to fix, theorize, and do something. We receive the other in faith that God is the one in whom both persons in the room "live and move and have our being" (Acts 17:28). Such a stance enables us to receive, with minimal fear and prejudgment, the different other.

Some who become seriously disabled write about entering a "new life." In midlife, Reynolds Price, the esteemed writer and professor of English, became permanently paraplegic and suffers chronic pain following cancer of the spine and its treatments. In his memoir, *A Whole New Life*, he writes that his best companions were those who were able to register with him what it meant that he was required to leave one life and enter a new one. For instance, one day when his condition seemed to be deteriorating he was with his cousin Marcia. He wrote: "I recall the sober look on her face as she stood by my bed that afternoon and said, 'We don't know what's going on here, do we? But we're riding it out. I'm with you straight through, for however long it takes.'"[4] Like Marcia, we who offer spiritual direction try to attend to whatever reality is present. This requires the same kind of honesty and commitment Marcia gave to her cousin Reynolds.

Supervisees often become trapped by the sense that they ought to appear fearless and offer concrete help. This exaggerated sense of professional obligation stretches the distance between director and directee and gets in the way of the directee focusing on knowing self and God better. A supervisor of therapists writes, "It has been my experience as a supervisor that many therapists drown their empathy or appreciation of the patient's struggle by worrying that they are not doing enough for the patient, or that they are doing the wrong things."[4] Marcia did not make that mistake. She remained focused on Reynolds's experience and honest about her own ignorance. Jesus asked no more—and no less—of his disciples in Gethsemane.

Jean-Dominique Bauby, editor of the French magazine *Elle*, sustained a massive stroke that left him completely paralyzed by "locked-in syndrome." He died less than a year later, in his mid-forties, but before dying, he dictated a book, telegraphing it letter by letter by blinking an eyelid, the one part of his body over which he had volitional control. He, too, refers to his new life.

Both Price and Bauby experienced radical change in their lives. They invited people to enter their new lives and get to know them. Their memoirs extend that invitation beyond their circles of friends. Bauby began dictating letters to those who knew him when he heard of others referring to him as a "vegetable." He wrote that one who referred to him in this way employed a "tone of voice [that] left no doubt that henceforth I belonged on a vegetable stall and not to the human race."[6] Bauby viewed himself as caught in a diving bell and writes that through correspondence, however laboriously produced on his end, nearly "everyone now understands that he can join me in my diving bell, even if sometimes the diving bell takes me into unexplored territory."[7]

Every person lives a particular life. The lives of some are markedly different because they were born physically different from most people. Harriet McBryde Johnson, a disability rights attorney with a lifelong muscle-wasting disease, writes about how little others understand her experience. She uses a wheelchair and cannot even "assume others have a basic comprehension of how [she moves] around in the world."[8]

Some people experience such extreme changes in their lives that it seems they leave previous lives and enter new ones. We recognize, as Reynolds Price insists, that each life, old or new, is whole. So those who enter "seemingly new" lives experience continuity with the life they've had to leave behind. After Christopher Reeve became a quadriplegic, rendered paralyzed and still, his wife assured him that he was still himself. He titled his memoir *Still Me*.[9] Those who accompany others strive to be with the person in his or her life, whatever the nature of it, alert to the movement of the Spirit, perhaps in a new form.

As we spend time with people, we get to know the "me," the core reflective soul, in the physical, historical, and social context. This is true whether the other has become physically other-than-normal later in life or was born this way, and whether the physical difference is visible or invisible. My son Andrew became deaf during his first year of life. For me, the experience was one of loss and grieving. He, however, did not experience loss. He experiences a distinct condition in life that presents some opportunities, obstacles, joys, and discontents, which I try to see and comprehend.

Andrew teaches me to understand his experience as a deaf person. When he was a little boy, he taught me that I needed to stop and give him my full attention if we were going to have a conversation. Because we were signing, I needed free hands, and because he was reading my face, I needed to be turned toward him. Many times Andrew actually pulled things from my hands, pulled me to sit next to him, and, hands on my face, turned my eyes on him. That was the only way we could have a genuine conversation. Stopping and turning are essential movements of attention. Often when I remind myself to stop multitasking and attend to another person, I feel those small hands guiding my face.

As a supervisor, I attend to the supervisee/director's accompaniment of the directee. Does the supervisee show understanding of how the directee experiences the world, speaks about the disability, understands it in relation to life with God and others? Can the supervisee distinguish personal feelings and theological concerns personally stirred up by the other's disability from the feelings and concerns of the other? Does the supervisee's sense of the "whole" new life expand as the other explores what the whole of it is? Is there a person-to-person ease in the relationship?

The psalmist affirms that God bears witness to our affliction and sets our "feet in a broad place" (Ps 31:8). Are we as supervisors standing in that broad place as we attend to supervisees who accompany others into diving bells, new lives, deaf culture, handicapped zones, and other distinct territories?

Fluency

Whenever we get to know another in a deep way, we learn to understand a language that is nuanced differently from our own. We learn what is meant by certain words, inflections, gestures, and pacing. To become fluent takes time. Attention and time help us get to a place where communication seems to flow with ease and grace, which is a state of fluency.

An issue of fluency particularly salient in direction with a physically disabled person is that of metaphor. There is a poverty of precise nontechnical vocabulary for illness and disability. Virginia Woolf claimed that "English which can express the thoughts of Hamlet and the tragedy of Lear has no words for the shiver and the headache."[10] As a result of this linguistic poverty, what we know about bodily experience often is communicated via metaphor.

Jean-Dominique Bauby writes of the diving bell in which he is encased. He also refers to the butterfly of his imagination that allows him to soar and travel. Metaphors illumine abstract concepts by linking them with more concrete ones. The most common metaphors reference our corporeality and so are crucial to any conversation about physical disability.

Umberto Eco, an expert in semiotics, claims that the most elementary universal linguistic feature, across all languages and common to the entire human species, is that which refers to our bodies. Not all cultures recognize notions of substance (for example, "the apple is red"), nor do all recognize the notion of identity (for example, "a = a"). But, writes Eco, all people and languages recognize human embodiment. We stand up, sit, or recline. We understand moving left or right, staying still, walking, waking, sleeping, using limbs to touch, kick, grasp, penetrate, and so on.[11] We also have embodied senses, memory, feelings, and speech. Human bodies breathe, grow, consume, shed, break, bleed, heal, and expire. These "normally" shared experiences are constitutive of language and culture.

In attending to another with physical experiences different from our own, we must be attentive beyond the usual confines of our culture and language. In discussing this with a supervisor of psychoanalysts, I was told that an analytic guideline is "Speak to each in the language he can understand."[12] In Christianity, we understand that one sign of the presence of the Holy Spirit is that "we hear, each of us, in our own native language" (Acts 2:8). God enables heart-to-heart communication that breaks down barriers, bridges linguistic, corporeal, and cultural distance, and gives voice to bodily experiences beyond our vocabulary.

We look for this growing fluency in supervisees, especially those who are directing the physically disabled. In spiritual direction, as we, or those we supervise, open to this broadening of linguistic understanding, our metaphorical vocabulary expands. This involves ethical and theological dimensions. As Eco points out, the language of embodiment "has become the basis of an ethic: first and foremost we must respect the right of the corporeality of others, which also includes the right to talk and think."[13] We extend our own experience of our bodily dignity and rights to others as we develop morally, and our moral understandings are suffused with bodily metaphors.

Ethical metaphors of corporeality populate Scripture. The people of Israel are told to "hear," "see," and "walk in the right path." Jesus repeatedly uses bodily imagery in moral ways: "Can a blind person guide a blind person?" (Luke 6: 39), "[B]lessed are your eyes for they see, and your ears for they hear" (Matt 13:16), and "Whoever follows me will never walk in darkness" (John 8:12).

The Catholic writer Nancy Mairs, who writes often about disability and her experience living with multiple sclerosis, points out that our language "demonstrates the extent to which physical vigor equates with positive moral capacities."[14] She lists some of these moral metaphors, including "Stand on your own two feet," meaning "Be independent"; "Keep your eyes open," meaning "Stay alert"; and "Look the other straight in the eye," meaning "Be honest." Just as the healthy body is used metaphorically to indicate moral "uprightness," so the disabled or ill body signifies moral depravity and sinfulness (in moral terms, for example, people are referred to as "blind," "crooked," "lame," and "sick"). Corporeality informs language, metaphor, morality, and spirituality.

As a supervisor of spiritual directors, I look for signs that the supervisee is trying to comprehend the language of the other. In particular, when the directee is disabled, I attend to the ways the director strives to understand the other's corporeality in fact and in metaphor. There are surprises as barriers are breached and bridges built. A blind man says, "Good to see you," causing the director to hesitate before responding in the same language, although the director does, in fact, see the directee. The hesitation marks the director's awareness of difference and sensitivity to the use of vision language with a blind person. Similarly, another director marvels that a woman with severely impaired speech talks of finding her voice, employing the same metaphorical understanding the director uses to describe becoming more assertive.

The supervisor also looks for indications that the directee is trusting the director with the feelings elicited by the experience of physical difference, and that the director is able to attend to those feelings. A director is moved to tears recounting her experience of listening to a directee in a wheelchair speak about how painful it was to hear a sermon about Psalm 1 in which all the points the pastor made were literalistic elaborations of how we are to *walk* with God. Another director speaks of struggling to be attentive and helpful as a directee with terminal cancer rages about verses in Scripture that claim our bodies are temples of the Holy Spirit. Increased empathy with the directee's feelings shows that the director is coming to know the directee better. Noticing nuances of language and metaphor are indications of the supervisee's growing fluency in the language in which the directee hears God and self.

In North American synagogues, "*Shema*," the Hebrew call to "Hear," is interpreted for the deaf with the sign for "Pay attention." The sign does not indicate the ears, but employs the physical metaphor of vision. It involves holding one's hands flat-palmed on either side of one's head and, wrists bending forward, pointing all fingers outward in the line of sight, as though directing vision into a channel between the palms of the hands. As supervisors, we direct attention. We hold focus on the subtle movement of God in the directee's life and, in particular, in the interactions between the director and directee. In doing so, we listen for the unique language of the relationship between the director and directee, as the director becomes increasingly fluent with the directee's growing and personal language of faith.

Responsibility

The words *care* and *cure* have the same Latin root, *curo, curare*, which means to cure, to take care of, to take trouble for, to be devoted to the anxieties and concerns of others, to heal and restore to health.[15] In time, the words *cure* and *care* diverged, the first concentrating on treatment and the endeavor to eradicate or reverse an illness, disease, or disorder, and the second having to do with the moral art of compassionately helping the other, both denoting kinds of responsibility.

In spiritual direction, we are concerned with compassionately helping the other, and in the restoration of wholeness by God's grace. It is our responsibility to God and to the other to respond to this call as we are able, drawing on the caring practices of our discipline. The philosopher Emmanuel Levinas writes that our experience of transcendence is implicated in our call to other persons; in fact, "the idea of the Infinite is to be found in my responsibility for the Other."[16] Our relationship with God shapes our response to the other, and our closeness to God is affected by our responsible relationships with others.

Lovingly entering into another's experience is to act responsibly to God's call. Bauby applauds those with the ability to enter the "diving bell" and claims that another's presence can "ease our burden a little when our crosses bruised our shoulders too painfully."[17] That is surely the call of the spiritual director, and the supervisor stands as one who, in turn, eases the burden borne by the supervisee/director. The community in which spiritual directors are embedded supports our responsiveness to directees. The supervisor is often the frontline representative of that community, serving as a guardian of competence, supporter of advocacy, and link to resources in the broader community of care.

In all cases, directors have a professional responsibility to refer the directee to health professionals who offer services needed by the directee, so we are familiar with referring people to psychologists and physicians. Disabled directees may need other resources. A supervisor may work with a supervisee to discover what services are available for a disabled directee. Supervisees may have an exaggerated ideal of the purity of spiritual direction that limits their human responsiveness to the other's needs. Letting a directee in a wheelchair know that a church is accessible and has a community of congregants in wheelchairs is a natural act of kindness, not a violation of the contemplative direction space.

In caregiving professions, there is a conversation about activity replacement as a form of care. A nurse helping a patient change clothes is an example, as is a teacher writing a story dictated by a dyslexic or nonliterate child. In both cases, part of the care is doing for the other what the other is unable to do. In spiritual direction with a physically disabled directee, activity replacement may involve the director going to the home of the directee, rather than the directee coming to the director.

In supervision, the meaning of going to the directee's home would be part of the conversation. Did the offer to go to the directee's home arise out of an understanding of the directee's experience that was tested in the relationship, or was it a unilateral decision on the supervisee's part? Was it offered tentatively, or was it imposed on the directee? Was it not offered or discussed, and if not, why not? If the supervisee did decide to offer and the offer was accepted, how does the visit affect the relationship?

Related supervision issues might have to do with maintaining a posture of hospitality in another's space, regarding the other with respect and not condescension, minimizing distractions in an unfamiliar environment, and holding the contemplative stance against the intrusions of the other's household. In the directee's home, the director is a guest in the home *and* the host to the holy space of spiritual direction. The supervisor can help the supervisee reflect on how it is to be both guest and host with the particular directee. The experience of being an itinerant director can be liberating, once the awkwardness passes. While we affirm that wherever we are, God is present, we still think of certain places as more conducive to experiencing God. Taking this art beyond our carefully crafted "temples" and direction rooms expands our capacity for noticing that presence. For the directee who is visited, it is an affirmation of God's presence in his or her ordinary life and physical circumstances.

It is impossible to predict and enumerate the variety of ways in which a director might be called on to respond to the special needs and gifts of a directee.

What a supervisor looks for is that the director is able to respond appropriately and caringly as situations arise.

Compassion

Compassion is essential to the caring stance. Without it, the relationship is not one of care. Experiencing compassion is not, however, a matter of merely hoping for a spontaneous feeling to well up. Just as psychotherapists learn empathy as a primary relational skill, so spiritual directors can mature in their ability to be compassionate.[18] Compassion is a kind of practical wisdom that is acquired and shaped by practice.

It is not a contradiction to claim that a Christian virtue is also a skill that can be practiced and developed. Jesus instructs us to "love one another." This is not a demand for forced emotion, like "be happy." Rather, it is a call to cultivate moral virtue and act in accordance with it. Aristotle, the great expositor of character ethics, wrote the following in his *Nicomachean Ethics*:

> [I]t is this [moral virtue] that is concerned with passions and actions, and in these there is excess, defect, and the intermediate. For instance, both fear and confidence and appetite and anger and pity and in general pleasure and pain may be felt both too much and too little, and in both cases not well; but to feel them at the right times, with reference to the right objects, towards the right people, with the right motive, and in the right way, is what is both intermediate and best, and this is characteristic of virtue.[19]

This responsive, caring attunement to the directee—passion and action—is what the supervisor is hoping to see and encourage in the supervisee.

A disabled directee once said to me: "You can imagine that I am the target for well-meaning, supposedly compassionate intrusions. Sometimes when I'm out in public, strangers will come up to me and ask about my condition. Christians can be the most offensive. Some will ask if they can pray for me, and I say, 'No, thank you.'" Looking intently at me, he said, "I've suffered this all my life."

People with visible disabilities fall prey to unsolicited and unwelcome attention from people who consider themselves caring. However the attention is intended, it may seem like pity, with the distancing and pathologizing projections we (not Aristotle) associate with the word.[20] The encounter is too much about and for the one initiating the action than it is about and for the one receiving it. In *The Screwtape Letters*, C. S. Lewis describes such an initiator as "being the sort of woman who lives for others—you can always tell the others by their hunted expressions."[21]

My directee, after telling me about being approached on the street with offers of prayer, went on to say, "The only time I let strangers pray for me is when they are very old."

"So out of compassion for the very old you let them pray for you, even though you find it offensive?" I responded.

"That's right," he said. I found myself visualizing the encounter—him in the wheelchair allowing an elderly person to pray—and I was moved by his kindness to strangers, kindness that went unrecognized. They had no idea what he was thinking and feeling as they prayed. It made me think about how lonely he has been in many encounters.

Psychologists Lyman C. and Adele Wynne have written of intimacy as the combination of trusting self-disclosure and communicated empathy.[22] My directee trusted me with this self-disclosure, and I hope I communicated attunement to his feelings, neither too much nor too little compassion, but the right degree, expressed in the right way, and stemming from the right motive (as recommended by Aristotle and exemplified by Jesus). The compassion did spring from my heart's response to his kindness, but that response was shaped—and continues to be shaped—by the careful, steady work he and I have done to enable me to know him as a person, learn his language, and understand the life he lives.

In taking this direction experience to supervision, I felt that my supervisor helped me hold that window through which we both looked at what had transpired in the session with my directee. Her help in holding that window enabled me to relax. I realized I had been straining under the weight of my earnest effort to be empathically attuned. I could feel the tension in my eyes and forehead, and I noticed the leaning posture of my torso. With my supervisor, I could sit with the tears I felt in response to my directee's experience—tears of sympathy for his experience of unwelcome attention, and tears of admiration for his kindness.

My supervisor's attention enabled me to feel more deeply what the session stirred in me. In the strain in her face, I became increasingly aware of the pain I had experienced as my directee's words evoked childhood memories of my handicapped mother being accosted by purportedly well-meaning strangers. I had watched her suffer others' unwelcome attention and the stigma of her difference. Remembering my mother magnified my appreciation of what my directee experienced and how he reacted to it.

Compassion derives from Latin words meaning "to feel" or "to suffer with." As my supervisor listened to me, I felt as though my mother, my directee, my supervisor, and I were joined together in recognizing a kind of pain that is not known by everyone. In the words of Scripture, it is as though, through God's tender mercy, "the dawn from on high [broke] upon us, to give light to those who sit in darkness . . . to guide our feet into the way of peace" (Luke 1:78–79). Sitting quietly with my thoughts, I felt that light and peace. My supervisor held me in that place of dawning awareness.

Jean-Dominique Bauby writes of something like this when his speech therapist, the one with whom he developed his system of communication, appears at his
door: "The invisible and eternally imprisoning diving bell seems less oppressive."[23]
Bauby was seen and known in the way many were seen and known by Jesus: the
hungry crowds, the leper on the road, the widow of Nain, the thief on the cross.
Attending to, feeling with and suffering with the other, dissipates theodicies that
would calculate blame and offer illusions of control. That is the kind of emptying
that true attention entails. We stand with the other, offering only ourselves and the
grace we have received, willing to see the other and the grace he or she bears.

It is this compassionate vision we hope to bring to spiritual direction and
supervision. It is, indeed, super-vision in that it goes beyond the analytical or clinical gaze of noticing the material details of Bauby's paralyzed body, to seeing the
butterfly that lives, fragilely and resiliently, within that diving bell. This vision
penetrates, illuminates, and transforms.

Pediatrician W. Thomas Boyce, in writing about this way of seeing, contrasts
our highly developed ways of seeing patients and clients "who come to us bearing
their all too visible frailties" with the vision of Christ. Christ's vision, he writes, is
"a redemptive view in which all of the wonder, hope, and humanity that each of
our patients bears along to us is not lost, but is seen."[24] To see the whole person,
the visible frailties as well as the vital spirit, is our commission and blessing.

Offering Christian Compassion

Christian compassion rests on the Passion. Supervisors help spiritual directors imitate Christ, who "became as we are" (Phil 2:7), human and humble, at
times afflicted with hunger, nakedness, poverty, sickness, and imprisonment, and
at all times loved by God and worthy of care. Awareness of our human limitations, capabilities, suffering, delights, finitude, and transcendence enables us to
recognize the humanity borne by those for whom we care. As the risen Christ
holds our hands with his pierced ones, so our hands hold the hands of those we
serve, as they, in turn, hold other hands.

This understanding is essential to supervising those who are spiritual directors of persons with disabilities. Jesus' insistence on the nonnegotiable unity of
love of God and love of neighbor refutes any impulse toward or argument for
marginalizing, stigmatizing, or victimizing the one who is different. He calls us to
see God's image in the other and, therefore, to love. A gift of Jesus' life and Passion is "a growing concern for victims everywhere in the world," such that
"[t]oday the victimization of ethnic groups, of women, of handicapped people,
of the very young and the very old, is coming to light."[25] Spiritual directors stand
in that light. That light enables us to come alongside others who are different. It
shines through the window supervisors and directors look through together,
regarding the spiritual direction of the disabled.

Notes

1. Author's paraphrase of biblical citation.

2. James Astor, "Some Reflections on Empathy and Reciprocity in the Use of Countertransference between Supervisor and Supervisee," in *Journal of Analytical Psychology* 45 (2000): 368.

3. Simone Weil, "Reflections on the Right Use of School Studies," in *The Simone Weil Reader*, ed. George A. Panichas (New York: David McKay Company, 1977), 49, 51.

4. Reynolds Price, *A Whole New Life* (New York: Plume, 1982), 79.

5. Diane Shainberg, "Teaching Therapists How to Be with Their Clients," in *Awakening the Heart*, ed. John Welwood (Boston: Shambala, 1983), 164.

6. Jean-Dominique Bauby, *The Diving Bell and the Butterfly* (New York: Vintage, 1997), 83.

7. Ibid.

8. Harriet McBryde Johnson, "Stairway to Justice: An Unguarded Civil Rights Landmark," *The New York Times Magazine*, May 30, 2004, 11.

9. Christopher Reeve, *Still Me* (New York: Ballantine, 1999).

10. Virginia Woolf, "Illness," in *The Body in the Library: A Literary Anthology of Modern Medicine*, ed. Iain Bamforth (London: Verso, 2003), 193.

11. Umberto Eco, "When the Other Appears on the Scene," *Five Moral Pieces*, trans. Alastair McEwen (New York: Harcourt, 1997), 20–24.

12. Paraphrase from a passage from the Qur'an ("Never did We send a Messenger except [to teach] in the language of his [own] people in order to make [things] clear to them." Chapter 14 ["Abraham"], Verse 4) and mentioned in private conversation by Dr. Janis Baeuerlen.

13. Eco, "When the Other Appears," 22.

14. Nancy Mairs, *Waist-High in the World: A Life among the Nondisabled* (Boston: Beacon, 1996), 56–57.

15. Edmund D. Pellegrino and David C. Thomasma, *Helping and Healing: Religious Commitment in Health Care* (Washington, D.C.: Georgetown University Press, 1997), 27.

16. Emmanuel Levinas, "Beyond Intentionality," in *Philosophy in France Today*, ed. Alan Montefiore (Cambridge: Cambridge University Press, 1983), 113.

17. Bauby, *Diving Bell*, 110.

18. For example, the mid-twentieth-century turn in mainstream psychoanalysis to "relational psychoanalysis" was propelled by Heinz Kohut, who viewed empathy as a clinical method in which persons can be trained. The empathic relationship is central to many psychotherapeutic theories, and professional training strives to cultivate empathic skill. See Kohut's posthumously published *How Does Analysis Cure?*, ed. Arnold Goldberg with Paul Stepansky (Chicago: University of Chicago, 1984), especially the chapter "The Role of Empathy in Psychoanalytic Cure.")

19. Richard McKeon, ed., Book II, Chapter 6 (Chicago: The University of Chicago Press, 1973), 1106b/15–24

20. For a contemporary critique of pity as a perversion of compassion see Hannah Arendt's *On Revolution* (New York: Penguin, 1991).

21. C. S. Lewis, *The Screwtape Letters* (New York: Macmillan, 1961), 123.

22. Lyman C. and Adele Wynne, "The Quest for Intimacy," *Journal for Marital and Family Therapy* 12, no. 4 (October 1986): 383–94.

23. Bauby, *Diving Bell*, 40.

24. W. Thomas Boyce, "Beyond the Clinical Gaze," in *The Crisis of Care: Affirming and Restoring Caring Practices in the Helping Professions*, ed. Susan S. Phillips and Patricia Benner (Washington, D.C.: Georgetown University Press, 1994), 148.

25. Rene Girard, "Satan," in *The Rene Girard Reader*, ed. James G. Williams (New York: Crossroad, 1996), 208.

APPENDIX A

CONTEMPLATIVE REFLECTION FORM

Directee's Code Name: Ed
Date of Conversation: 12/3/04
Directee Session: #16

Director: Carrie
Supervision Visit: #15
Supervision Visit Date: 12/20/04

1. In a prayerful and reflective context, think about the directees with whom you are currently working. Choose a direction relationship to reflect upon with your supervisor that you think would be helpful to you in some way. Decide upon one session on which you want to focus.

2. Using words and phrases, give a brief description of the life context and characteristics of the directee—those that particularly contribute to an understanding of the session upon which you are focusing, e.g., married, male, pastor, 45 years old, 3 teenage children, recent surgery, outgoing, energetic, active, etc.

    Directee is always busy, I would say driven. He is in his mid-thirties, single, and in the process of changing jobs. His childhood was less than happy, with demanding parents. He is very bright and capable of self-reflection. His workplace is one of conflict. He is able to own his part in the conflict.

3. What did you notice about the directee in the direction conversation that is particularly striking to you?

    He is able to identify his personal pain but is having trouble getting a sense of healing. I am struck that his issue of letting himself be deeply loved by God may be my issue, too.

4. What did you notice about yourself in the direction conversation that is particularly striking to you?

    I had the thought "is this my issue?" go through my head, but then I tried to stay with him since he was in a very painful place.

5. Of all the things you could notice during the direction session, where did you see glimpses of the gifts, fruits, or movement of the Holy Spirit? For example, signs of life, freedom, joy, compassion, solidarity in suffering, justice, enhanced self-identity before God, ability to stand in the truth, invitation, consolation, a "new word spoken," etc.

    I saw signs of freedom/growth in his ability to realize he was part of the problem. I admired his strength in staying with a very painful burden in his life. I noticed he intellectually could verbalize God's love for him, but then seemed to "lose" the thread. I felt very sad that he did not seem to grasp God's love for him, just as he is.

6. Key Part of the Conversation:
    Choose an area of the direction conversation that you feel drawn to discuss with your supervisor. Write up two pages of the dialogue, as you remember it, in the four-column format. In the left-hand column, enter the dialogue. Place your feelings beside the place in the conversation where you noticed something in you. In the next column, add thoughts you may have had. Add any body observations about you or the directee in the last column. This CRF is about what was evoked in you during the direction session— for example, your "inner movements," feelings, images, physical sensations, desires, "interior senses," convictions, beliefs, self-understandings, or self-perceptions.

7. The Issue: (focus question)
    What is the issue regarding your experience as Spiritual Director that you bring to the supervision session, and why do you bring it? The issue you bring is about YOU. It concerns your own interior movements, and it is **this issue that lies at the heart of the supervision session. Please spend time contemplatively reflecting upon this. Make this an activity of prayer.**

Is my own inability to accept God's unconditional love a barrier for my directee? Is my anger also a problem?

8. At the Close of the Supervisory Time:
    Share with your supervisor (and note below) any new awareness gained through the supervision process that might help you in your next session with this directee.

    Do you have any questions for consultation? What are they? Remember, consultation questions deal with things such as "How could I have helped the directee stay with his or her experience more?" or "I sensed that this person should be referred for counseling . . . how do I do that?"

(This form was developed by instructors for the Diploma in the Art of Spiritual Direction program at San Francisco Theological Seminary. It may be used or adapted according to professional needs with the expressed consent of the director of the Program in Christian Spirituality.)

Director, Program in Christian Spirituality
San Francisco Theological Seminary
105 Seminary Road
San Anselmo, CA 94960
dasd@sfts.edu
(415) 451-2838

APPENDIX B

Sample Dialogue for Contemplative Reflection Form

Director: Carrie
Supervision Visit: #15
Supervision Visit Date: 12/20/04

Directee: Ed
Date of Conversation: 12/03/04
Directee Session: #16

Dialogue	Feelings of Director	Thoughts of Director	Body Responses Director	Body Responses Directee
* EI: I had an awful day. I had a blowup with my coworker.	I'm tired but centered and open.		Feel my body relaxing.	His face is flushed.
* CI: Do you want to tell me about it?	Expectant			
E2: I have been having problems with this person and finally we both just blew. I told him how I felt and he told me. It was good in a way, because I think it will lead to our getting beyond our logjam, and I'm looking forward to talking with him tomorrow. (pause . . . Ed tears up)	Sad for him			Tears in eyes
C2: (I hand him a tissue box and wait . . . then ask gently) What is happening now as you remember this?			Bodily sense of holding the other.	

* "E" is Ed, the directee. "C" is Carrie, the director.

Dialogue	Feelings of Director	Thoughts of Director	Body Responses Director	Body Responses Directee
E3: I feel sad all of a sudden. It's as though God is trying to say something more to me.	Compassion			
C3: Something more?				His body closes in, he hunches over and cries softly.
E4: You know I think God is saying to me I can't leave this job, as painful as it is, until I get past this one thing about myself. When I was a child, my dad was always bugging me, and I felt like I needed to be perfect. So when J. got so angry, it felt like a personal attack on my credibility.	Moved, sad	Perfection, oh that condition.		
C4: You're full of anger, yet you feel that you are being called to stay put in a painful job situation because there's an opportunity to move beyond this lifelong pain and anger here.	Amazed at his strength.			His face is red.
E5: Yes, and I want to get past this place. I don't want to be angry all the time. When I am so angry and have such high expectations, it is difficult to feel loved, even by God.			I feel my stomach sink. I get this "knot" when I feel unloved and angry.	

Dialogue	Feelings of Director	Thoughts of Director	Body Responses Director	Body Responses Directee
C5: It is hard to feel loved when we are so angry and have such high expectations of ourselves!		Boy, I have this problem, too. (I say a prayer that I can pay attention to him and deal with my own stuff later.)		
E6: I know God loves me, I know it's okay to deal with all this anger but somehow I can't seem to feel that love.			My body feels lighter.	
C6: You want to feel God's love even when you're angry.		I remember when I was angry a lot.		
E7: Yes, but mostly I get stuck in putting myself down or being very frustrated that I don't let God's love in.				
C7: What would it be like to experience God's love in the midst of being angry?				
E8: Being angry and feeling God's love at the same time. Hmm . . . I've had this experience . . . feeling anger and God's love together . . . (quiet). It's quite a contradiction in terms, don't you think?	Excited at this potential new understanding.			

Dialogue	Feelings of Director	Thoughts of Director	Body Responses Director	Body Responses Directee
C8: Sure. *And* a gift—to know both of these things, your anger and God's love, together!				
(there is about five minutes of silence)	Peaceful		Gentle groundedness	
E9: This is amazing! I feel this light-colored mist falling on me . . . Now it is falling on my coworker too . . . I feel like I'm wrapped in God's arms . . . Hmm. . . . I'm beginning to think I can use this "mist" when I need to remember how much God cares for me, angry or not!		Notice that God is there for him and his coworker.		Body seems to jolt out of hunched position.
C9: I notice that your whole body is sitting up and open now. When you came in you seemed hunched over.			My "knot" is dissipating.	
E10: Yes. I have a resource now to help me when I am angry. I can remember and see myself surrounded by the mist of God's love.	Grateful for God's love and spirit that breaks in to help us.			

This sample dialogue may be used or adapted according to professional needs with the consent of: Director, Program in Christian Spirituality • San Francisco Theological Seminary • 105 Seminary Road • San Anselmo, CA 94960 • dasd@sfts.edu • (415) 451-2838

APPENDIX C

ABOUT THE CONTEMPLATIVE REFLECTION FORM

The Contemplative Reflection Form (CRF) functions as a guide to help a director carefully reflect on a particular spiritual direction session or relationship. It is designed to provide appropriate background information for the supervision conversation and to help focus the conversation around a particular issue. It is meant to assist the director and supervisor in entering into a dialogue that fosters the growth and development of the director as a spiritual director. The CRF is the *starting point* for a supervision conversation.

1. Choosing a session:
    This statement invites the director to think about and consider his or her experience of directees and direction sessions in a prayerful context, consciously reflective of the presence of God.

2. Description of the directee:
    This statement invites the director to give a brief description of the life context and characteristics of the directee. This helps call to mind the person of the directee for the director and gives the supervisor general and helpful information about the directee.

3. The directee:
    This question asks about the directee and what is striking in this particular direction session. There are many things a director might notice about the

189

directee, such as the directee's conceptualization or image of God; the strongest feelings expressed by the directee; shifts in the physical, nonverbal language of the directee; dimensions of experience that were absent from the directee's self-presentation; the arenas of life that a directee speaks about or does not mention.

4. The director:
This question centers on the director and what was noticed about himself or herself in this particular direction conversation. Directors might notice their strongest feelings, places where they felt blocked in hearing the directees, their affective responses to new awarenesses or deepened experiences of God, what they think about directees or their narratives, strong physical sensations, things they noticed, things they missed.

5. Contemplative Listening/Movement of the Spirit:
The director is asked to become aware, in the session, of the directee's being drawn, in the moment, more deeply or intensely into experiencing God's presence. (Does the director notice the presence of God or movement of the Spirit in the direction conversation? Is he or she aware of "shifts" or "transforming moments" in the direction conversation?)

6. Choose an area of the conversation:
In light of the above, the director chooses an area of the conversation that he or she feels drawn to discuss with his or her supervisor. The director writes up this portion of the conversation. The dialogue is written in the left-hand column. The director puts his or her thoughts in the section for "thoughts" and feelings in the section for "feelings." In the column marked "body," the director puts his or her physical sensations. In the final column, the director notes any body movements or reactions of the directee.

7. *Keep the Focus*:
Directors are asked to reflect carefully on the area of focus they bring to their supervisors, as this constitutes the heart of the supervision session. Directors are asked to bring to the supervisor an area of focus that is about them. They select a part of the direction session to write about for supervision because *something was going on inside them at the time*. The director is encouraged to note particularly the listing of his or her interior movements in the center columns of the dialogue form. Here are some examples: "When the directee talked about her mother's death, I moved the conversation away from that subject. I felt butterflies in my stomach." "I sound like a teacher here." "I have a hard time with this person's fundamentalist theology." "When the directee talked about Jesus' warm embrace,

I wanted desperately to feel God's warm embrace right then. I was distracted by this thought and lost the thread of the conversation." These examples show that the focus area selected from the dialogue has to do with what was going on inside the director.

8. Consultation questions (if any):
    Here the director writes down any questions for consultation that he or she may have as a result of this direction session.

9. At the end of the supervision session, the director discusses with the supervisor what was learned and what, if anything, he or she would do differently. The director then notes on the supervision form any new awarenesses gained as a result of the time spent in supervision.

(This form was developed by instructors for the Diploma in the Art of Spiritual Direction program at San Francisco Theological Seminary. It may be used or adapted according to professional needs with the expressed consent of the director of the Program in Christian Spirituality.)

Director, Program in Christian Spirituality
San Francisco Theological Seminary
105 Seminary Road
San Anselmo, CA 94960
dasd@sfts.edu
(415) 451-2838

APPENDIX D

REFLECTION QUESTIONS ON "THE GIVEN AND THE GIFT"

The purpose of the following questions is to assist the reader in paying attention to both the givenness and the gift of his or her own sexuality, as well as how the reader's responses to the erotic may be a help or a hindrance to his or her ministry of direction. Some or all of these questions may be appropriate for supervisors to use in their work with directors.

Beginning to Pay Attention

To what or to whom do you find yourself—your physical self—attracted?

Which of your current directees do you find most attractive? Why?

How comfortable are you with your own body? What do you like about your body? What do you not like?

Where and in what situations do you experience the most pleasure with your body?

Where and in what situations do you experience the most discomfort or pain with your body?

What is your sexual-life history? Whether or not the relationship involved genital pleasure, who are the people with whom you have shared the intimate desires of your heart, mind, soul, and body? Within these relationships, where or when did you feel closest to God—or farthest from God?

Have you ever experienced abuse or misuse? Have you ever abused or misused another?

Naming the Erotic

In my "glossary-in-progress" in chapter 6, I give, adopt, or adapt names for spirituality, the erotic, sexuality, intimacy, and spiritual direction. What "names" or definitions would you give to each, and how would you describe the relationships among them?

Paying Attention: Sexuality as a Given

Who taught you what it means to be a "man" or a "woman"? What did they teach you? How?

What makes you happy about being a woman or man?

What do you not like about being a woman or a man?

In their book *Primary Speech*, the Ulinovs list aspects of sexuality about which people pray (pp. 76–77). Look at this list. Have you ever prayed about any of these things? Which ones? Have any of your directees ever talked about any of these issues or asked you to pray with or for them about these issues? What was your response?

What issue or issues would you rather not hear about from your directees? Can you say why?

Paying Attention to the Gift of Sexuality

Read or reread the Song of Songs, perhaps using one of the contemporary translations by Marcia Falk or Bloch and Bloch.

Imagine yourself as the spiritual director of the young woman or man of the Song. How would you respond to their expressions of desire for one another?

What is the most extraordinary or even foolish thing you have ever done for the sake of someone you loved?

Regardless of whether Jesus ever experienced physical/sexual intimacy with another, how easy or difficult is it for you to think of him as a sexual being? Is there some aspect of our humanity that Jesus did not incarnate?

Are there ways of responding sexually to others that do not embody or mirror the Spirit of Christ?

Paying Attention to the Gift of Sexuality within Spiritual Direction

When have you experienced yourself as being *desirable* to God? How did/does God let you know this? Have you ever described this experience to anyone else? Have you ever talked to your own spiritual director about this?

Have you ever resisted God's efforts to urge, draw, or invite you into a deeper relationship? How did/do you resist? Have you ever talked to anyone else (including your spiritual director) about your resistance?

How do you tend to image God? Male, female, or other? If the Spirit were to touch and hold you with human hands, would it be as a friend? Parent? Lover?

Are there any important relationships in your life of which you have never spoken in spiritual direction? Which ones? Why?

What internal signals do you have that let you know when your directee is speaking of something that really matters to him or her? Are these signals fairly reliable?

How does your own director help you to "articulate and clarify" your desires? How does it feel to you to be heard and assisted?

Have you ever felt yourself aroused by one of your directees? How did you respond to your own arousal?

Have your own longings or desires ever been awakened by the longings or desires of your directees? Have you ever felt a "sympathetic vibration"? Have you ever felt jealous of a directee's relationship with God? Who was the directee and what was the occasion?

Paying Attention to the Problems

Is there someone—or some group of people—that you would not be open to serving as a spiritual director? Whom? Why? What does this limitation say about you?

Is there something important about yourself that you feel you cannot share with your spiritual director, but would like to? What signals have you received from your director that keep you quiet?

Have you ever expressed some matter of great personal importance or intimacy to your director and had it dismissed or belittled? If so, how did this feel to you?

Look over the names of your present and past directees. Are there any directees whom you have never discussed with your supervisor? Are there any directees whom you have repeatedly discussed with your supervisor? Why?

To the extent that you are aware, have you ever "distorted the reality" of your own director? In what way? How did he or she respond?

How do you recognize transference? Have directees ever seemed to "distort" your reality as their director? Who or what did he or she expect you to be that you were not? Did you talk about this with your supervisor?

When was the last time you found yourself enmeshed in countertransference? How did you recognize it? What did you do?

Do you ever touch your directees? How? When? Do you have any directees for whom touch from you would not be appropriate? Why?

CONTRIBUTORS

MARIA TATTU BOWEN, PH.D., holds a degree in Christian spirituality from the Graduate Theological Union, in Berkeley, California, and a Master's of Applied Spirituality from the University of San Francisco. She has extensive experience teaching, lecturing, writing, and ministering in both Roman Catholic and Protestant settings, including the Diploma Program in Spiritual Direction at San Francisco Theological Seminary. She has worked as a spiritual director since 1985 and has supervised spiritual directors since 1996, seeing in her practice laypeople, seminary students, clergy, and religious women and men. For more information, please visit her website at www.mariatattubowen.com.

MARY ROSE BUMPUS, R.S.M., PH.D., is a Sister of Mercy of the Cincinnati Regional Community. She has been a spiritual director for twenty-five years and a supervisor of directors since 1995. She currently serves as Assistant Professor of Christian Spirituality at Seattle University's School of Theology and Ministry, where she teaches courses in the art of spiritual direction and supervision. Bumpus is a former director of the Diploma in the Art of Spiritual Direction Program at San Francisco Theological Seminary, and she also writes and teaches in the area of biblical spirituality.

JOSEPH D. DRISKILL, PH.D., is Associate Professor of Spirituality and Dean of the Disciples Seminary Foundation at Pacific School of Religion. He is also a staff member of the Lloyd Center, where he does spiritual direction. His interests include the interface of spiritual direction and pastoral care. Driskill holds ministerial standing with the Christian Church (Disciples of Christ) in the United

States and Canada and with the United Church of Canada. He has pastored churches in Missouri, Kentucky, and Saskatchewan and served for twelve years as a campus minister. His publications include *Protestant Spiritual Exercises: Theology, History, and Practice* (Morehouse, 1999); *Ethics and Spiritual Care*, coauthored with Professor Karen Labacqz (Abingdon, 2000); chapters in *Religious and Social Ritual: Interdisciplinary Explorations* (SUNY, 1996); and *Still Listening: New Horizons in Spiritual Direction* (Morehouse, 2000).

SAMUEL HAMILTON-POORE, M.DIV., is a Presbyterian minister and spiritual director. He lives in Mason City, Iowa, with his wife and three children. He received his Master's of Divinity at Duke Divinity School, and a Diploma in the Art of Spiritual Direction at the San Francisco Theological Seminary. Hamilton-Poore has worked in the area of spiritual direction since 1996.

HUTCH HANEY, M.T.S., is the chair of the Department of Counseling and School Psychology, College of Education, Seattle University. In addition to being a counselor educator, he has a master's degree in theology and has taught multicultural pastoral supervision in the School of Theology and Ministry, Seattle University. He is the coauthor of *Basic Counseling Responses* and *Basic Counseling Responses in Groups* (Brooks/Cole-Wadsworth, 1998/2000), and has authored a chapter with Cleo Molina in a forthcoming book on the teaching of social justice.

REBECCA BRADBURN LANGER, D.MIN., is an ordained Presbyterian minister who has worked in the area of spiritual direction for more than twenty years and has been the coordinator of supervision for San Francisco Theological Seminary for the last three years in the Diploma in the Art of Spiritual Direction Program. Before that, she worked in congregations and a spirituality center in Pennsylvania while doing retreats nationwide. Langer did her training in supervision at Mercy Center, Burlingame, California. She is particularly interested in the intersection of visual art and spirituality. She is a wife, mother, and grandmother.

ELIZABETH LIEBERT, S.N.J.M., PH.D., is Professor of Spiritual Life at San Francisco Theological Seminary and a member of the doctoral faculty in Christian spirituality at the Graduate Theological Union in Berkeley, California. She has worked as a spiritual director and supervisor for many years. Liebert coauthored *The Spiritual Exercises Reclaimed: Uncovering Liberating Possibilities for Women* and *Retreat with the Psalms* (both Paulist Press, 2001). She is currently at work on a book that has grown out of her classes on discernment.

CLOTILDE ("CLEO") MOLINA, ED.D., is a lifelong learner, educator and consultant whose focus is primarily in the areas of diversity and leadership. Raised in Southern California as part of a large bilingual, bicultural Mexican

American family, and having been married into families with distinctly different cultures, Molina has a passion for understanding and describing differences. She earned a doctorate in Educational Leadership, a postmaster's certificate in transforming spirituality at the School for Theology and Ministry at Seattle University, and bachelor's and master's degrees in educational psychology and bilingual education from the University of Washington. She has focused her work on facilitating the development of individuals and communities within the context of a multicultural, interrelated world.

JAMES NEAFSEY, D.MIN., has worked as a spiritual director, supervisor, retreat leader, and teacher of Christian spirituality for many years. He has been a staff member of several formation programs for spiritual directors in Northern California, including programs at Mercy Center in Burlingame, and the Bread of Life Center for Spiritual Formation in Davis. Neafsey also teaches spirituality courses as an adjunct faculty member of the Pastoral Ministries Graduate Program at Santa Clara University.

SUSAN S. PHILLIPS, PH.D., is a spiritual director and supervisor in Berkeley, California. She is the executive director of New College Berkeley, an affiliate of the Graduate Theological Union, committed to the continuing education and formation of Christians for lives of discipleship. Also a sociologist, Phillips teaches about caring practices and spirituality at several seminaries in the United States and Canada. She is a wife, mother, and Presbyterian elder.